Cracks in the Pedestal

PHILIP GREEN

Ideology and Gender in Hollywood

Cracks in the Pedestal

University of

Massachusetts Press

Amherst

Copyright © 1998 by
The University of Massachusetts Press
All rights reserved
Printed and bound in the United States of America
LC 97-21775
ISBN 1-55849-119-8 (cloth); 120-1 (pbk.)
Designed by Mary Mendell
Printed and bound by Braun-Brumfield, Inc.

Library of Congress Cataloging-in-Publication Data
Green, Philip, 1932–
    Cracks in the pedestal : ideology and gender in Hollywood /
Philip Green.
        p. cm.
    Includes bibliographical references and index.
    ISBN 1-55849-119-8 (cloth : alk. paper). — ISBN 1-55849-120-1
(pbk. : alk. paper)
    1. Women in motion pictures.   2. Women in television.   3. Feminism
and motion pictures.   4. Feminist film criticism.   I. Title.
PN1995.9.W6G74   1998
791.43'652042—dc21   97-21775
                                                                              CIP

British Library Cataloguing in Publication data are available.

CONTENTS

ACKNOWLEDGMENTS

This book grew out of my interaction with the students in a Smith College seminar, "Ideology, Politics, and Culture," which I have been teaching for the past decade. My thanks go to all those students (only some of whom I was able to acknowledge by name in the text), whose caustic, witty, and insightful commentaries on Hollywood films and network television bear necessarily unacknowledged traces on virtually every one of its pages. I was also inspired by an unsurpassed learning experience, Deborah Linderman's Smith College Faculty Seminar on the Teaching of Film, and by many stimulating conversations with Linderman about cinema in general and various movies in particular. In addition, I benefited greatly from the comments of Laura Green, Robert Green, Barbara and Leonard Quart, Ben Singer, and Elizabeth Young. The entire manuscript was read by Susan J. Douglas and Joel Kovel, whose comments were greatly appreciated; and for the University of Massachusetts

Press by a superlative copy editor, Betty Waterhouse. Clark Dougan, my editor at the Press, first had the idea for this book; I've been helped immeasurably by his encouragement, guidance, and friendly criticism.

About all these people I must of course say, in the conventional phraseology, that I thank them for their constructive assistance but that I take full responsibility for any mistakes, which are mine alone. There is one person, however, to whom I cannot offer that comforting boilerplate clause without being totally dishonest, for to do so would be to convey much less thanks than I owe her.

The first draft of the manuscript that was to become this book was a shapeless mass of hundreds of pages, arranged in no particular order, and making no particular point. Subsequently, during a period of several months, it took the shape it now has out of a process of dialogue and intellectual exchange with Gina Rourke, then a Smith College Ada Comstock Scholar. Her Smith College payroll voucher described Gina as a"research assistant," but this is like describing Michael Jordan as a "basketball player." I've often wondered what I may have done to deserve Gina; but then, what did Chicago ever do to deserve Michael? My recollection is that my first assignment for her was to make up a bibliographic card file for me, to "look for repetitions in the text," and to give me her ideas about any pages that "might be in the wrong order." What I received instead (in addition to that card file, which she completed, including the hunting down of incomplete references, in about a tenth of the time it would have taken me), was the first of a continual series of marginal comments, mini-essays, and e-mail messages, which eventually came to cover almost the entire manuscript. She treated every one of my thoughts, sentences, and even words, with the full respect that is given only by demanding perfection; made certain that I confronted all the hard issues I'd been carefully evading; and in general showed as fierce a dedication to preventing me from making a fool of myself in public as might be expected if the work were in part her own. And so it is.

Cracks in the Pedestal

Introduction

This is a book about gender, ideology, and mainstream visual culture—the cultural commodities produced by the multifold institution we call "Hollywood."[1] Specifically, I shall be looking at how male-dominated Hollywood (and it remains male-dominated despite the rising number of women in executive positions) has responded to the feminist revolution of the 1970s. I focus on Hollywood's treatment of gender, sexuality, and the institutions, especially "the family," within which our notions of gender and sexuality are embedded and take on active life.

My thesis, briefly, is that Hollywood's confrontation with feminism is rife with slippages and pregnant with evasions. On the one hand, in the contemporary "postfeminist" era, patriarchal traditions in visual culture are seemingly challenged yet ultimately reproduced. Yet at the same time the unrealized challenge leaves residues, residues that alert us to the existence of a seismic cultural change that is far from being consigned to the dustbin of history. The concrete detail of this book, following a prefatory discussion of ideology and visual culture, is therefore divided into two parts. Part I consists mostly of descriptions of how Hollywood movies and television programs—mainstream, or dominant, American visual culture—produce and reproduce our most familiar images of sexuality and modes of gender identity. This discussion, at the same time, begins to suggest those slippages and evasions in the reproduction of dominant ideology. These are picked up in Part II, which highlights resistance, ambiguities, ambivalences.[2] It concludes with a discussion of several genres that are to be found mostly outside mainstream Hollywood but have recently begun to be colonized by it. These include martial arts and other action films in which physically tough actresses replace their more familiar male counterparts as the protagonists; rape-revenge films in which unsympathetic rapists are hunted down and killed by their victims; and the new version of film noir, in which powerful and murderous women weave elaborate plots to destroy a succession of enfeebled men. In these genres a sense of sexual contestation, though obliquely expressed, is unmistakably present. In this discussion, I take a somewhat different tack than do those cultural critics whose focus is more on the allegedly unproblematic reproduction and strengthening of cultural hegemony.[3] My central thesis, in contrast, is that the contemporary production of visual culture takes place under conditions prominently structured by the feminist cultural revolution of the 1970s.

Because my purpose is to characterize the ideological aspect of an entire cultural domain, unlike many of those who do academic film studies and cultural studies I have not worked outward from an in-depth focus on particular films or genres (or television programs or genres). Instead I attempt to describe how certain techniques for the creation of ideologically inflected narratives—the linkage of physical appearance to moral destiny, the determination of who lives and who dies in suspense stories, the appearance of social criticism which is then canceled by a narrative's conclusion—work across genres (and even mediums). However, I do not intend to prove, nor is it possible to prove, that by some standard or other (which never could be agreed to by all commentators) an observable proportion of Hollywood products have one ideological character or another. There are many commentators (most of them on the political Right) who explicitly or implicitly attempt to do just this by piling up examples, but the multitude of examples merely disguises the arbitrary, ungrounded empiricism of this approach. Statistical generalizations about Hollywood are even worse, as no research team no matter how indefatigable can encompass its impossibly overstuffed past, let alone its overflowing present.[4] Nor is it possible to make up a supposedly representative sample of Hollywood movies, for there is no criterion by which one set of movies is more representative than another. For all these reasons, the strongest claim I make about the never-ending stream of cultural commodities, is to use modifiers such as "most," "usually," or—above all—"typically." That deliberately vague sort of claim is intended to be subject to check by anyone who has seen, or is going to see, a very large number of movies and television programs in all genres.

Moreover, the Hollywood text is a historical text. No film or television segment can be understood outside of its time and place, and comparisons across time and place (especially given the longtime existence of the Hollywood Production Code) are otiose. In that sense, my discussion of visual culture is not intended to be fully historical; by the time I could finish such an account, it would already be the year 2000 and everything would have changed once again. It's impossible to guess what Hollywood's orientation will be by the time these words are published, except that it will not be what it is as I write them.[5]

In any event my chief interest is not "whether" (which can be verified by any trip to a mall or evening spent in front of the television set) but "how." How does Hollywood produce its ideological texts (or textual moments) when it does produce them; more to the point, how should we go about being prepared to recognize them? The texts change over time but the techniques remain roughly the same, and I have therefore paid greatest attention to the films and television programs that display those techniques most revealingly. What follows is nothing like a "complete guide" to Hollywood and gender (which in any event would have to be a guide to Hollywood and almost everything else). Rather, I look at exemplary and in some instances possibly less familiar techniques and examples of Hollywood's ideological construction of gender and sexuality at work: a sort of reference guide to future watching. This is a narrow focus, of course, which leaves it to others to explain how movies and television produce meaning in general.[6]

Therefore, this is a book about what cinema and television are saying to people, more than it is about what people are learning from them. As such it is written from an epistemological realist standpoint. I assume, that is, the existence for any given "text" (literary or cinematic or televisual), an objective ("real") textual content independent of and beyond the particular meaning that I or any other viewer may assign to it. The texts are really "there," they are not *only* the results of a transaction between my ideological consciousness and an unstable textual reality. Of course they are that as well: in Pam Cook's words, "On the one hand, there is the empirical spectator whose interpretation of film will be determined by all manner of extraneous factors like personal biography, class origins, previous viewing experience, the variables of conditions of reception, etc. On the other hand, the abstract notion of a 'subject position,' which could be defined as the way in which a film solicits, demands even, a certain closely circumscribed reading from a viewer by means of its own formal operations."[7]

It may often not be possible to elaborate on this "demand," or "solicitation," beyond the capsule descriptions given in film and video guides. But it is there nonetheless.[8] I shall not be providing an argument for this "realist" position, however, simply because there are no absolute arguments for it—or against it. Fundamental epistemological propositions are utilitarian. It is not possible to do ideological analysis, if that is what one wishes to do, from a nonrealist standpoint; the concept of ideology is useful only to compare social myths with social realities.[9]

As ideological critique, so understood, is always at least loosely derived from Marx's historical materialism, a neo-Marxian work such as this one necessarily falls outside the mainstream of American feminist cultural studies in general, and feminist film studies in particular. That mainstream, though often touching upon Marxian theoretical practice, is rooted in a psychoanalytic theory ultimately derived instead from Freud: a different kind of materialism altogether, though equally critical as practiced by feminist cultural theorists.[10] This choice too has a utilitarian justification. "Ideology" has meaning only as an account of an individual's transactions with a structured social whole, but psychoanalytic theorizing always stands in danger of reducing social relationships to a mother-child dyad, or a nuclear family triad, and thus vitiating the concept of ideology.

Certainly, we should hope that some cultural critics will continue to prefer the discourse of psychoanalysis, since ideological critique by itself is incapable of generating certain kinds of fruitful understandings that psychoanalysis can achieve: identity formation, psychosexual narratives of the self, and transactions within the subconscious strata of individual minds. Nonetheless, unless the ideological differences in a group of men that numbers among itself, say, a neo-Nazi, a conservative Christian fundamentalist, a free-market Republican, a New Deal Democrat, a socialist feminist, and an anarchist, can be so explained by it, we must at some point leave psychoanalytic theorizing behind. The account of narrative and iconographic structures and conventions that follows in this book is therefore intended not to *displace* psychoanalytic critique, but to supplement it in a field for which its explanatory powers are limited.[11]

These reservations notwithstanding, I have borrowed heavily and eclectically from many psychoanalytically oriented feminist cultural critics, and have been greatly influenced by some, most especially Laura Mulvey, Linda Williams, and Carol Clover.[12] However, psychoanalysis is not merely one theoretical approach among many. Like Marx's, perhaps even more so, it is a discourse in and of itself, a way of knowing, an episteme. My borrowing, therefore, is in a sense illegitimate, and can only strengthen my own argument (if it does so at all) the way anecdotes strengthen a case the truth or falsity of which already stands on other grounds.[13]

Put another way, as a book about what cinema and television are saying, mine is primarily about the *production* of visual culture, and only secondarily about its consumption.[14] By "production" I refer not only to the economic institutions within which visual culture is created and by which it is distributed, but also, and in context more directly, to visual culture "as a system of representation through which individuals experience and understand their world."[15] This focus on cultural production and representation entails, as another consequence, that I also largely eschew (while again eclectically borrowing from) the kind of methodological approach that has come to be known as audience response analysis.

An outgrowth of, but a step away from the abstractions of, psychoanalytic theorizing, audience response analysis in the field of visual culture focuses on the interactions between texts and concrete spectators. In contrast to ideological critique, it plays a pivotal role when we wish to engage the "problem" of spectatorship, especially female—and particularly black and lesbian—spectatorship, which tends to be neglected by psychoanalytic theory's concentration on a generalized version of the (white) male psyche.[16] How do we in fact, whoever we are, *perceive* the way we are being represented? That is an open question. The assertion I shall be making, that Hollywood serves an ideological function and that its individual products have an ideological content, should in no way be conflated with or assimilated to the quite different proposition that each or any of these products itself has a discernible and variable psychological or ideological effect. I take it as axiomatic that there is no direct route from what a communicative expression says to what a reader or viewer sees or hears, and so we can never safely infer either from the other. As the audience response theorists suggest, we cannot assume that a particular cultural commodity has a given ideological effect any more legitimately than we can assume it has a counterideological or subversive one. To the extent that any remarks I make about the content of film and television imply the positioning and judgments of cultural spectators other than myelf, they would have to be supplemented by relevant studies of concrete spectatorship.[17]

At the same time, the focus on spectatorship can lead us up a blind alley. Thus I have refused to adopt the postmodern standpoint from which the cultural field is seen as (among other things) a realm of plurality, play, and multiple meanings, where members of different subcultures are seen as appropriating cultural commodities for their own subcultural—sometimes even subversive—purposes. This may happen from time to time. To make too much of it, though, is to substitute a legitimate insight about the ubiquity of power and the freedom with which it circulates, for the quite separate truth that there is an enduring material *structure* of cultural power to which those of us who merely consume cultural commodities are subject.[18] With this substitution, the possibility of transformative critique, real subversion, or the justification of revolutionary change simply disappears. Why bother, when anyone can generate her own critique by "appropriating" *Seinfeld,* as if mild amusement had somehow become socially defiant? Carried to this point, epistemological subjectivity justifies political passivity.[19]

In contrast to the emphasis of those who deploy either the audience response or the postmodern paradigm, my interest is in how the persons who have come to be authorized to represent us to ourselves, are using that authorization. I start with two major assumptions, both of which are so obvious that we ought to demand a great deal of contrary evidence before we consider them successfully refuted. First, because Hollywood is a creator of dreams and fantasies and purveyor of ideologies for the American people, as well as a multibillion-dollar industry at the heart of American life, it must to a great extent be representative of that life, neither apart from it nor opposed to it. Conversely, commercial mass culture is produced by people who, outside the disappearing realm of communal folk art, are not and cannot be identical with their audiences. In a capitalist world, where production even of art is for an impersonal marketplace, to make one's living by speaking to others is perforce to be a different kind of person than one who only listens. To get close to an accurate depiction of what Hollywood is and does, requires not a compromise between these two contradictory propositions, but recognition of the truth in both of them. In this book I shall examine how that contradiction works itself out in practice in one very central arena of ideological reproduction *and* contestation. In sum, the monopolized structure of production is permeable, and I shall emphasize its permeability. But if we think, as we sometimes do, that we are uncovering "subversion" in the midst of this core social sector, that subversion will usually have much more to do with the contradictory conditions of cultural production than with any genuine attempt at counterideological statement. In the first instance Hollywood is a force for social stability and must be understood as such.

For the most part, therefore, I shall be attempting to decipher manifest and latent ideological meanings in the cinematic and televisual texts that daily confront us so overwhelmingly—independent of any particular psychological effects those texts might or might not be supposed to have. For me, the single most important "effect" of mass, commercial, visual culture is that some people are producing it whereas others only consume it. Who these producers are, and how exactly they differ from the rest of us, is not important. What is important is the nature of the capitalist market as an instrument of domination (see Chapter 5). In short, ideological critique is a branch of democratic political theory; it leads to the demand that ideological (and institutional) monopolies be broken up, or reappropriated by excluded groups and classes.[20] Audience response theory and postmodernist analysis, quite differently, most often lead to an appreciation that visual culture is not always so monolithic as it seems, in that socially marginalized members of the mass audience are quite capable of transforming textual meanings for their own purposes. The demand and (within limits) the appreciation are both justified, it seems to me, but those who express them have different purposes in mind.

Finally, even an epistemological realist must acknowledge that the first of the two positions described by Pam Cook, that of being an "empirical spectator," fundamentally modifies his (or her) reception of "the text that is there"; and that therefore some self-styled guides to the real are more trustworthy than others. The proof of this pudding is always in the eating; as a concept "ideology" is unabashedly both diagnostic *and* normative. To say of a given communication that it is "ideological" is to say first, that it makes a partially mistaken claim about the world; and that the world (the aspect of it under discussion) could and *should* be different than it is. To take one very relevant example, my vis-à-vis, having read the chapters that follow, says that the family is naturally a harmonious institution, and that visual culture ought to reproduce that harmony. I reply that that is an ideological statement, for the family is also a realm of conflict. But I mean more than that he is mistaken about the family; in contrasting "conflict" with "harmony" I am also implicitly subjecting our understanding of "the family" to an evaluative norm, probably a norm of equality. Otherwise, how could I know whether we are observing harmony or conflict in the first place? But my own norm of equality is not some personal, idiosyncratic invention. It arises from the same culture we are both evaluating, and included as an essential component of that culture are the very visual texts I am analyzing, which are also a part of our, and my, consciousnesses. They speak through me at the very moment I (allegedly) "analyze" them; as Michael Taussig puts it: "To take social determination seriously means to see oneself and one's shared modes of understanding and communication included in that determining. . . . [I]t calls for an understand-ing of the representation as contiguous with that being represented, and not as suspended above and distant from the represented"[21]

Thus, at one and the same time I am both analyst and analysand, viewer and viewee. The pages that follow will provide evidence, or not, of my trust-worthiness as a spectator, but much of that evidence will not be accessible to any particular reader (as a totality it is presumably accessible only to myself).[22] Thus it is also important to know just who is the particular viewer and critic of North American visual culture who calls himself "Philip Green"; to engage in ideological criticism is not an innocent activity, and the interpretation of mainstream visual culture that follows can in no way be an innocent interpretation. Forty years ago, speaking of his own movie reviewing, the critic Robert Warshow remarked that "a man watches a movie, and the critic must acknowledge that he is that man."[23] If we remember to change the personal pronoun when it's inappropriate (it's perfectly appropriate in this case), that injunction is never out-of-date, especially when ideology is the subject.

To begin with, the analysis contained in these pages is only ostensibly about gender rather than about race and class. It is not possible to separate the analytical elements of a social system from one another. The realities to which those terms refer are inextricably intertwined, and no discussion of the one is possible without explicit or implicit commentary on the others. Race and class structure the social meanings of gender and sexuality, as they in turn structure the social meanings of race and class. In that light, what is on the one hand a rational principle of selection (you can't write about everything at once) is on the other the suppression of a reality that is always there even if I am not (or some other person is not) noticing it.

In this case, too, the presence and (relative) absence correspond to another kind of social reality.

I am a person who inhabits one out of many possible subject positions in the contemporary United States. My viewing is necessarily the viewing of a white, heterosexual, American male academic who does not share the subject position of repressed or marginalized peoples, and who in practice therefore accepts the various terms of a multifold privilege that he theoretically criti-cizes.[24] As a certain kind of political and academic man, attuned primarily to written accounts of other people's experiences, and having taught for years at a college for women, I can be at least *intellectually* aware of the ways in which educated white women see visual culture. I have somewhat less perspective on how, say, educated black or Latino or Asian persons see the culture, and much less on how working-class people of any background do so; the latter groups receive fewer opportunities to produce commentaries on the ways in which they are represented by others. So there are millions of people who quite predictably might see cultural commodities very differently from how I (or other white feminists such as Linda Williams or Carol Clover) see them. No reading of mass culture by persons such as us is complete unless an integral part of it is a reading by other women and men who, because of their radically different social positioning, might have radically different interpretations of the life on which the material is based.[25]

Mine therefore in no way pretends to be such a complete reading. On the other hand, awareness of a gap in understanding itself can be at least a corrective of a negative kind. I have tried not to understand cultural commodities too quickly; not to suggest that gender is somehow the only correct starting point for a discussion of cultural representation; and not to forget that whatever understanding I do finally come to, emanates from a position and a perspective that are more than my own, but less than everyone's.[26] Still, these are inescapable limitations, and I make no pretense of having transcended them. Given that caveat, as an interpreter I have been trained primarily by two kinds of cultural exposure. The first is by years of immersion in Marxian and then in feminist cultural criticism and political theory; and introducing such criticism and theory to sympathetic, insightful, and forceful female students. The second is by even longer years of immersion in "Hollywood" itself, mitigated perhaps only by an intensive (though certainly not equally intensive) immersion in the commodities of not-Hollywood (such as *Sweetie, The Vanishing, The Scent of Green Papaya,* and others briefly mentioned in chapter 1). Ideologically (leaving aside potentially dissonant aesthetic responses), the viewing of that culture passes through the political lens of an uneasy (and possibly unsustainable) amalgam of Marxian and feminist liberatory ideals. It also passes through the often overpoweringly sentimental lens of visual culture itself. I am a passive consumer of the culture I critically anatomize below, a stance for which I helpfully forgive myself in advance by purporting to be aware of what I am doing, or not doing; and by advertising this self-awareness here.[27]

Inescapable limitations, indeed, can even be an opportunity. As all serious observers of Hollywood have understood since the publication of Laura Mulvey's seminal work on dominant cinema, her psychoanalytic concept of "the triple male gaze" is the key to an initial understanding of the production and consumption of visual culture (cinematic visual culture, at any rate). The triple male gaze is the gaze of the camera, which (via the cinematographer/

director) chooses what is to be shown on the screen; of the male protagonist on the screen who directs our gaze to the female objects of his gaze; and, most crucial, the gaze of the *male* viewers in the audience, whose fantasies it is uniquely the intention of classical cinema to activate. As Mulvey described it, male voyeurism therefore controls both what is shown on the screen and what is seen emanating from the screen.[28] All difficulties aside (and I shall be alluding to some of them in subsequent pages), this once-revolutionary theoretical paradigm now seems so necessary that it is hard to imagine what the study of visual culture might have been like in its absence. However far we may go beyond it, Mulvey's recognition of what has lain at the core of classical cinema is essential. Without it, we would be ignoring the most salient aspect of cultural reproduction—somewhat like discussing the political economy of professional sports without mentioning men. One sees the worst results of this kind of ignorance, for example, in the polemics of the anti-Hollywood Right, who manage to locate the "cause" of Hollywood's obsessive pursuit of violence and sexuality in some alleged "liberal" disposition of cultural "elites," without ever even faintly noticing that it is almost entirely men who are engaged in this pursuit.[29]

However, if what I have described as my central thesis is correct—if the contemporary production of visual culture takes place under conditions prominently structured by the feminist cultural revolution of the 1970s—then the production and content of the triple male gaze ought to be changing. But how? Since dominant visual culture is created in large part to be seen by men, it is crucial to understand just what it is that men see when they look at it: to create, so to speak, a spectatorship theory for men. Here the problem arises: For the most part, women (and it is largely women who have constituted the field of post-Mulvey film studies at its best in the United States) can only conjecture how to create this theory. For it is also true that, as Warshow might say, a woman watches a movie, and the critic must not forget (but often does forget) that she is that woman . . .

On the whole, from the psychoanalytic perspective, women's idea of what men see is derived largely from Freud (usually via Lacan), whose key concepts (especially that of male castration anxiety) are often subjected to a double (and doubly dubious) attribution. First, it is assumed that they apply more or less indiscriminately to men in general, who become subject to a kind of essentialism that would be considered unacceptable if applied to women *and* that enables the critic to avoid acknowledging that she is a woman watching these films (and television programs). Second, and more critical, it is often implicitly assumed, in the absence of anything the layperson might recognize as evidence, that there is a direct link from this general psychic formation to particular visual images, and thence to the ideology of male domination and female subordination.[30] That is, from subconscious states of mind almost primitive in their simplicity, the psychoanalytic theorist deduces attitudes toward complexly articulated systems of social relationships, which are then summed up in gross categories ("men's consciousness," "patriarchy") that may conceal more than they reveal.

My own experience, contrarily, has been that as fruitful as the psychoanalytic approach has proven to be for film studies, and for my own understandings of visual culture, I in fact sometimes do not see (or at the level of consciousness do not think I am seeing) exactly what it is that I am alleged to be seeing. For half a century I have been an avid beneficiary of the triple male gaze in my own watching, but what that gaze sees and enables me to see has changed significantly during that period. It should be useful, therefore, to point to those contemporary occasions when one male viewer may provide a different account of what the contemporary male gaze sees (and, inferentially, has constructed for its own consumption).[31] Do not forget, however, that this gaze also has a historical context. Mulvey's intervention was just one intellectual contribution to a women's liberation movement that had created, and—even after its decline into "power feminism"—is still creating, a gender disturbance (that "seismic cultural change" referred to above) that has thrown all previous modes of cultural understanding into confusion. This book is a report on some outcomes of that disturbance.

PART I   Foundations of Social Order

1 Ideology, Gender, and Visual Culture

The role that visual culture plays in modern societies is given by the very
nature of those societies, and by the peculiar supporting role that ideology
does and must play in them. An ideology is the ensemble of beliefs and
practices that support a (partially) fictitious sense of community among the
members of any organized human group.[1] In Althusser's phrase, it "represents
the imaginary relationship of individuals to their real conditions of existence."[2] Because understanding of the world is a *lived* understanding of the
conditions of existence, no version of that understanding will be completely
false; as refracted through ideological lenses, however, understanding is incomplete and inadequate because uncritical of the totality of that existence.[3]
As long as the world is not utopia, this dialectic of acceptance and rejection
remains an unavoidable aspect of individual consciousness. As Jacqueline
Rose, arguing for the contribution of psychoanalytic theory to an understand-

ing of the processes of (female) identity formation, puts it: "[T]he unconscious constantly reveals the 'failure' of identity. Because there is no continuity
of psychic life, so there is no stability of sexual identity, no position for women
(or men) which is ever simply achieved."[4]

This instability of identity entails also a basic instability in our relationship
to the world. Ideology is a response to that instability. From our earliest
moments, ideological discourse prepares us for the social roles we are likely
either to inhabit or to *desire* to inhabit. Before we have even encountered them
we learn to recognize them as plausible repositories of our consciousness and
action. But our lives are full of contradiction, pain, and self-abasement, some
(though not all) of which is *unnecessary*—is "surplus repression," in Marcuse's
phrase.[5] If we suspected this to be true of such basic roles as wage worker,
professional, employer, housewife, father, mother, we might not be able to
commit ourselves to them with our full being. Ideological discourse, if it is to
be successful, must keep this suspicion from crossing our minds too often;
must hide from us potentially unsettling recognition of the fault lines in our
own, socially inscribed identities.[6]

Visual culture is just one of the ideological apparatuses that convey the
positive message and obliterate the negative one, but it is one of the most
important: aside perhaps from our familial interactions (which often "work"
a lot less well than cinema and television do), it is the most credible. The
genius of ideological discourse (unlike the didacticism of propaganda) is to
conceal opposition, to paper over the gap between it and affirmation. We
might say, epigramatically, that propaganda is always recognizable by its presence, whereas ideology is discoverable primarily by its absence. When ideological discourse "works," it does so by the apparent lack of any effort to promote
it, by seeming to be just a believable story about real people and their lives.
Visual culture is thus an ideal material for ideology to work with, for in
successful visual culture we meet "real people," in the process Althusser calls
"interpellation." The viewer is interpellated ("hailed," as, quintessentially, by a
policeman when walking down a street) as a *subject,* as the bearer of a familiar
social role, or rather one that has become familiar over time through the
operation of ideological apparatuses that confirm the real conditions of existence.[7] Whatever social roles are eventually to receive us, visual culture is
capable of presenting these roles as *natural,* and also of confirming us as
passive subjects rather than social actors when confronting those conditions.
And it does this without lecturing, browbeating, or disciplining us.[8]

The kind of visual cultural commodity that performs this social role most
insistently is that produced by the complex system to which we commonly
give the name "Hollywood." In the sense in which I use it here, "Hollywood"

denotes a style even more than it designates a location. This style, manifestly aesthetic but underneath resolutely ideological, is now instantly recognizable anywhere in the world, and can be produced by film industries thousands of miles from the United States.

The primary characteristic of the Hollywood style is that the commodities of dominant visual culture appear before us as objective evidences of the world, rather than as subjectively authored interpretations of it. As such they are also incredibly expensive in comparison with the products of ordinary visual culture, due to the immense and complicated effort required to create an invented replica of the human world so persuasively "real" that it looks as though it's simply been filmed in passing. In this way, the creators of Hollywood's commodities are necessarily entangled with owners and managers of financial and commercial capital. Both the style and the institutional position mesh with the intention of ideological discourse generally, which is to present social institutions as natural and normal, without it seeming to be the case that anyone outside ourselves is actually engaged in making the presentation: exactly what Hollywood at its best accomplishes. At the same time, the Hollywood style is in a sense not recognizable at all to most people, as the intention of the makers of dominant visual culture is to create a style defined by being the lack of a style; that is, by not calling attention, in any way whatsoever, to its origins in idiosyncratically individual acts of creation.

This apparent objectivity is the effect that "Hollywood" aims at, and the other primary characteristics of the Hollywood style flow logically from this one. They are, first, dedication to a commonsense version of realism in the depiction of the social world; second, a humanistic psychology that assumes the comprehensibility of motivation; third, a linear historical determinism according to which precedent conditions are always the cause of apparently related subsequent conditions; fourth, a moral idealism, equally committed to determinism and comprehensibility, which presumes that all social contradictions can be resolved, thus excluding tragic and ironic accounts of human action; and finally, a naturalistic mode of acting that by virtue of its insistence on being imitative of "real" behavior manages to convey all of these assumptions without critical question or comment.[9] To paraphrase Annette Kuhn, this is the ideology of the visible as evidence of the truth.[10] Politically, Hollywood is far from monolithic, and fragments (usually no more than that) of a counterhegemonic worldview are often visible in its productions. Rarely if at all, though, do any of those productions escape from the confines of Hollywood style as summarized here; thus any profound social critique is unavailable to them.[11]

What I am calling "realism" is not just a matter of narrative style. In

Hollywood the term encompasses much more basic decisions about representation that might better be called not "realistic" but literal-minded. There is no *artistic* reason, for example, why males should be played by men, females by women, superficial racial labels made into social identities. To say that that is the way life "really" is merely begs the question. Imagination, difference, and contingency, are not aesthetic but social categories.[12] The visual culture of Hollywood suppresses all of these.

Another way of understanding all these stylistic decisions taken together is that they result in the effacement of all traces of authorship from the stories constructed out of the raw materials of their creation. To be sure, cinema and television are strikingly different in this aspect as in many others. Throughout this book, I shall regularly be adverting to their difference, but almost as regularly explicating their origins in a common source. So in this case, films (conventional films) erase their authorship by presenting narratives of apparently seamless construction projected from an unseen point behind the viewer, whose own dreamlike imagination then functions as the source of whatever is visible on the screen (which is also the impersonal location from which all sound seems to emanate).[13] The image seems to have no point of enunciation, no author except ourselves as we vicariously identify with the camera's standpoint, no authoritative viewpoint except that which we come to inhabit in the familiar shot / reverse shot sequence: the meaning of the look—our look—confirmed by the reaction of the person who has been looked at.

Dominant television, though often making similar use of the shot / reverse shot strategy, quite differently confronts viewers with a myriad of constantly shifting viewpoints, none of them obviously possessing exclusive authority, all of them regularly interrupted by commercials.[14] Here, authorship is hidden not by erasure but by confusion and multiplicity.[15] Even more, television's relentless domesticity—which in sitcoms, soap operas, and family melodramas renders the site of narrative action indistinguishable from the viewing site that audiences inhabit as they watch it—further conceals any traces of authorship or artistry that might work to defamiliarize visual pleasure.[16]

In either event, though, the result—the naturalization and normalization of someone else's vision of daily life—is usually the same. Indeed, to recognize this outcome of the Hollywood style, especially insofar as it determines the presentation of masculinity and femininity, it is probably necessary to immerse oneself in those cultural products from around the world that refuse its embrace most ostentatiously: films such as *Shadows, Chimes at Midnight, Celine and Julie Go Boating, Les Carabinieres, Aguirre: Wrath of God, Jeanne*

Deilman: 23 Rue Scribe, Lancelot du Lac, Salvatore Giuliano, Variety, The Man Who Envied Women, Occasional Work of a Female Slave, Joan of Arc of Mongolia, The Bitter Tears of Petra Von Kant, Four Adventures of Reinette and Mirabelle, Ordet, Daughters of the Dust; or television programs such as *Pennies from Heaven, The Singing Detective, Berlin Alexanderplatz,* or *Heimat.* Only in its visible absence can it easily be seen.

A few examples may make this distinction clear. In Hollywood's version of the gender wars, Mary Wollstonecraft's and John Stuart Mill's vindication of the formal legal equality of women is never seriously in question, although (see Chapter 4) that does not prevent Hollywood productions from recuperating the centrality of "the family" one way or another.[17] What, by comparison, is "said" about the same subject in the French/Vietnamese film *The Scent of Green Papaya?* In it, a woman spends her entire life in domestic servitude of one kind or another, while living amid surroundings of great beauty and peace. At the end we see her sitting under the seemingly benevolent eye of a statue of the Buddha, apparently at one with herself and the world. An apologia for the submission of women: except that at this very final moment of the film, and for the first time in its decades-long sweep, we hear on the soundtrack the passing of jet planes and the sound of distant gunfire. Is it then instead an ironic commentary on her beatific acceptance of life, perhaps? Or do I just want to believe that because of my own views about equality and the Vietnamese War? Those questions are unanswerable, but it is quite possible to imagine alternative endings that would leave us in no doubt. For example, suppose the film ended not with guns and planes but rather tranquil music on the soundtrack? Or the woman's image dissolved to one of her husband making love to another woman? These would be clear signifiers of ideological resolution or counterideological critique, respectively. To have omitted them and their like is not necessarily to have made a better film, but it is to have made one that distinctly and distinctively refuses ideological closure, and is in that sense a very "un-Hollywood" film.

In contrast, to see how consistent Hollywood style can be, even in the service of counterideology, one can do no better than to compare Jane Campion's first full-length feature film, *Sweetie,* which was made in New Zealand on a low budget, with her first expensive "Hollywood" film, *The Piano;* or George Sluizer's Dutch film *The Vanishing* with his Hollywood version of the same story. In making these contrasts we begin to see how a dominant ideology can be reproduced without anyone's making an apparent attempt to reproduce it.

The Piano is a clearly feminist film with a "strong" heroine who struggles against and survives the full weight of gender oppression. It is also almost painterly in its invocations of the surreal beauty of a dreamscape, and again quite atypical in this respect. Underneath, however, *The Piano* is a traditional Hollywood film, complete with a tremendously attractive star; a White Knight who comes to her rescue; a Black Knight of horror-story dimensions; and inscrutable natives who stand in for a mysterious but finally humanized "nature." The protagonist herself demands nothing but bourgeois equality; that is, the right to be recognized as an individual with rights. Therefore in 1993 an audience can anachronistically identify with her, secure in its feelings of moral rightness; and secure also in the knowledge that nowadays talented women (such as themselves) are unlikely to be forcibly prohibited from pursuing their talents merely because of their womanhood.[18]

Sweetie delivers no such easy identification. Torn between a manipulative protagonist and her grossly obese, dysfunctional sister (the eponymous Sweetie), our attention can never find a secure, emotionally satisfying focus. We are quickly reminded that, in Susie Orbach's words, "fat is a feminist issue." But in what way exactly? In Sweetie's case, the answer is certainly unclear.[19] All in all, the family these sisters inhabit is a nightmare of bad faith and disarray that looks utterly irredeemable. Where the oppression *The Piano* visits on its protagonist seems to cry out for remedial legislation about the marital rights of women, the oppressiveness of Sweetie's milieu does not seem amenable to any benign rearrangement of social institutions or redefinition of "the family."

This is not to say that *Sweetie* is apolitical, or that it supports a position of skepticism about the utility of feminist reform or revolution because of the tragedy of individual lives. A viewer who sets out to watch both films from, say, a socialist feminist position might well, as I do, find *Sweetie* more politically urgent than *The Piano*. It is quite possible to argue, with Trotsky, that the historic task of socialism (feminism) is to raise the lives of men and women from the level of a fate to the level of a tragedy. If that is so, then the tragedy or general messiness of individual lives may remind us that at least we should try to remove the *additional* oppression that malignant fate (in the form of the avoidable poverty, inequality, and so forth, which are visible in the film) visits upon them. It is not, however, possible to relate this reminder to any particular stance taken by the characters within the film, or suggested by the terms of its closure. In this, *Sweetie*, unlike *The Piano*, forestalls ideological recognition, and leaves us to think our own political thoughts.

The two versions of *The Vanishing* provide an even more striking contrast. In the Dutch original, as the male protagonist attempts to track down his vanished woman friend, who may have been kidnapped and murdered, we the viewers become progressively more uneasy and disoriented because it is not at all clear whether he's a "good" man or not. Worse, she may not even have been a "good" woman, and the killer, as we eventually discover, is not obviously coded as a worse man than the boyfriend. He does not, in S. J. Perelman's famous words, enter wearing a black hat, and then dismount from a stage-coach and kick the nearest dog. Whom are we rooting for? *What* are we rooting for? If this were *Sleeping with the Enemy* we'd know where we're at. We don't want Julia Roberts's family reunited, because it's an antifamily, and we'd rather have no family at all than a family built around domestic violence. We want the ideology of the family united with an American individualist ideol-ogy to which women (if they're as attractive as Julia Roberts) have finally been admitted. But in *The Vanishing* we've no idea where we're at and the dénouement, perhaps the most horrific to be found in any movie ever pro-duced, is all the more unbearable because we've never known what to expect or where we were heading. Here the absence of ideology is the absence of meaning as well, and all the harder to bear because of that. *The Vanishing* is a horror story, but quite unlike Hollywood horror stories. It is not about terrors of sexual identity, or good-looking women being stalked by a monster. There are no monsters in it, only ordinary people, and the fundamental decency of ordinary people is *not* recuperated. Its absence of meaning, its true horror, is nihilism, the absence of meaning for everyone regardless of race, creed, or gender.

In the Hollywood version, by contrast, we are immediately drawn into the villain's viewpoint, which is so clearly villainous that it will therefore continue to be so no matter how much he is presented as a loving father, and so forth. The film eventually turns into a familiar version of the chase, in which—for this is contemporary Hollywood—our clueless but fundamentally good "hero" has to be rescued from a horrible death by an intrepid, resourceful, and unappreciated woman. She is the misunderstood hero in his (her) new, universal (white) guise, especially recognizable in an American context be-cause she is clearly presented to us as "nothing but" a waitress. That is, her social-class membership is clearly "lower" than that of our middle-class hero, and her appearance as a morally superior knight in slightly tarnished but shining armor confirms the peculiarly American version of class transcen-dence as inverse snobbery: Who needs equality since lower is better anyhow?[20] But just when we're in danger of forgetting where we're really at, ideology comes to the rescue (and unintentional comedy replaces the real terror of the original). Our female hero, who to this point has outthought and outfought the villain at every turn, conveniently turns her back on him so that finally the real "man," who seconds ago was on the verge of terminal suffocation, can rise from his grave and save her from strangulation with—at last—his fifteen seconds of heroism. Although we can never securely infer how an audience is receiving an intended ideological message, surely anyone who has failed to receive *this* message is culturally impaired.

The original version deprives us of a hero, and the price of this is that we are also deprived of a heroine. But we can't help asking as we slink from the theater, Is heroism what we should be looking for in the first place? *The Vanishing,* that is, doesn't offer a moral critique of its characters, as ideological films always do (see Chapter 3). It offers a critique of conventional *moviemaking* as a way of understanding the truth about the world. Although these three non-Hollywood movies in fact do not (as contrasted with some of those in the earlier list) have clearly identifiable authors recognizable as some other person outside our own dreams, they still evade the normative outcome of the Hollywood style. Making us look at what is crooked instead of straight, apparently alien instead of superficially familiar, indecipherable instead of ostensibly clarifying, they forestall any desire we might have to read them as objective evidences of the world.

In contrast, the Hollywood style, which calls up processes of identification in the case of film, and of recognition in the case of television, is identical with ideological discourse. In the attempt to engage our moral sympathies in a "realistic" narrative, fictional or nonfictional, about the (re)constitution of community, and about what is "natural" and "normal" within that community, the works of creative consciousness that make up the field of visual culture are saturated in ideology. Within the unique historic settlement we call "America," the need (of those with power) to uphold the dominance of the dominant ideology, determines not only the source of whatever problem is to be resolved and the social ambience that is taken for granted, but even what comes to be considered an "accessible" narrative style. Most generally, the primary enterprise of modern (but not modernistic!) storytelling, with its realistic social and psychological surfaces, linear narratives, sympathetic protagonists, and emotionally satisfying endings, is implicitly ideological by virtue of its structure alone, without regard to the necessary ambiguities of any particular narrative content.

The notion that human life makes sense, that social forces are comprehensible, and that "happy" endings are normal, conveys a secular version of the sentiment that "God's in His Heaven / All's right with the world." Marx's description in *Capital* of the mystification of the process by which labor creates surplus value, gives an almost identical picture of the way in which an illusory image of a harmonious labor process is substituted for a hidden reality of exploitation.[21] We, as cultural consumers, are interpellated as "citizens" of (subjects in) this harmonious world. It is a world both capitalist and patriarchal; it is also a racially constituted world. As men and women, we are reassured that we are bound together by a fundamental sympathy recognized in the institution of marriage and the family. As citizens of diverse social backgrounds, we are told in every possible way that only "whiteness" gives access to the highest level of rewards. And as economic subjects, we not only find that our cultural milieu is structured so as to reward passive consumption, but we are also assured that there is ultimately nothing to be active about.[22]

Furthermore—and this is crucial—all this happens, so to speak, behind our backs. Ideological narratives (or narrative fragments, or stereotypes) treat the imaginary world of social harmony as though it really were the natural and normal world, without acknowledging their own function of defining what is "normal" and "natural" within that world. Sophisticated viewers (a term that has no connotations of education or "culture," but merely of a general skepticism in the face of other people's stories) are aware that this is happening, but still will get so caught up in a skillfully told story that at least for the moment they will forget that someone else is defining their world for them.

To be sure, film and television again pursue interpellation in quite different ways. To paraphrase one of Althusser's comments about ideology: we do not speak the film; the film speaks us. And we do not even know we have been spoken. Television does not seem to emanate from within ourselves, but is simply the "real" upon which we are eavesdropping. It is just there being life. And even though we know that life is not a sitcom or soap opera or police drama, even while we may laugh at their silliness, they still seem to be about American people leading American lives. This is even truer of such science fictions as Star Trek, in which the protagonists' attitudes are not only not futuristic, but are usually (as in their uninflected liberal pluralist humanism) about twenty years out of date in the here and now: "Tomorrow's stories, yesterday's headlines." Better, television at its most effective is not even about American people leading American lives, it just is American people leading American lives. On sitcoms especially, the lead characters often play themselves—Roseanne, Brett Butler as Grace, Carol Burnett, John Laroquette, Mary Tyler Moore—and mug the camera whenever they deliver a particularly funny line. Roseanne in particular, or perhaps Roseanne in particular, "reads" her diegetic character, or herself, in the light of the exegetical autobiography with which she and *TV Guide* regularly regale us. So the unalloyed naturalism of television interpellates us as inhabitants of the same world it is bringing into our living room.[23] Watching films, contrarily, we seem to be inhabitants of a world created by ourselves.

In either case, what kind of inhabitants? Into what social roles are we interpellated by these cultural commodities? Above all, we are interpellated as consumers of culture rather than as its potential creators. Commercial television makes the connection literally. The viewer is there to watch and then to buy, and nothing—a point to which I shall return—is to be allowed to obstruct that linkage. Movies are much different; they are works of art, not advertisements. It is perhaps stretching a point to compare the average products of dominant cinema with the classic literary works analyzed by Terry Eagleton, but "the ideology of the aesthetic" is, in cruder form, dominant cinema's primary structural determinant.[24]

It follows that we are interpellated as passive social spectators rather than social actors. Movies that are the products of dominant cinema, and television, do not demand that we engage in action.[25] They encourage us to enjoy, to take pleasure in, even the most horrific of socially realistic narratives: and to watch more movies and more television. Again, they accomplish this in quite different ways. Television's ideology is that of distraction rather than of the aesthetic, but though the "couch potato" may seem more a figure of fun than does the movie nut, the social results of the two preoccupations aren't all that different. In the midst of a bitter divorce we can enjoy a weekly narrative of family unity.

In this light all of Hollywood's cultural productions may be viewed as a single metatext (or two metatexts, since television has a different systemic form). For those millions of us who've grown up with no other visual culture, the effect of this metatext is so powerful that even its occasional deviations merely remind us of the "big picture" that they are deviating from. However, we have to remember that just as telling a story is only one possible way of entertaining us, there are also many possible ways of telling a story. In fact, not every linear narrative is linear in the same way, nor, to invert Tolstoy, is every happy ending happy in the same way.

The metatext, then, is not merely a series of artifacts to be passively consumed; it is more complex. On the one hand, it is a system for accustoming us, to the point that we become compulsively familiar with it, to a *single* way, out of all the possible ways, of telling a story. However, all stories are not the same story. If they were, people would read them or watch them at random. And all stories do not render us passive consumers to the same extent, or in the same way. We must go on to ask, What are the recurring features of the ideological worldview of modern patriarchalist capitalism, as practiced specifically in the United States (the source of most of the available feature films ever produced, as well as the most widely watched television programs)?[26] What enables this worldview to represent a familiar, recognizable moral universe, inhabited by individuals whose lives for the most part can be lived happily without recourse to destabilizing political interventions?

First, the distinction between modern capitalism and earlier social orders is that in the former the relationship between people (both male and female) and society is more problematic, or at least is conceived of as being more problematic. Ideological reproduction—the reproduction of that way of thinking which leads us to believe that it is *right*, not merely necessary, to go to work, or to stay home and care for the children; or to obey the law out of a sense of duty rather than of fear—is therefore uniquely important in modern capitalist societies. However, at the same time it has built-in limits.

The most crucial of these is that the heroic entrepreneur, "a man alone," whose entire way of life is an affront to the normal conventions of social behavior and moral decency, must be praised and encouraged. He is after all the man who, mythically at least, makes capitalism work. And yet there is an obvious price to be paid for letting him go his own untrammeled way, or treating his behavior as wholly acceptable. Not only the commodities of visual culture but an astonishing proportion of modern American cultural productions of all kinds (Abstract Expressionism in painting, for example) begin with a recognition of that essential conflict at their core.

Capitalism itself is hardly ever directly eulogized in mainstream visual culture. There are few narratives about the beneficent effects of private ownership of the means of production; the benevolence of the wealthy; and upward social mobility through hard work. At first glance this seems strange. If the United States is a capitalist society, and if "the ideas of the ruling class are in every epoch the ruling ideas," then why do not the dominant cultural institutions of this nation produce glorifications of the ideas, and practices, of capitalism and capitalists? Why does the heroic entrepeneur appear metaphorically as the asocial individual but only rarely as an actual businessman? Why are there so many cinematic stories in which the beneficiary of upward mobility actually benefits from a lucky break in the Horatio Alger tradition (*Breaking Away, Flashdance*), but hardly any true paeans to the unambiguous benefits of toil in cinema (or on television). Why are there so few unalloyed celebrations of the corporate and industrial milieu, except in the academy and in the press?

Probably the most important reason for this strange absence of the businessman-hero is that success stories without conflict make boring stories, and conflict plays an uneasy, not to say dangerous role in the world of capitalist mythmaking. Narrative conflict usually requires an antagonist, or hostile force, or even enemy. But who now is that to be? It cannot be other social groups or classes because then an unpleasant truth about capitalist political economy—that it is *not* a world of harmony, common interests, and benevolence—would begin to be revealed, and potential audience segments might be alienated. Labor unions are a natural antagonist of capitalists, after all, but there are more organized workers than there are capitalists: they watch more TV and go to more movies. Generally speaking, if labor unions are to be vilified that can only be safely done by showing them as the enemy of workers themselves, not of capitalists (e.g., *Blue Collar, Hoffa*). If there is to be an enemy of the system, that enemy must be safely alien: heretofore, Communism as the disparaged alternative *(Moscow on the Hudson, Streets of Gold, Ninotchka)*. But these are inevitably stories that legitimize the *nation*—the United States *as* a capitalist society—more than they directly legitimize capitalism as a wonderful social system that just happens to be located in the United States. We are led to focus on communal institutions within which the world that capitalism has created can be validated, without the questionable claims of capitalism (including the real, but infrequent, existence of upward mobility through hard work) themselves being too directly, unbelievably, and dangerously asserted. Indeed, the only genre in which the skill-intensive production of commodities is regularly exalted is the contemporary adventure movie (as *Top Gun*, or any of the films of James Cameron), with its relentlessly boyish enthusiasm for high-tech weapons of mass destruction.

This is not to say that capitalism is not central to American visual culture. Quite the contrary: among all capitalist nations the United States is the most oriented to the subordination of other values to consumerism and its pleasures, rather than the virtues of social hierarchy, and it is through the loving depiction of consumer products that its ideological case is made. Proponents, say, of nuclear power should not be upset by the absence of feature films or television dramas responding to *The China Syndrome* or other anti-nuclear power films. In a fictional narrative, lectures about acceptable risk factors or the proportion of the nation's power grid drawn from nuclear energy plants would drive even the most devoted proponents of nuclear power to the nearest exit (as happens to many of *Moby Dick*'s would-be readers, for example, after a few of Melville's lectures on whaling). It is the devotion to and dependence on the American standard of living implicit in every Hollywood production that makes whatever such case there is to be made. The surface of virtually every American film is lush and dreamlike even when the life of down-and-outs is its ostensible subject matter; thus we can never really accept a Hollywood film as having come to grips with material deprivation of any kind. Just when we think we are being treated to a hard-hitting exposé of the lower depths we must be most aware of this powerful variant of the ideological illusion. As for television, its life and its ethos are relentlessly middle-class, so that (race very occasionally aside) no social problem can ever be seen as totally unsolvable, no persons (e.g., gays) totally unassimilable, and no lives lived as the waking nightmares that so many American lives are.[27]

The social conflicts specific to patriarchalist capitalism as a social order are therefore to be repressed; they return in other forms. But visual narratives rarely proceed in a straight line to an explicit ideological point; if that's what we wanted we could read an essay. Therefore, dramatic (even comic) fictions usually describe an uncertain and suspenseful trajectory.

Once, the individualism/community conflict was the most common example of this trajectory, at least in cinema (not nearly so much in episodic television, which perforce takes a different view of the passage of time). The predominant convention was played out as a movement from individualistic rebellion or withdrawal, to the protagonist's eventual reconciliation with (and defense of) the social order, the family, and so forth.[28] Works that were ideologically conventional thus invariably ended in a paradox. This paradox is brilliantly concealed in what we come to think of as "good" or "artistic" or "sophisticated" films. (*Casablanca* is by now Hollywood's most treasured example of this paradox at work). However, it is also embarrassingly revealed in what are then called "bad movies": movies that, for example, have endings that seem randomly tacked on in order to resolve a mess that no one associated with the production ever understood in the first place. The paradox lay in the implication that autonomous individuals can exist within a social framework without surrendering their individuality, *either* to that social framework *or* to collectivist rebellions against it. Deflecting our attention from the paradox by depicting a believable resolution to a conflict that might otherwise plausibly be seen as irresolvable, was (and still is) the underlying intention of all concrete ideological production. This is the context in which Boy Meets Girl, Buddy Loses Buddy, Parent Regains Child, and so forth. Our very deep cultural attachment to the whole notion of *individual will* and the rightfulness of its self-realization (a notion that, as Hegel points out, hardly existed through most of human history) ensures the existence of conflict.

In the contemporary era, however, repressed conflicts tend to return in a different form. Most prominently (in particular as racial conflict tends to be most visible in its comparative absence from the screen or the set), they return in the form of solvable dilemmas of sexual intimacy. The successful businessman and his reward of profit is displaced by the heroic white, male, individual actor whose reward is a beautiful woman. Today, the integration of the rebellious hero has been superseded by the theme of the transformation of independent women into dependent members of a heterosexual dyad (as Melanie Griffith in *Something Wild*, Jane Fonda in *The Morning After*, or Meryl Streep in *The River Wild*) a theme that is, inter alia, also much more amenable to the constraints of television's domesticity.

Within this framework, familiar social cleavages that threaten social integrity, such as cleavages of gender, class, and race, constitute the thematic material out of which a narrative will produce the anxiety of initial disharmony and the satisfaction of ultimate reconciliation. Specifically, ideological discourse in visual culture produces stories about three versions of alleged social harmony: (1) The Family, that is, the integrity and necessity of conventional (heterosexual, monogamous) domestic life; (2) The Community, or threats to "law and order" by its domestic enemies; by aberrant social injustices that are eventually overcome so that the general interest in maintaining law and order can be restored; or by conflicts of race, class, or ethnicity that turn out to be only apparent; (3) The Nation: war or civil strife (especially the Civil War), and alien enemies. The primary (not the sole) ideological element in the content of cultural commodities is best conceived of as the attempt, in the face of individualist (very rarely socialist) doubts, to make the *family*, the *community*, and the *nation*, seem natural and normal. Family, community, and nation are seen as the core components of an imaginary social whole, within which the autonomous individual can find both independence and mutual dependence.

Of course, film and television narratives do not necessarily point our way to what they are doing. Very often instead, genre films or television episodes that seem to have no strong ideological content contain what we might call ideological inserts: religious services at the death of a minor character (there are no nonreligious funerals in Hollywood, and hardly any secular weddings since the days of screwball comedy); reverential funeral services for dead policemen; the nerdy boy-next-door on sitcoms, who helps us delineate the character of "real men"; casual references to "carpetbaggers" in Westerns from Hollywood's classical period (there are also no decent Reconstruction politicians); nationalistic racial stereotypes ("Arab" terrorists); bad endings for sexually aggressive women (who lose their heads in horror movies, but in melodramas or comedies only lose out in the heterosexual sweepstakes), and so on. In some genres, monsters and mutants may be introduced, or aliens from otherwise, but the humans we see are as recognizable and stereotypical as apple pie. This normalizing, naturalizing impulse in dominant culture is so unquestioned that in the movie *Aliens* the Chicana intergalactic marine Vasquez is made to suffer jokes about "illegal aliens." An arbitrary political boundary that will probably be effectively nonexistent within fifty years is projected hundreds of years into the future by a bad pun. So the ideology of family, community, and nation is casually, but not trivially, reaffirmed in the midst of what otherwise seem to be quite unideological genre narratives.

But both thematically and iconographically, "family" and its eventual recuperation forms the resolute core of this worldview. It is the Family that is the heterosexual dyad, that stands at the heart of this ideological discourse. Within the bonds of familial heterosexuality, ambiguities of individual and community, national loyalty and intimate loyalties, are meant to be reconciled. In the aftermath of the women's liberation movement, with all the strains it put upon the very ideal of that reconciliation, the politics of sex and gender has become central to visual culture. In most American cultural production, and especially in mainstream visual culture (for it is the most industrialized of all the cultural arenas), the idea of the sexually hierarchical family as a necessary moral unity, under strain, under attack, even in serious question, but finally reaffirmed, stands out as the central theme. In movies as diverse as *Aliens, Little Man Tate*, and *Lorenzo's Oil*, Hollywood cinema (and television even more so) regularly attests that happiness, or even survival, can only be found within some version of the family and normalized sexuality—just when we were beginning to think that such a resolution will be impossible.

As I've already suggested, this aspect of the social order is never really separable from the other elements of a class/race/sex/gender system. For example, the frequent evasion of racial confrontations where we might ordinarily expect them, highlights otherwise concealed truths about the cultural meanings of sex and gender. What are we to make, for instance, of the snowblinding whiteness of Woody Allen's vision of New York City (e.g., in *Annie Hall, Manhattan, Hannah and Her Sisters, Bullets over Broadway, Manhattan Murder Mystery, Broadway Danny Rose, Crimes and Misdemeanors*)? Since these are essentially romances, it's difficult to avoid the conclusion that this absence has the same meaning as does the nonexistence of interracial families on television or in cinema generally; the disappearance of all but high-status minorities from soap operas; or the lily-whiteness of such ensemble sitcoms as *Friends* or *Seinfeld*. In its palpable longing that "the Other" will just go away, and in its revelation of a white racial consciousness inseparable from our notions of love, heroism, and public life, this absence embodies the most basic material meanings of our social order in its very lack of embodiedness.

In this way, as we shall see in discussing such genres as female action films or rape-revenge films, or the particular ways in which the social order is recuperated from incipient criticism in mainstream Hollywood productions, issues of gender are illuminated by the manner in which race and class are addressed or ignored while depicting them, and vice versa. At the same time, confrontations over sex and gender are also recognizable as the core of an ideological constellation in their own right (the same version of the sex wars, for example, appears in sitcoms written by African Americans for African American audiences as in those written by white scriptwriters for white audiences). It is this constellation that is the subject of the detailed discussion of visual culture which follows in the rest of the book.

Two final contrasts will make this centrality of the family and sexuality clear. The mise-en-scène and narrative of English films, soap operas, and so forth, invariably emphasize class differences above all others (although liberal feminist notions of the centrality of gender discrimination have begun to make inroads, as in the British *Prime Suspect* series). Furthermore, English films about "law and order," whether celebratory of class rule or critical of class oppression, never raise the possibility, as does a long and noteworthy tradition of Hollywood movies, that legitimately organized law enforcement might actually be dispensable. There are few or no "outlaw heroes" in English cinema; the figure of the outlaw hero requires for its historical significance an assumption of "classlessness" that most English people would find extraordinarily presumptuous.

In comparison to English films French films, at first glance, seem to be overwhelmingly about sexual tension and disorder. However, they are not thereby more "American." In fact, because the French do not have so strong a tradition of liberal individualism as do Americans, French movies are rarely so edgily combative about ordinary sexual relationships as is almost any American film, even one made before the period of contemporary feminism (think of Hepburn/Tracy, or any movie with Cary Grant or Barbara Stanwyck or Judy Holliday). Female jealousy of male philandering is a staple of French movies; the derogation of men as a gender composed of childlike, clueless, macho, self-satisfied chauvinists, is only occasionally to be found in them. It is not too much of an exaggeration to say that whereas in French films political confrontations almost always have a sexual undertone (see, for example, *The May Fools*), in Hollywood films sexual confrontations are invariably politicized. In this politicized form they appear with astonishing frequency. But it is the absences and evasions that follow on their appearance which tell us the most about the cultural politics of the gender wars.

2 Erasures

Ideology represents, variously, a reflection of, accommodation to, or justification of, the way our material lives are organized, by us or for us. Ideological themes, emphases, and biases are not plucked out of thin air, and are not arbitrary or isolated. Any concrete discussion of gender and ideology in visual culture, therefore, has to begin in an understanding of the political economy of visual culture.

The most fundamental way in which Hollywood conveys the ideology of a harmonious community precedes any narrative messages that visual culture more or less delivers. Rather, a potentially divided audience is sutured together, like films themselves, by a twofold effacement: first, of the industrial means of production of cultural commodities; and, second, of, more specifically, women's role within that industry.

The basic effacement or erasure of the means of production takes place both within, and without, cinematic and televisual texts. Within the text (diegetically) labor—that is, its conditions and especially its conflicts—simply does not appear. Although "equality of opportunity" is endorsed by everyone in a general way, the irreducible and palpable fact is that the capitalist mode of production—even the "postindustrial" mode of production—requires relatively few bosses and very many, many workers. If all the latter were really to become bosses, or independent professionals, the entire raison d'être of capitalism would disappear. The single incentive that distributes work effort among the successful members of a capitalist society is the incentive to be at the top of a hierarchy of power and wealth. Take away that incentive and some other, presumably utopian ethical incentive, would have to be found to induce such people to take responsibility for organizing productive activities. "Everyone knows" that class hierarchy and its necessary outcome, class conflict, are really inevitable and indispensable in such a society. Everyone knows this, but most of us deny that knowledge most of the time: more than on anything else, ideology depends on the denial of this knowledge. Just as my divided consciousness as a meat-eating sentimentalist erases knowledge of slaughterhouses at mealtimes, so my divided consciousness as a privileged consumer in a capitalist society that I think unjust, erases knowledge of Phillipine (or Californian) sweatshops as I put on my shirt in the morning.

The different ideological apparatuses—schools, churches, newspapers, political parties, and representative bodies—make their distinctive contributions to the organization of these essential acts of erasure. Hollywood is among the most important of these. As a collectivity we probably spend more time consuming infotainment (as Benjamin Barber calls it) from Hollywood than from anywhere else—but never for more than a few minutes at a time.[1] It is mostly only for purposes of establishing plot or ambience (e.g., *Dirty Dancing, Breaking Away*), that Hollywood shows us means of production in operation. Even less, except on very rare occasions (*Norma Rae, Blue Collar, Matewan,* a few episodes of *Roseanne* in its early years), does it show us the *social relations of production* that give life to the interaction of people with machines, or each other (except occasionally at the level of interaction among professionals). One would never know how much the protagonists of our cultural narratives depend on the work of others; just as protagonists never go to the toilet, they never have to arrange the conditions under which their social activities take place. This is as true of "progressive" movies or television shows as of more conventional ones, and as true of the new feminist genres as of the old masculinist ones. So *Rollover*, a film in which Jane Fonda more or less single-handedly takes on the forces of global capitalism, begins with a shot of an office cleaning woman who then disappears from our view never to be seen again, while Fonda's acts of female agency go on without her.[2]

In Hollywood, the actual goods we live on and through get produced, distributed, and consumed without visible labor on anyone's part, like manna from heaven. The people who consume those goods are never shown as being in any relation at all to the people who produce them—not even, save an occasional episode of *Roseanne* or *Grace under Fire*, the relation of knowledge that there *are* such people. "There," Marx wrote in a chapter of *Capital* entitled "The Fetishism of Commodities and the Secret Thereof," "a real relationship among people appears as a mysterious relationship among things."[3] He was writing about classical economic science (or ideology), but describing Hollywood fictions even better.

It is not only labor that disappears from the metatext. So too does any hint of class conflict between capital and labor. Class itself does not disappear. Working-class men (there are few working-class women in Hollywood's text, other than housewives) appear from time to time, on beer ads and in police stations and in minor roles, instantly recognizable by their ethnic accents and their beer bellies. For the most part, though, Hollywood is relentlessly middle-class or more than that, establishing no values that can't be subordinated to consumerism and its pleasures. Especially on television but in cinema too, no one is ever really shown working, and television land is inundated with teenagers driving fancy cars who never seem to have to worry about money. Although Hollywood occasionally lets us see the wolf at the door, he always goes away in the end.

As for class conflict, it appears occasionally, but then only in sublimated form as *ressentiment*, or status envy, expressed not so much in overt declarations as in narratives and iconographic tone as a whole. One of the mainstays of the American ideology of community is inverse class snobbery, an almost vulgar-Marxist notion that hard-working people are somehow more morally upright, more reliable in a tight corner, than rootless urban sophisticates with money and professional careers. What the metatext tells us over time, from *Born Yesterday* through *The Beverly Hillbillies*, the television series *Love and War* or the movie *Dumb and Dumber*, is that lower is better, is authentic.[4] Diegetically, what stands for "higher" class in the critical sense is not so much possessions or power as it is intellect. Scientists are dangerously Promethean (as in any science-fiction movie of the 1950s); professors are jokes; lawyers are brilliant actors in the courtroom but are never shown being analytical; conspirators against the world in adventure movies are always more intellectual than anyone else around. If a character with an educated accent admires classical music or high art in your presence, hold on to your wallet. Typically, the capitalist villain of Michael Crichton's novel, *Jurassic Park,* is motivated by scientific hubris in the movie version. Science itself is accordingly reduced in stature. The novel's most exciting scene is one in which a nerdish girl is redeemed and becomes the book's hero, by virtue of the genius (lovingly detailed) with which she masters a computer program to restore power to the park, while the raptors beat at the door. In the film the raptors are the stars, and her heroism is reduced to a brief mumbo jumbo of key strokes and muttered asides. This refusal to see the excitement of intellectual mastery has nothing to do with what is "cinematic," and everything to do with ideology.

Conversely, lack of educated intelligence equals practical and moral wisdom. The epitome of a long line of films and television shows in this tradition is *Forrest Gump,* which gives us the simpleton as sage. It is typical of *Forrest Gump,* and of the strategies of such films generally, that its hero is made a wealthy man by the outcome of a hurricane, a direct, ideological inversion of the material truth that hurricanes always bring social devastation in their wake, and that the poor (who are their most frequent victims) are invariably made even poorer by them. There is no satire intended here. Forrest is the ultimate commentator on an essentially benign culture in which his view of events and institutions always turns out to have been the correct one, and the view of critical intellectuals badly mistaken. The theme of this movie is borrowed (to put it charitably) from the earlier *Being There,* in which another simpleton becomes adviser to the president by saying nothing or making meaningless pronouncements at the right times. *Being There,* however, satirizes American institutions without always sentimentalizing Americans. Quite to the contrary, *Forrest Gump's* sentimentality is also its communitarian ideology, as is that of the similar *Dave,* another version of inverse snobbery in which the "ordinary" man makes a better president than the real one.[5]

This inverse snobbery—itself completely inauthentic as it is always penned by educated authors—appears in many forms and genres. For women, it is very often the wise-cracking waitress who stands in for virtue and practical wisdom. We meet her in *It Could Happen to You,* in which a policeman leaves his greedy wife for a more charitably inclined waitress with whom he has agreed to split a winning lottery ticket; or *White Palace,* in which Susan Sarandon gives James Spader a crash course in sexual pleasure and ethics as well; the American version of *The Vanishing; Thelma and Louise;* the television series *Laverne and Shirley* and *Cheers,* and the more recent *Strange Luck* or *Mel's Diner.* What is most important about the figure of the waitress (or the similar figure of *The Nanny*) is that, whatever her material difficulties, she is never shown as having the questionable relationship to her own womanhood that is always in the foreground for "professional" women. The pejorative stereotype is translated into Hollywood's version of social reality. And social class disappears, to be replaced by the healing powers of sex.

Above all, however, it is the law and order genre, whether in the form of the police procedural or the courtroom drama, that establishes Hollywood's uneasy amalgam of classlessness and status resentment. On both television and the large screen, the police procedural is central, and not merely because of the way in which it constantly lectures us about soft judges, the victimization of decent people, the inexplicable malevolence of violent criminals, the degeneracy of drug culture, and so on. The most important function of the police story is as a multilevel drama of social integration. The police station is the only place in American society in which men (and women) are shown actually doing blue-collar work.[6] The factory and the construction site are virtually nonexistent; the store exists only to be robbed. (Typical in the absence of real work is the sitcom *Wings*, which takes place in and around an airport, and yet hardly ever shows anyone working—not even the coincidentally beautiful mechanic, who seems to have arrived direct from the modeling studio.) Men working hard (a few surgeons aside) are *police*men. So by the magic of Hollywood's alchemy lead is turned into gold: the police, once seen as enforcers of class conflict, material emblems of social disorder, become miraculously and mysteriously transmuted into the signifiers of a united, universal community. Also, in recent years every station house has a black chief or inspector; every D.A.'s office, a (white) female prosecutor. The dirty little secret of the law as white man's law becomes enshrouded in a cloak of symbolic affirmative action —though with all that we will look long, hard, and unavailingly for any movie or television episode in which "the law" looks even remotely like an emanation of, say, black women. There is still no mistaking where "the law" comes from.

Above all, in film after film (*Someone to Watch Over Me, The Big Easy, Sea of Love, Physical Evidence, Criminal Justice,* the made-for-TV *Revealing Evidence* and *Criminal Behavior,* and the TV series *NYPD Blue*), the classless society is again cemented via sexual exchange, unbelievable in the real world, between male cops and female professionals (usually prosecuting attorneys). Thus not only are class barriers overturned, but what might otherwise seem pretty clearly to be a loss of male occupational privilege is recuperated by, as Stanley Aronowitz puts it, "the status conferred upon masculine sexuality and its powers by society."[7]

Exegetically, the same rule of smoothing out class differences and suppressing class conflict holds to perhaps even more effect. Just as all traces of authorship outside the fantasies of viewers themselves are effaced by Hollywood's production techniques, so too its productions efface all traces of the means of production that have created them. The film and television industry is one of the major employers of wage labor, often exploited wage labor, in the United States. It has a long history of labor disputes, of the bloody and brutal suppression of strikes, of corrupt union-busting campaigns.[8] But all of this too is elided when the credits roll at the end of every film or television program (though much less extensively on television, where time is too expensive to waste on identifying carpenters and key grips). Not only has a finally harmonious community been depicted within the narrative, but the impression we are left with is that this depiction is itself the work of a true community of management (producers, distributors, director, and so forth) and workers, who have come together voluntarily to produce this labor of love, this entertainment, for us to enjoy.

Jane Feuer has described how certain 1940s MGM musicals starring Gene Kelly, the Left populist answer to Fred Astaire, are so constructed that at the end the people, the "little people," come together to produce a play, or a show, or just to celebrate together in acts of spontaneity that suggest the creation of a true popular democracy. We would never know, unless we think very hard about it, how much hierarchy and authoritarian discipline went into the production of that illusion of spontaneity.[9] This is a metaphor for everything that Hollywood does. Here, now to paraphrase Marx, a real social relationship among people appears as a mysterious relationship among works of art. What Laura Mulvey suggests about commodity fetishism in the age of consumerism is especially salient in understanding Hollywood: "the invisibility of the workers' labor is just as essential for the commodity's desirability as the visibility of the artisan's labor is for a craft object."[10] Imagine how movies or television programs would look to us if the final credits came with an exegetical flow chart, the wages, salaries, and point shares of every contributor being attached: how quickly all illusion (and with it, desirability) would disappear.

This double erasure or effacement of the means of production is only the first step in creating this fetishized world of ideological illusions. Another, equally crucial step follows on its heels. Men create dominant visual culture: that's why it's dominant. This condition is true across the board, though it has different, and perhaps profounder, consequences for cinema than for television. Let us consider one simple material fact about cinema. Of the 1,794 feature films released in the ten-year period 1983–92, women had directed only 81, or fewer than 5 percent. Even this figure represents a significant upsurge in women's participation in filmmaking: in the thirty years from 1949 to 1979, women had directed fewer than .2 percent of released feature films.[11] Although there are no comparable statistics for television, an impressionist account developed over many years of watching is that it may be even more sexually exclusive at the directorial level.[12] Women have always had a much greater participation as scriptwriters in Hollywood, especially on television, but still not nearly so great as men's. In any event, the writer is responsible only for what we hear, not how we hear it nor what we are looking at as we listen.

Whatever is being said, in movies at least what is more important is that the voice comes not only from the images on the screen but from the darkened theater itself, joining the light that comes from over our shoulder as a kind of news from nowhere. But that "nowhere" is the spectacle, the images, and these have been chosen by the men who direct and the men who photograph (there are virtually no female cinematographers in the history of film) with the very intention of eliminating the authorial effect, thus making the movie seem an unauthored fantasy from the depths of "our" own psyche. Not all movies are fantasies, and moviemakers may work very hard to make a particular movie seem "realistic." However, commercial moviemakers will hardly ever (perhaps never!) work hard to prevent the very acts of viewer identification that are the historic source of cinema's mass appeal. And because these are constituted not by the recognition of a social situation or a landscape but rather by the recognition of a *person,* they are necessarily inflected by gender and sexuality.

Gender and sexuality in turn are never represented literally (as might be, say, the canyons and monoliths of Monument Valley), but are acted out. Almost always, no matter what else is happening on screen, they are a partially phantasmic projection. When we see players on a screen interacting sexually, we are seeing not just any unreality, but the particular unreality of *men's* sexual fantasies. Again this is not so true on television: sexual fantasy, even sublimated sexual fantasy (the staple of sitcom world), is rarer there, as much more of the intended audience is female. As I've noted, one of television's most popular genres, and the genre most imbued with sexual fantasy—day-time soap opera—is very often created by women; but again, never at the directorial level. However, the communicative core of commercial television is not episodic fiction but advertising, which is saturated through and through with sexual fantasizing: so much so that anyone who turns the sound off during the ads will often not have the faintest idea what variety of product is being advertised by the soundless parade of sexy models across the screen. The vocabulary of these ads—voyeurism, the association of sexual attractiveness with power, the presentation of heterosexuality as a hunt for prey—is primarily a male vocabulary.

All this being so, maintaining the illusion and desirability around which dominant visual culture is centered depends not only on the erasure of all traces of the means of production from the culture's final products, but also on the blotting out of all traces of the equally crucial exploitation of the bodies of women, upon which Hollywood's illusion of glamour depends. The "triple male gaze" is, as Mulvey argues, what produces the "dream factory's" dreams.[13] Without glamour, the voyeuristic appeal of films to men and women both, as well as the mesmerizing quality of much of television, would disappear.[14]

The illusory world of glamour is framed by men and deployed by men, and the hierarchy it naturalizes is the domination of men over women. But the *labor* that creates that world is actually the labor of women, Hollywood women. That labor too, the role of women in reproducing the social means of production, is subject to a double erasure. To begin with, much of the labor that does not appear on screen (see my comment above) is women's labor— the actualities of mothering, cleaning one's own and other people's houses and workplaces, and so forth. There is also an erasure of essential labor that takes place not only offscreen but even outside the formal boundaries of the film and television industry.

It's not just that for every Julia Roberts or Michelle Pfeiffer there are hundreds of ill-paid actresses with nothing to show for their work but walk-on roles in scanty clothing and high heels, or body doubling in nothing at all. It's rather that even for every one of those there are hundreds more who work as prostitutes, "models," exotic dancers, topless waitresses, hard-core performers, mistresses, and supplicants on casting couches. This sexual reserve army, moreover, has two additional functions. First, by its very existence it renders the bodies of all women (even the allegedly powerful and independent Roseanne Barr), subject to the authority and disposal of men, not only over their conditions of labor or (notoriously) their sexual availability, but over the very size of their breasts or shape of their legs, and how these will be displayed to the world. Only a few female performers in the history of Hollywood have attained enough wealth and power to escape the sex trap. Barbra Streisand and Roseanne Barr come to mind today; yet even Roseanne, who has made a (sometime) countercultural career out of genuinely flaunting bodily excess in the face of attempts to rein her in, felt compelled for whatever reasons, and however cynically accepting she may sound, to subject her body and face to the pains of cosmetic surgery, and to wind up looking as though she's been skinned alive.[15] Second, it subjects women in visual culture to the tyranny of age, so that women who were once major performers (Elizabeth Taylor, Brigitte Bardot, Jane Fonda) tend to disappear from view at an age when male actors (e.g., Sean Connery and Clint Eastwood, both of whom are older than those three actresses) are just coming into their own as heroes and sex symbols. Yet what the rest of us see of that tyranny is only the residue that becomes, in different ways for men and for women, the stuff of our day-dreams. This is the most decisive erasure of all.

One more material fact emphasizes the dual erasure to which women are subjected in visual culture: in 1994, in one public library with a large film video collection, of the first one hundred films I counted in various genres (excluding horror), eighty-four starred men (according to the list of credits). Many listed two or three men in the credits before finding room for any woman, and the majority listed five or six men before finding room for a second woman. Of the sixteen movies starring women, almost all were come-dies, and most of those had female comics (either Goldie Hawn or Whoopi Goldberg) in the lead. Four films titled Nadine, Roxanne, She's Having a Baby, and Working Girl, all starred men.[16] Only two films (Big Business and Little Man Tate) starred two women, and one of these was the only one of the hundred directed by a woman (Jodie Foster). Putting aside that film and The Dead, in which John Huston gave top billing to his own daughter, we could say that in this sample (which there's no reason to believe is unrepresentative) six out of every seven films directed by a man stars at least one man. In many of these films, as well, nothing about the narrative per se demands a male lead. Movies such as Groundhog Day, or Ghostbusters, or Back to the Future, or Witness, would tell the same story were gender roles in them reversed, or were male protagonists replaced by females.[17] When one of Hollywood's most gifted and attractive actresses, Susan Sarandon, who through most of The Client has sustained an otherwise lifeless film, has to be rescued at the end by an eleven-year-old boy, we learn something about the relative place of women.

Too, most of the women in these films clearly exist only to be looked at and symbolically possessed. An inspection of the cassette covers shows that virtu-ally all of them in any genre feature a woman in a sexy pose, a stripteaser, a murder victim, a girl friend, or someone else quite peripheral to the narrative of the movie inside. These covers are advertising, and what they advertise is the availability of women—or rather, they reiterate it almost as a generality irrelevant to the particular context. The central experience of the films them-selves, though, appears to fulfill some other purpose. There is something that has to be added, then, to Mulvey's discussion of "scopophilic fetishism" as the essence of dominant cinema.

Mulvey's general point is that (dominant) cinema, with its erasure of its own material source and consequent appeal to the viewer's unconscious, is *formally* a voyeuristic activity. The triple male gaze is a specification of the intended voyeur's gender. Yet the men who inhabit this standpoint most profoundly don't satisfy it (if it can be vicariously satisfied rather than merely titillated) with the productions of mainstream Hollywood. Instead they view either hard-core, or—with a little but not much more social acceptability— the dozens upon dozens, perhaps hundreds, of R-rated movies produced since the abolition of the Production Code in 1962, in which the narratives are flimsy excuses to undress women as often as possible (among innumerable examples, note *Bedroom Eyes, Bedroom Eyes II, Night Eyes, Night Eyes II, Indecent Behavior, Indecent Behavior II*). From what mainstream Hollywood apparently considers the predominant male standpoint, most films are only secondarily direct appeals to male voyeurism. Primarily, they are daydreams of accomplishment and heroism. Not the look but the *act* is their appeal to audience (male but perhaps even female) identification.[18]

What is true of films is also true, in a different fashion and to a different extent, of television. Sitcoms and soap operas are aimed at a segmented female audience, and women therefore star and appear in them in comparatively large numbers. But the dramatic fictions that one might think could be targeted at a more representative adult audience, are just like films in this respect. In one week of 1995, for example, of thirty-seven primetime series episodes on all cable stations available in western Massachusetts, thirty-two were primarily devoted to the exploits of a man, or two men.[19] In only one, *Under Suspicion*, was a woman really the protagonist; that is, the person who carries out the significant action that we are supposed to focus on. And even *her* agency was questionable: she was a line policewoman whose cases were assigned to her by male bosses.[20] More generally, about two out of every three players receiving listed credit in *TV Guide* on primetime television are male (a ratio found also in Hollywood cinema). In 1987 the National Commission on Working Women found that a fifth of new TV shows had no female characters, and that "in many others women characters (were) incidental."[21] Like black people from a Woody Allen film, if not so dramatically, women vanish from sight. This is hardly surprising. Movies and television programs (domestic comedies aside) take place in public space, and the public order is still overwhelmingly male. The naturalizing force of visual ideology, the literal-minded reading of "reality" that mainstream culture engages us in, merely confirms this.[22]

Voyeurism as such is a double-edged indicator of male power; the power of the gaze is considerably less than total.[23] Cinematically this seeming contradiction is resolved most successfully not in the figure of the hero as womanizer or stud (as Mulvey's analysis would at first glance seem to require), but rather in the figure of the laconic hero who rejects domesticity for his larger obligations. If he can't have women whenever he wants them, better not to want them at all. An endless roster of leading men from Cooper to Eastwood (of whom the most representative figure is Henry Fonda / Wyatt Earp in *My Darling Clementine*) give witness to his preeminence. The buddy movie, the road movie, the cop movie, the war movie, the gunfighter Western, even many sitcoms with working men and homemaking women, or with unbelievably chaste male leads, are all variants of this figure, variations on a theme.[24] Women are peripheral figures, or childbearers for some other man (e.g., Van Heflin in *Shane* and *3:10 To Yuma*) who does useful work but not the most compellingly urgent work. Or, they may be shadowy figures who are thinly drawn substitutes for the truly sexual woman whom the hero must renounce (compare Grace Kelly and Katy Jurado in *High Noon*). Or, they are simply rejected by the hero with minimal regret (as in *Clementine* or in Randolph Scott / Budd Boetticher's *Decision at Sundown*).

The male gaze is as much a way of reducing women as it is of desiring them, and so can often be satisfied by simply dismissing them from view. As Peter Biskind and Barbara Ehrenreich put it: "Whenever we cast our eyes up to the silver screen, wherever we look—at figures riding tall in the saddle, crouched in foxholes, careening down mountain roads in fast cars, or even cowering in the kitchen—we see men. One urgent and consistent theme that stretches through Hollywood films . . . has been masculinity."[25] And many of these men, including those whose iconography seems much more "masculine" than that of the endlessly deprived buffoons of sitcom land (say, John Ritter) are themselves surprisingly chaste: especially if a film is to be considered "serious." The male viewer's identification with the male protagonist is not meant to be compromised by competition with him for the female. Most of the time, identification is with one of two males who are competing *with each other* for the female.

Here too we have to add something to Mulvey's discussion of voyeurism; as she herself has acknowledged, it does not account for the apparent pleasure *women* take in looking at "attractive" rather than "unattractive" other women. (Has any woman said that *Mildred Pierce* would have been more satisfying if Ann Revere or Thelma Ritter had played Mildred instead of Joan Crawford?)[26] As their ads reveal, television shows such as *Central Park West* or *Courthouse* or *Savannah*, in which all kinds of sexual coupling are rampant by traditional standards, and on which the average level of female pulchritude makes most movies look austere, are aimed primarily at women. In part, women may enjoy their own depiction as vicarious sex objects, since being a successful sex object is still the most economical way for a woman to get ahead in patriarchalist society. Also, women enjoy revelations of their own excess, so stifled and restricted in (American) real life. But also, the emphasis on female attractiveness is not about sex at all. It is rather about *property*. The aging, used look of the once-glamorous Helen Mirren in the various versions of *Prime Suspect,* or even more the seedy, debauched look of Lynn Redgrave (once a very sexy Xaviera Hollander) as an unsympathetic reporter in the British series *Calling the Shots,* are unthinkable in a Hollywood film or television production. The female icon, from Rita Hayworth to Melanie Griffith, is not primarily what men can *look at* (a minimally satisfactory activity); she is what men can, they hope, *buy*.[27] The male viewer is interpellated as he who strives to possess her; the female viewer is interpellated as she who longs to be possessed by the right man. The great female icons of classic cinema, I think, gave women a viewing pleasure that Mulvey does not account for, by virtue of spending so much cinematic time *not* being possessed, before the final (and dubiously credible) clinch. Otherwise man as competitor, woman as prize, is the underlying structure of much Hollywood drama.[28] Conversely, when women compete for men (unless they are coded as the bitch-villainesses of soaps) the prize is not to have the man but to be had by him.

Thus one (male) television executive remarked, anent a "new (1994) season" of series featuring mostly aggressively active men, that "we've got action for the men, and sex for the women."[29] Who exactly are meant to be the voyeurs? In fact, for women the rule of acceptable social behavior is the corollary to the male rule of look but don't touch: look desirable and be desired. Thus women can vicariously enjoy the sex appeal of other women.[30] However, what is here called "sex" has its limits: the rule for women is, enjoy being desirable, but don't look too desirable; and don't allow yourself to be touched, except by the man whose behavior has been legitimated by the standard of the times. The woman who violates *that* rule is a slut: a word for which there is no male equivalent in the English language, because there is no male version of that social role.

This female contradiction is unresolvable. As Bette Davis so nicely puts it in *Now, Voyager,* "Don't let's ask for the moon when we have the stars." Today, women are more sexually active in cinema and on television than they once were, but sexual *agency* is a different matter. Active (female) sexual agents in cinema (for obvious reasons they appear with much less frequency on television) are most often depicted as sex workers: prostitutes, strippers, and so forth. They are shown as pure objects of either voyeurism, or of violence, or of both. In the thrillers and police procedurals that they briefly inhabit (before dying), we rarely even learn their names, and would not recognize their faces if we saw them in another such movie the next day. Less often, they are secondary characters who are doomed to be losers or worse (as in horror movies or high-school comedies); or golden-hearted whores who demonstrate their hearts of gold by finally becoming "not-whores," by surrendering their sexual self-determination. *Pretty Woman* is the most well known example of this genre, although *Mighty Aphrodite, Leaving Las Vegas, Showgirls,* and *Milk Money,* are not far behind. It reaches a kind of apotheosis in the made-for-cable *Bad Girls,* a Western starring some very serious actresses (Madeline Stowe, Andie MacDowell, and Drew Barrymore), in which not just one but *four* golden-hearted whores, who can outride and outshoot every man in the Colorado Territory, manage to avoid consensual sex for the entire film: three of them riding chastely off into the sunset while the fourth prepares for what has all the look of a virginal marriage. Female agency has its very clear limits.[31]

All this being the case, in dominant cinema or television there can only rarely be a *heroine* the way there is a hero: a figure who encompasses both desirability and sacrifice, the way the hero (Shane, Rick Blaine) can encompass both desiring and abnegation. Even Ripley in *Aliens,* who except in her nightmares is totally in charge of every frame she's in, is seen as a sexual being only very briefly (see Chapter 8). In dominant cinema and television most heroines are, like Sigourney Weaver, beautiful, or at least exceptionally attractive. They are, as Mulvey says, the voyeuristic objects of desire; but because we (the men in the audience) desire to possess them rather than to be like them, they are rarely its active expression. Like ownership and control of its means of production (unsurprisingly), the ideology of the metatext is male. Individual idiosyncratic texts peck at it, but do not dent it. So the means of production and the means of reproduction (using the latter phrase as a double entendre rather than in the sense Marx and Engels intended for it) form a perfect tandem in visual culture, in the way it is produced and in the stories it tells.

Nevertheless, the sexual double standard is more than sexual. It has a meaning that can't be reduced to either eros or psyche. It is about action, work (but not really productive work) in the world, adventure—all of which belong to men. By reducing women to the objects of a look, the triple male gaze confirms the ideology of separate spheres as much as or even more than it satisfies male sexual desire.[32] As for women, looking at other women being looked at by men (as John Berger puts it in his British TV documentary *Ways of Seeing*) is training for the role of consumer, the other half of capitalism; just as the role of passive sex object is the other half of patriarchy. That linkage is or at least has been the heart of dominant cinema. "Men dream of women," Berger remarks, and "women dream of themselves being dreamt of by men. They are there to feed an appetite, not to have any of their own." On television sitcoms or family dramas *(Blossom, Beverly Hills 90210)* the issue of sex for girls is whether they should allow it; for boys (only rarely) whether they should take it. Concomitantly, it is invariably men (sometimes even young men, as brothers) who make the final decision for "their" girls: the mere object of an appetite lacks the requisite knowledge or character to judge it authoritatively.

This differentiation, though it is certainly less visible than it used to be, is also the mainstay of television advertising, which means effectively network television as the prop for advertising's worldview. Times have changed. Men and women now both drive cars, but even the women driving cars are carefully selected to be the kind of women valued by men. In fact, male and female icons are *both* selected for their conformity to the scale of male value: active and rugged-looking if they are men, sexy if they are women. Sometimes the women in ads appear to be active persons (we might see a woman on her car phone doing what passes for business on television). But they are also professional models and thus objects of male voyeurism; television advertising remains an impregnable bastion of scopophilic fetishism. Conversely, it is predominantly women who clean floors and keep shirt collars white, while ads for certain products (beer, for example) keep the world of rugged action *in the world* still carefully in view for *men*.[33]

In this sense also there remains an effective proscription against the career woman, and especially the *single* career woman. Comedies such as the earlier *Mary Tyler Moore Show* or *Murphy Brown* more recently seem to contradict that generalization, but though the MTM empire during the 1970s generated occasional exceptions, these women usually carry their domesticity with them. They make public events happen much less often than they solve the relational conflicts around them.[34] What is very rare on television (early *Roseanne*, before its depoliticization, being the most obvious exception), is the depiction of a woman working *because she has to*. That Peg on the long-running *Married with Children*, for example, could actually not work and not be interested in working, is incredible; better to make fun of her obsessive nail manicuring and incompetent cooking than to suggest that women might have a *necessary* role in the labor force. And could the point have been made any more directly than it was, for example, during the series *Twin Peaks*, in which any woman who stepped out of the traditional female roles of homemaker or waitress was instantly corrupted by drugs or sex? Or than it was in the 1995, made-for-Lifetime-TV film *I Want Him Back*. In this film a couple whose marriage was broken up by the wife's careerism reconcile after their daughter's marriage. Meanwhile, the first ad featured an opera singer explaining that her marriage stayed whole despite her career because ready-to-serve meals enabled her to take good care of her husband.

If it's hard to equal that confluence of images and dialogue for sending a message, still the point gets made over and over again on television. Nor is it really a "point," but more an ideological version of the social real, present, again, in what is absent. On all the family melodramas, sitcoms, soap operas, and even workplace dramas (the courts occasionally excepted) of television land, there is no society. There are only relationships.

As for cinema, whatever it is a career woman does, she can be shown doing it, but again voluntarily rather than out of economic need—and very often she is still not to be shown getting away with it. If they are not actually killers themselves (such as Glenn Close in *Fatal Attraction*) very often tough female professionals somehow wind up in the arms or under the knife blade of a dangerous man (think of *Suspect, Jagged Edge, Defenseless, Blue Steel, The Morning After*).[35] In dominant cinema's version of unconventionality, as in *Black Widow*, the single career woman can even wind up—almost but not quite—in the murderous arms of another woman. Or, finally, she can be treated with contempt, as was Sigourney Weaver in *Working Girl*.[36] Whatever the trajectory her treatment follows, 1987s *Baby Boom*—Diane Keaton choosing motherhood in rural Vermont over a career in the big city—expresses a choice that Hollywood will rarely repudiate.

In classical Hollywood cinema productive spinsterhood repudiated itself. Now it kills or is killed. The extraordinary fate of Diana Muldaur on *L.A. Law* —falling down a conveniently empty elevator shaft—made explicit that the woman who can't be assimilated to patriarchal institutions on their terms must be eliminated, one way or another. As for married career women with children, their alleged inadequacy as wives or mothers also turns up regularly both in cinema (e.g., *The River Wild*) and on television (e.g., *The Marshal*): the reward for a return to a reasonable domesticity being their husbands' (or even ex-husbands') loving arms.

The same theme is conveyed in small ways as well as large, in lighthearted comedy as well as melodrama. Watching "teen" television, for example, one is left wondering how all those hard-hitting female prosecutors we see on shows such as *Law and Order* ever got to law school in the first place. On teenage shows, girls, white or black (e.g., *Family Matters*), are rarely interested in anything but sex or "relationships." Boys, even when portrayed as sexually obsessed, are often already career-oriented, if only to an athletic career.[37] But then, even the independent-minded Maggie on *Northern Exposure* was more wistful about missing relationships than she was dedicated to any particular activity, including her beloved flying. The ideological message of all these texts is roughly the same. Women are meant to be separated from the means of production—just as they are. The domestic labor they are otherwise destined for is neither portrayed nor valorized. As in conventional economics, or in the institution of wage labor that economics whitewashes, women's work takes place offstage. Except when it can be depicted as either emergency care or moral instruction, it is not worthy of our serious attention. Women's real labor consists of being looked at.

This is the message of the metatext of television and movies. Nonetheless, that metatext is rife with exceptions and fissures that I shall take up in subsequent chapters. Women of action abound; as do, to a lesser extent, women sitting behind desks and ordering men around. More and more, as the 1990s progress, public space seems to welcome women, at least token women, to its embrace. Still, every time that we think we are in the presence of one of those exceptions, witnessing one of those fissures, we need to look again: for things are often not exactly as they seem at first glance.

3 Ideological Destinies

American-style pluralism, which has been at the heart of dominant ideology since the end of World War II, is a shifting, expanding, and basically progressive conception, constantly under pressure to incorporate newly legitimized groups and identities within its scope. Mainstream visual culture especially, by nature of its need to appeal to the widest possible audience, depends on and must incarnate the strongest available version of liberal tolerance as its ideological core.

To return to an earlier example, the invisibility of black people in Woody Allen's movies and in so many televisual milieus, and whatever implications we can draw from that invisibility, is still a far cry from what used to be expressions of straightforward racial domination. These have been replaced by more subtle signs of a racial hegemony that no longer relies on discrimination and denigration nor, in its public face, even finds discrimination and denigration acceptable.[1] We need only try to imagine proposing a film project calling on Denzel Washington to play a buck-toothed rapist or cheerfully incompetent idler, or Whoopi Goldberg an eyeball-rolling domestic servant, to realize how quickly global generalizations about Hollywood's treatment of minorities can become outdated. Similarly, we cannot imagine a network teleplay in which homosexuality is simply mocked by the protagonists, with no recuperation of liberal "tolerance." In the 1990s, the bounds of the normative family may occasionally even be extended to encompass, say, gay couples (as on television's *Northern Exposure, Roseanne, Friends,* and *Mad about You*).

What remains constant, though, is the insistently assimilationist character of Hollywood's (and America's) pluralism, and a concomitant delineation of "acceptable" insiders from "unacceptable" outsiders. Hollywood's heroes are hardly ever racists, and middle-class black professionals abound (sometimes in extraordinarily unrealistic numbers), but images of the urban decay that heroized policemen deal with are predominantly images of people of color. Even in the 1996 television season—"the year of the gay"—gay men and women take their place in relative profusion as objects of comedy, liberal toleration, or understanding; but not as the iconographic idols who give a narrative its moral center. And though hardly anyone makes believable on-screen speeches about how a woman's place is in the home, women whose place is outside the home tend to get murdered (or to become murderers) with alarming frequency.

It is the *structure* of ideology in this sense, rather than the historical vagaries of its overt inclusions and exclusions, upon which we should focus. The products of Hollywood change over time, because so does the society (and the world) that consumes them. But change occurs within recognizable boundaries. Although the democratic capitalist *Zeitgeist* is constantly in flux, the United States always remains a democratic capitalist society (to the extent that that is not a contradiction in terms). The same is true of Hollywood. Whatever the nature of its commodities at a particular time, its primary social function of expressing normative dreams and fantasies and communicating ideologies, has never changed, and neither have the basic techniques of visual narration that accomplish this function.

Nonetheless, "exceptions" and "fissures" cannot be avoided; the metatext constantly calls itself into question. There are inherent limits to the directness and forcefulness with which ideological discourse can be deployed. If it begins to verge on propaganda it will usually lose its credibility. How is an often unpleasant reality to be handled? The answer is twofold. First, cinema and television promulgate an interpretive code that enables us to "read" visual culture in an emotionally reassuring way, even when in the presence of what looks superficially like moral failure or ambiguity. Second, narrative itself is structured in such a way as to take account of unpleasant realities while producing satisfying outcomes (see Chapter 4).

As to the interpretive code, the most important of its conventions are those that establish a crucial double linkage, of iconography to moral character, and of moral character to social destiny. Where character is ambiguous (as in *The Vanishing*), no one's fate stands for anything, and we can deduce nothing about the social order from it. But in Hollywood's visual culture, the protagonists (and even incidental characters) almost always meet (or enjoy) the fates that they seem to merit. We learn how to separate the deserving from the undeserving, often at a glance.[2]

One aspect of the code is purely visual. "Glamour" has to do with much more than a surfeit of beautiful women. The word represents a series of choices that are made in almost every Hollywood film and television program. The hero looks like a hero, not a character actor; his beloved is attractive by accepted social standards or even beautiful. The female lead is not only more than ordinarily attractive. If she is nonwhite but starring in a movie made primarily for white audiences, she will be relatively light-skinned and have facial features recognizable as close to a "European" standard (Angela Bassett, Jennifer Lopez, Cicely Tyson). If a female star is not attractive by conventional standards, we are watching a comedy; in a drama she could only be a secondary character.[3] Not only that; she never has a hair out of place. She can be on the run for a week from gangs of assassins and still wind up looking exactly like Julia Roberts in *The Pelican Brief,* wearing perfectly matched outfits and made up like . . . a movie star. This is Hollywood's visual dissonance at its peak. Just as Hollywood's lower depths usually look comfortable, so its victimized women usually look as though they're on the way to the bank with a million-dollar paycheck (perhaps, if they've looked really miserable for a moment, with a detour to an Oscar nomination). *Baywatch,* that compendium of Hollywood's attitudes toward its own glamour, sums up this ideological coding perfectly when Mitch, the male lead, says of the dying Tracy, "How can someone so beautiful be dying?"[4]

On the other hand the female must not be too beautiful without also being able to convey a sense of vulnerability: what separates the girls from the men. Thus the inescapably tough, independent, and icily beautiful Theresa Russell, paired with Burt Reynolds in *Physical Evidence*, becomes the active element in the romantic dyad, and the whole movie drifts askew. By its conclusion, a film that began with an ugly death has become a comedy, as she kicks the villain to his death down a flight of stairs, at the foot of which Reynolds lies helplessly out of the action, mugging for the camera. In the end, *Physical Evidence* might as well have been a Cynthia Rothrock martial arts movie (see Chapter 8), for all the chance it had of appealing to a mass audience trained in the Hollywood version of romantic sentimentality.

Sometimes not looks of any particular kind but merely gender is enough to establish destiny. For example, horror movies follow the rule, as enunciated by one film critic, that "being frightening means, almost by definition, frightening a woman."[5] Even here, though, a woman thought to be "homely" by casting directors will not find it easy to get the role of victim, which is typically reserved not for the underattractive but for the oversexed. The fascination of serial murder, as in *Wild Palms* or *Silence of the Lambs* or *Henry: Portrait of a Killer* (and the multitude of their sleazy imitators) is almost always the serial murder of *good-looking women.*[6] By comparison, what men do to boys can only rarely be spoken aloud. It's hard to avoid the suspicion that *that* kind of sexuality is considered too "sick" to be represented in public; rape is somehow more "normal."[7] And of course precisely *because* women are threatened by men, they need protection from them.

These are all ideological choices. They confirm sexual hierarchy. The tough, rugged man can take care of things—especially of "his" woman. As soon as we see an attractive female protagonist, a rugged man of action, and an ordinary looking man of thought (usually wearing glasses), we know which one she will wind up with; or rather, which one will wind up with her. If we ask, How can it be reassuring to most men that someone utterly unlike themselves wins the female prize? the answer is that we can now think of *our* prize, whoever she is, as what we deserve. We have not been deprived (of Nicole Kidman or Rene Russo or Julia Roberts or whomever) by lack of money or lack of status, but by simple lack of looking like or acting like a *hero:* a lack that can't in any way be blamed on "society."

Again, to feel the full force of the code we need to observe what happens when it is ignored. The films of the French director Coline Serreau (who found herself unable to work under the regime of dominant cinema even in France) provide a recent counterexample. In her *Romuald and Juliette* the eponymous heroine is an overweight black cleaning woman who attracts the hero because of her humanity rather than her looks. In *La Crise* the only person who responds sympathetically to the hero's quiet desperation is a self-proclaimed racist. Once the connection between the conventional evaluation of persons and the conventional evaluation of social outcomes is fractured in this way, it is the ideological link that is really broken. In *La Crise* we cannot say that because the racist is a good man, therefore racism is a good thing. The film gives us no grounds for believing that: nothing else it does validates racism (even the "racist" himself excludes his Arab friends from his attack, further suggesting the confusion and ambivalence of human motives). As for Juliette, she could not be the sexual heroine of a Hollywood film because her portrayal resolutely refuses being the stuff of fantasy. Whatever daydreams a man might have in her cinematic presence will take him into ordinary life and its obvious limitations, rather than allowing him to transcend it in an ideologically fantasized utopia.

In contrast, the ideological statement of Hollywood movies inheres in what is absent: the class (and racial) boundaries of worldly success for men. When we men (I cannot presume to speak for women here) are in the world of what we have been taught to recognize as female glamour, *everything* else we see is to at least some extent transformed by it. Robert Altman's film *Short Cuts*, for example, is developed from a series of short stories by Raymond Carver, stories that in their groping and barely articulate minimalism cast an unsettling light on American life. The film, however, feels less like an interwoven collection of California lives than like a passing parade of Hollywood beauties, and any man watching the screen concentrates on them as his visual experience, whatever else he may be seeing. Similarly, *Thelma and Louise* broke new ground as a female "buddy movie," and the television series *China Beach* was innovative in its depiction of women's relationship to war. But in both of them the immense attractiveness of the female stars limited the extent of their novelty for male viewers, and perhaps even for many of those female viewers at whom they were primarily aimed.

Conversely, to be a "hero," a man on the screen can engage in almost any behavior that still leaves him available as the credible object of a female search for fulfillment. "You're a ruthless bastard" can be a compliment as easily as a criticism; in some genres, more easily. "You're a ruthless bitch" can almost never be a compliment, and in fact there is no male equivalent for that epithet. Even a female protagonist meant to be admired for her toughness is also reminding us, the audience, that she is *different,* and she carries her difference with her like an unmistakable threat. A man, say, firing an underling remains the particular man that he is, good or bad. A woman (e.g., Sigourney Weaver in *Working Girl* or Linda Fiorentino in *The Last Seduction*) can never fire an underling, or engage in any other "male" activity, without standing in for all women, and so causing a discussion about what it's like working for a woman, how do women handle authority, and so forth. As long as expectations are still marked by the underlying structure of patriarchalism, equality of representation has a double-edged meaning for women.[8] There may, for example, be all sorts of reasons having little or nothing to do with misogyny why the killer in a suspense movie is made to be a woman: to appeal to male fetishism (see Chapter 9) with a character other than the protagonist's wife, to have a lead role for a popular actress, and so forth. But in context that representation is also necessarily misogynistic in some degree or other: no neutral presentation of women is possible.

In this respect, perhaps the most revealing statement Hollywood makes about sexual hierarchy lies in the way that love scenes in R-rated movies invariably contain a moment in which the hero picks up his lover and carries her to bed: a feat beyond the carrying capacity of most men's backs (at least those who are not lovers of 110-pound sylphs). These scenes also almost always conclude, after much egalitarian to-ing and fro-ing, with the man on top and the woman underneath: a position less accurately described as "missionary" than as "ideological." To see a woman on top and staying there tells us that she is probably a killer (e.g., *Basic Instinct*). The knife is about to come out.

On television, with its enfeebled narratives and iconography, this kind of linkage is not so obvious, but it is still noticeable if one looks for it. On the putatively "feminist" *Under Suspicion* (which was created by a woman but as usual had many episodes written by men, and all directed by them), an internal affairs policewoman, after subjecting one of her male colleagues to a viciously defamatory interrogation, comes on to him in a bar after she's cleared him. During the interrogation we've seen her only at a distance in a darkened room, and she has seemed to be very sexually attractive. Now we see her in close-up: her complexion is bad, her features are much sharper than the usual standard, and she looks a good deal like a classical witch (shades of Glenn Close in *Fatal Attraction!*). His rejection of her is understandable for many reasons, but watching these scenes we realize that her sexual behavior, not her interrogatory style, is the aspect of her character that we, with him, are meant to reject. Conversely, the female protagonist—his equally unchaste lover—is comparatively diffident in his presence, and even finally has to plead with him for his sexual favor: although at the station house she gives no quarter to fellow cops or suspects. She is almost beautiful, but not so much so as to be an irresistible siren—for then she would be out of control and no longer our heroine. The line is not just fine; it's a razor's edge.

By and large, men signal their manliness by refusing to give in to the demands of circumstance. Women signal their femininity by exhibiting a willingness to do exactly that (compare Gary Cooper and Grace Kelly in *High Noon*). What women do not do, though, without treading on what is instantly defined as dangerous territory, is initiate sexual activity (except when the narrative is clearly coded as a comedy of role reversal such as *What's Up, Doc?*). The sympathetic womanizer, such as Ted Danson on the television series *Cheers*, has no female equivalent. Even on the more or less countercultural *Northern Exposure*, Janine Turner's most memorable sexual choice is her decision to go into the wilderness alone and free herself from sexual entanglements.[9]

Appearance and behavior are separable, but linked. Sometimes appearance stands in for behavior, even though in principle it is not attached to any particular behavioral style. For example, the presence of an overweight man or woman (using the term in its social rather than medical sense) in a romantic lead role, indicates that we are in the presence either of a comedian or of a "working-class" representation *(Marty, Roseanne, Only the Lonely)*. In Hollywood, being obese is a form of deracination, or worse. In one 1995 episode of *The Simpsons* Homer deliberately becomes grotesquely fat in order "to get on disability." In ads for diet supplements the gross is magically converted into the beautiful.[10] Can we imagine Danny De Vito as Kathleen Turner's wife and Michael Douglas as his lawyer in *War of the Roses*?

No more, similarly, can we imagine a gay man or woman as the hero in an adventure story or thriller, performing all the hero's normal functions of saving women and children and the like, but turning an uninterested shoulder to opposite-sex smolderings from rescuees, sidekicks, and so forth. Movies such as *Longtime Companion, Philadelphia*, and *Making Love*, present themselves as domestic "problem" movies and pleas for tolerance. They are invariably about loss rather than accomplishment (though *Torch Song Trilogy* could be summed up, perhaps unfairly, as "boy gets mother"); they are most definitely not phantasmic bids for the surrendering of identity. Among Hollywood's "gay" movies and subplots, only Donna Deitch's *Desert Hearts* dares to follow the trajectory of a classical romance *tout court*, as girl meets girl, girl rejects girl, and girl finally gets girl. But Patricia Charbonneau is tastefully beautiful, just as is Patrice Donnelly in *Personal Best*. Iconography is destiny. When Hollywood introduces us to a lesbian heroine who is one hundred pounds overweight, has a mannish haircut, hangs out in leather bars, and is on the run from malevolent killers because she has come into possession of a secret document that will change the course of history, we'll know that the code has been overthrown.[11] Even less exotically, the first time we see Sigourney Weaver defying fate with a 5'6" man by her side (or register her true height next to that of, say, Mel Gibson or Sly Stallone), we will know we're in for a different kind of movie experience. It's not likely to happen soon.[12]

Morality is also destiny, particularly in the realm of the Law. The negative work of "abolishing" class and class conflict is not by itself enough to establish a believable *and* ideologically correct world. Absence requires a contrary presence to be "here," so the positive work of affirming the mythically harmonious community must also go on within visual culture. Most fundamentally, dominant ideology is confirmed by the dual equation of the moral order of the universe with the legal order, and the family relations, of the particular community known as the United States.

As to the first, the equation of law and morality is confirmed overtly in *romans policiers* and courtroom narratives, but also and more generally in any consideration of guilt and innocence, crime and punishment. The overall approach (though it can be occasionally breached since the elimination of the Production Code) is that the handling of these is finely calibrated to keep a kind of Golden Rule firmly in mind: Crime Does Not Pay, but Human Decency Is Always Appropriately Rewarded. From *I Am a Fugitive from a Chain Gang* to *Unforgiven*, the lesson Hollywood always teaches us is that formal legalism is too rigid to be an effective social cement. At the same time, real moral obloquy must never go unpunished. The Law must not be flouted. Even protagonists who have engaged our deepest sympathies must pay the price the Law demands (think of *The Defiant Ones* or *Lonely Are the Brave*).

The Rule, however, makes the most effective ideological statement when its application is not immediately obvious (as is all too often the case), but requires us to think through what we have seen in order to make a believable link between it and our knowledge of conventional social morality. Conflict is essential to the Hollywood narrative style, but oversimplified versions of conflict become worn out; more complexity is necessary to keep our attention. Thus the familiar narrative figure of the misunderstood hero, who commits crimes that turn out not to be crimes; kills accomplices, but only in self-defense; lets apparent criminals escape, but only because their crimes are not so serious as some injustice that has been inflicted on them; pulls off some enjoyable caper and gets away, but loses the swag. (A 1994 television movie called *Sex, Love, and Cold Hard Cash* should be seen as a compendium of all these thematic codes.) Again, a prostitute can be a heroine (*Pretty Woman*, or *Sex, Love, and Cold Hard Cash*) as long as we never actually see her with any man but the hero, to whom she is faithful. The code, of course, is different for man and woman. He must behave like a hero; she must behave like the kind of woman who deserves a hero.

One made-for-television movie of 1995 illustrates the Golden Rule nicely, as commercial television is even more careful than dominant cinema when it comes to the fine calculation of moral linkages. What if the "hero" of a crime story is a woman? What happens to the code then? *The Desperate Trail*, an anachronistic Western starring Linda Fiorentino, is so convoluted that paradoxically it illustrates the Rule with perfect clarity. The moviemakers were trapped by the fact that the movie exists only as a follow-up to Fiorentino's incredibly successful role as a cold-hearted, destroying bitch in *The Last Seduction*. Here, she must be as hard as nails and yet, the genre being what it is, a sympathetic hero. In the commercial mainstream, women, unlike the kind of men impersonated by Charles Bronson and Clint Eastwood, are not supposed to be hard as nails, for that seems like an inversion of the moral order. What is to be done?

Just as detective stories are about, as one critic put it, our pleasure in finding out "what will have happened," so this movie is chiefly about our finding out who will have deserved to die; that is its only real suspense. A veritable killing machine with a gun in her hand, Fiorentino dispatches so many men that by the end of the movie we've lost track. Gradually, though, we learn that she is a "battered woman" who has murdered her abuser (well, two abusers, as she lets us know in an offhand remark; though any man who would dare to lay a finger on her should really be considered mentally impaired). As for the men she kills while on the run, they are not exactly bad men, but three of them are gamblers who are trying to kill (quite reasonably, one might think) her card-stacking partner. The rest are unfortunate enough to be members of the posse that is chasing her on behalf of an unprofessionally vengeful U.S. marshal who, we even more belatedly will find out, was the father of one of her abuser/victims. Her recently acquired partner, meanwhile, is a bank robber (and cardsharper) who steals in order to support the younger brother he once accidentally crippled. So just as she's really a good woman, he's really a good man: but not good enough, as it turns out. He, after all, is a "real" criminal. She's just suffering from an extended case of battered women's syndrome. At the end, therefore, he must die—but only after saving her life by killing the lawman, so that her hands remain clean enough (the posse members being cowardly opportunists rather than "real" lawmen) to take the reins as she rides off into the sunset (with or without the swag is unclear by this point). This "Dirty Harry" version of moral linkage might not meet with everyone's approval, compared with the simpler moral code of earlier Westerns. Some viewers will get up and walk away from the set as soon as she guns down the gamblers. But still the ideological linkage is perfectly clear in the end.

It becomes even clearer when contrasted to the moral coding of another narrative about a battered woman, the 1995 movie *Woman Undone*. In this movie, a husband, enraged by his wife's infidelities and by her announcement that she has had an abortion without consulting him, drives her into the desert to kill her.[13] He has beaten her before this but, as far as we know, only since her first infidelity; and we never see him do more than slap her, nor is she ever even mildly bruised. While resisting him, she knocks him out, takes the gun with which he'd intended to shoot her, and runs away. Recovering, he chases her down in the car. While trying to run her over, though, he crashes into a rock wall, and is hopelessly trapped beneath the steering wheel as the car flames up around him. In agony, he asks his wife to shoot him, and she does.

Everything I have just described is the story she tells to the jury that is weighing a charge of first-degree murder against her. They hear no other firsthand account, nor do we the audience. Nor is there any circumstantial evidence against her that isn't perfectly accounted for by her story. There is also not the faintest evidence of premeditation in the prosecution's alternative reconstruction of the events. Yet the jury finds her guilty as charged. Under these circumstances, it is impossible to have any doubt (reasonable or otherwise) that the authors of this tale have found her "guilty," not of murder but of unacceptable behavior. This conclusion is strengthened by the fact that at the very end we learn that she will be eligible for work-release in *four* years, and that her ruggedly attractive lawyer has fallen in love with her. Four years seems ridiculous for first-degree murder, but in Hollywood's moral world it is just about right for two illicit affairs and one "unauthorized" abortion.

Of course, in a story that didn't end with the husband's death, that sort of behavior would not lead to a jail sentence. Payment of some kind, however, would have to be exacted. Unlike Linda Fiorentino in *The Desperate Trail*, this woman has violated *other* moral rules than the one against killing. Killing, oddly enough, is the one transgression about which dominant culture has always been relatively relaxed. What matters is not whether you kill, but whom you kill, and why. In this case the female protagonist's defiance of patriarchal codes is willful, rather than merely a response to an injury done her. In this movie too, our pleasurable attention is devoted solely to finding out what will have happened, and then retrospectively rewinding the movie in our heads to see why what happened had to happen. Making ideological sense of this kind is perhaps visual culture's greatest accomplishment.[14]

Different genres, of course, may be coded quite differently. The horror genre defines horror precisely as the triumph of evil, but most horror movies uphold the established order, in that the horror they recount is never social but rather individually pathological.[15] In this genre, the code often clearly determines, if not who shall die, then who shall kill. *Fatal Attraction,* which follows the structural trajectory of the conventional horror film, is a perfect example of this kind of linkage. The film had various endings, but in none of them does Michael Douglas succeed in killing Glenn Close. That could simply not be allowed to happen, for if he were strong enough to do that, then what was his problem to begin with? Male weakness in the face of predatory female strength is excusable, even ineluctable; turn him into a man of strength and nothing was forgivable. Chuck Norris and Clint Eastwood do not get seduced by vampires. Only Anne Archer, the good wife, can perform the required deed, for her strength resides solely in her determination to save her family, and is therefore pure.

Other than deliberate social satires such as *The Player* or *Bob Roberts,* the films that have fully violated the negative side of the Golden Rule can be counted almost on the fingers of one hand (no such television episodes could escape the eye of the censor). In addition to one or two "big caper" movies *(Gambit, $),* they are usually movies about female killers, most notoriously *The Last Seduction* and *Basic Instinct.* The fetishistic pleasures of male masochism seem to be the only ones allowed to controvert The Law. However, since such films lack any invocation of female solidarity (unlike the oppositional films of the Dutch director Marlene Gorris), they are effectively quarantined as random examples of amorality: really as, again, horror movies.[16] The Law is mocked, but is not overturned.

As for more direct invocations of the link between law and morality, these occur mostly through the idealization of the police, and so also of essential masculinity in the person of the policeman. In any social order the police perform a dual function of both protection and repression. It is a self-imposed duty of the makers of visual culture to erase the latter function as carefully as they erase the means of production. Above all, against the reality that we (the public) very often fail to discover "the truth" behind any criminal process, courtroom dramas and police stories alike systematically and easily discriminate the "guilty" from the "innocent," so that "criminals" can be safely demonized and walled off, socially and morally, from the viewing audience. In this metatext *we,* the innocent viewers, are regularly reminded of our distinctiveness from *them,* the malefactors, the outsiders.

Most of us, with part of our minds, know that social status, political power, access to or denial of instruments of coercion, and the random exigencies of individual fate often determine who we are and what we do; that we are sometimes one thing and sometimes another; and that "crime" is often, as the criminal middleman in *The Asphalt Jungle* puts it, "just a left-handed form of business enterprise." [17] The ideology of "law and order" elides these uncomfortable possibilities, stitching together our divided consciousnesses and reassuring us that our communal unity is "real." More crucial, by putting centralized coercion, police *power,* at the core of representations of "community," the genre also elides the possibility of noncoercive forms of community: those suggested, for example, by the popular institution of carnival, or by voluntary cooperation among workers, strikers, neighborhood residents, or women.[18] Instead, force or anarchy, the "thin blue line" or the streets taken over by "them" (guess who?) is the only choice the metatext gives to us. And in putting force first the metatext necessarily puts men first. No matter how many token women may be shown participating in the processes of legalized violence, women can never pass the implicit test of physical equality.

At first glance this affirmation of community through the law enforcement genre might seem to present a paradox. "The apparatus of state coercive power," in Gramsci's words, " 'legally' enforces discipline on those groups who do not 'consent' either actively or passively (to the general direction imposed on social life by the dominant fundamental group)." [19] Too much and too visible enforcement must make the state seem less like a democratic state and more like a police state. Why then do the visual media emphasize rather than deemphasize its role?

The answer is that much of the most important coercive work of the police has never been shown on television or in dominant cinema. For example, the police "neutrally" enforce the laws that give private owners and their representatives total control over access to the means of production, and also (which often amounts to the same thing) serve "the state" in its reified form whenever it comes into conflict with the workers who actually perform its functions. Thus the police regularly function as strikebreakers. Clearing a path for replacement workers and preventing effective picketing (let alone the seizure of workplaces), they are *always* on the side of management. Similarly, in cities and suburbs the police provide special patrols in the neighborhoods of the wealthy, not just to prevent crime but to keep out unseemly looking civilians. Much of this work is done as moonlighting, *in* uniform during off-duty time. Another regular task of the police is the harassment of women (those small entrepreneurs labeled "prostitutes"). This task is accompanied by expressions of virulent misogyny (on the part of male police), just as the similar but much more intense repression of racial minorities is accompanied by expressions of virulent racism (on the part of white and sometimes even Hispanic police). With the exception of racial repression, all of this activity is simply ignored by the media. Even that last is shown only in the form of policing "criminal" activity (usually involving drugs), never as the unceasing harassment and violence it actually entails. It goes without saying, finally, that the unmitigated vocabulary of scatology, obscenity, and pornography which composes the actual discourse of most police work (and of military action as well), and which is directed almost entirely at women and racial minorities, remains unheard: even during the carefully edited versions of "real" police work that the viewing audience is allowed to see.[20]

Instead, dominant visual culture turns the policeman into that mythic figure, the lone hero of the detective story; and stories of social division enforced by violence become stories of justice reconciled with law. The community remains whole, except for random and usually pathological "criminals" who are not like the rest of us at all. Identifying with repressive force, we therefore become the repressors as well—and so can no longer identify what "we" are doing as repression. We are helped in this direction too by the constant references, in police shows and movies, to "soft" judges, and criminal "scum" who've been acquitted and "put back on the streets" because of "technicalities" (as in warrantless searches or coerced confessions). So Hollywood obliterates the *problem* of police authority, of the Hobbesian state, and leaves "criminals" and good people confronting each other unequivocally once again. Seen in this light, movies such as *The Desperate Trail* actually perform an essential function. In extending the category of "good guys" more and more widely (in the present case to women), while narrowing the range of vice more sharply, they enable the greatest possible number of us to interpellate ourselves as the former. So doing, we can identify with the ideology of law and order even while deploring this or that application of it.

It's not that rogue cops (or army officers) can't be found in mainstream visual culture; there are a plethora of them. But in the law-and-order movie or television series, these villains function as scapegoats whose behavior does not call the system into question. The scapegoat will usually be clearly designated as a "psychopathic" or simply "corrupt" cop.[21] Almost always (even in Charles Burnett's unyielding portrayal of institutionalized racism, *The Glass Shield*), it is the law that rides to the rescue of the law. At the same time, the law-and-order narrative is replete with racial stereotypes, such as the ubiquitous black drug dealer / pimp, or macho Hispanic juvenile criminals. These have the effect of specifying terms of communal integration and unification (minorities should shape up their own behavior) that do not question the good intentions of the community as a whole, nor of the white, mostly male, police who are taken to represent the community.

The equation of morality with "the family" and conventional sexuality poses somewhat different problems. Iconographic coding draws on our already established knowledge of the code; it cannot develop or resolve plots. Narratively, how does Hollywood ideologize sex and gender relations? The answer cannot be, simply by showing the "normal" approvingly. To claim this would be to misunderstand the attribution "ideological." If every depiction of a functioning family or a happily heterosexual couple were to be called "ideological," then in effect we would be saying that of any description of ordinary daily life. It's not so much that this is an implausible usage (Althusser would defend it), as that the unavoidable inference of a negative moral judgment leaves the critic (the daughter of parents, let alone often the partner of another adult and the mother of her own children) out in Archimedean moral space without solid ground to stand on. It's crucial to understand the ideological family not as the "normal" family simply depicted, or even valorized, but rather as the "normal" family (and "normal" sexuality) reconstituted into a special site of moral privilege: not as necessary human unity but as coercive ideological symbol.

In the Hollywood metatext this ideological symbolization appears as a series of instantly recognizable "families." Some embody moral virtue exclusively (recognizable by the perky, cute, preternaturally wise, loved and loving children who inhabit them); others ("social problem" movies) raise the specter of familial inadequacy until the family is finally recuperated. Yet others depict it as a source of evil and are therefore instantly recognizable as horror movies. Any particular movie or television program may be more subtle than this (or less). What merits the attribute of "ideological," regardless, is the *gratuitousness* of a depicted linkage between moral virtue, physical survival, and membership in a "family." A single example, drawn from films in different genres, will illustrate the meaning of "gratuitous": an example of what knowledgeable viewers call the "death warrant."

In the movie *Aliens*, almost all the men involved in what one calls the "bug hunt" are ineffectual. Physical, intellectual, and moral power are exercised primarily by two women, Ripley (Sigourney Weaver) and Vasquez (Jeanette Goldstein), and an android in male shape (Lance Henriksen). Ripley and Vasquez are different, however: whereas Ripley is manifestly a woman in a traditional male role, the sexuality and even gender of the muscular Vasquez are ambiguous. When Ripley, after spending almost the entire movie in body-concealing fatigues, finally strips for action, the camera's gaze, and that of every male in the audience, is on her bosom: until this moment it has been present only by its absence.[22] Vasquez, conversely, is in a real sense always stripped; although she is much more buxom than Ripley, up to the moment of her death the camera's gaze is always centered on her uncovered biceps, as well as on the immense weapon she cradles in her arms.

When we first meet Vasquez doing chin-ups, a male marine sarcastically asks her, "Hey Vasquez, have you ever been mistaken for a man?" To general laughter from almost every woman in the audience, Vasquez replies, "No, have you?" But the joke is double-edged. It only makes sense (that is, it is only funny) because of the assumption (shared by James Cameron the screenwriter and his audience) that masculinity is naturally defined by muscular physique and physical prowess. Because of this expectation about the "natural" and, correlatively, the "unnatural," we know that the unmanned male will die before Vasquez, but we also know that she has just signed her own death warrant. She will die heroically, saving a lesser male from a hideous living death, but die she will. Even in the best of causes, this is one transgression that Hollywood always punishes. (As though in homage to tradition, the creators of *Star Trek II* killed off series regular and future feminist martial-arts expert Denise Crosby almost as soon as they had introduced her).[23]

Ripley, conversely, is cast in the classic cinematic mold of the reluctant hero who, disillusioned with compromise and corruption, has retreated from a career of activism. From Rick Blaine to Will Mummy, from Bogart to Eastwood, the reluctant male hero's moment of truth comes in his recognition of an obligation to defy evil. If Ripley were a man, then the moment in *Aliens* when she takes over the platoon's armored car from its inexperienced commander, in order to rescue the trapped members of the group, would be such a moment; and that is how it feels to enthralled viewers. But Ripley's social reintegration has in actuality come earlier, with the platoon's discovery of Newt, the ten-year-old survivor of terror. From that moment of discovery on Ripley is clearly defined secondarily as the best soldier on the screen, but primarily as Newt's mother, the only member of the group who can communicate with a young girl. (Vasquez, in contrast, has no interaction with Newt: dead again). It is as a surrogate mother that Ripley becomes a whole person, after the trauma of her earlier experience with the hideous aliens (in *Alien,* in which she is the only survivor and the only wholly effectual member of the spaceship crew as well). It is as both mother and "wife" (to the wounded and helpless marine, Hicks) that she, unlike Vasquez, survives. The "real woman" lives, for Hollywood can never allow a child to go unmothered.[24] The ambiguous woman must die, for Vasquez is too far gone into "masculinity" to be recuperated for the sexual order.[25]

Put another way, the ideological point is not simply *who* dies; that could be explained at least partially without reference to *sexual* ideology. That is, in this narrative Ripley / Sigourney Weaver is both iconographically and thematically the leader, the commander, whereas Vasquez is proletarian muscle. How could Ripley be the *individual* hero if she has this or any other professional fighter (as opposed to a mere comrade) standing at her back when high noon comes? Note that Hicks, the sole surviving male marine and Ripley's would-be lover, is himself completely disabled at the moment of final confrontation. In contrast, when Will Kane's Quaker, pacifist wife shoots one of his enemies in the back at the climax of *High Noon,* this does not detract from his heroism against overwhelming odds but rather reaffirms the centrality of the family bond. *High Noon,* though, is about family as a substitute for community; *Aliens* is much more abstract in its embrace of "family." So the point of Vasquez's death is not *that* she dies but rather *why* she dies. The ideological message in this and similar films (there are many) is given by the antecedent social identity of the subordinate character who is chosen as the sacrificial victim.

We also cannot afford to forget that Vasquez (the character, not the actress) is a Latina, as the movie constantly (and anachronistically) reminds us. Non-white men and women have always stood for "the body" in Hollywood iconography, beyond masculinity and femininity into pure lust. Gradually Hollywood has begun to find roles for black men—Denzel Washington, Lawrence Fishburne, Morgan Freeman—that fit them into familiar images of patriarchy, including the universal hero/savior, that used to be reserved for whites. What chiefly makes this development possible is the extent to which white audiences have been encouraged to associate black men with a positive masculinity through the selling of professional sports.[26] Women have not been subject to any such campaign, though. The color of commercialized female sports heroism (Rebecca Lobo, Martina Navratilova, Katarina Witt) is almost entirely white.[27] Correlatively, the peculiar phenomenon of Whoopi Goldberg aside (and even she has been a fetishized or comic figure in most of her roles), Hollywood still manifests an inability, even on television series oriented to black audiences, to find roles for black women beyond a limited range of stereotypes: nurturer, Amazon, lust object. The options available to Hispanic women have until recently been even more limited.[28] Unsurprisingly, in a society divided by boundaries of class, gender, and race, the death warrant is overdetermined.

Consider again the similar distinction that is central to a minor thriller, *Survive the Night,* seen by almost no one except on video. In this film Stephanie Powers, her daughter, and her sister Helen Shavers are relentlessly pursued through the wastelands of the Bronx by a murderous gang. Even before meeting the two women we know that at least one must survive if the daughter does, for once again Hollywood will not leave children without an adult to care for them—unless we are watching a horror movie, which will have its own recognizable conventions (e.g., particular children as the spawn of the devil). The children we meet in *Pixote,* or *Shoeshine,* or Buñuel's *Los Olvidados* will never be met in a Hollywood production; the ideology of the family cannot sustain a confrontation with their existence. The survivor, then, need not be the biological mother, who might be a criminal, a hopeless addict, or something similar. But in *Survive the Night* it must be one of them.

Iconographically, there is a clear difference between the two potential protagonists, though they are both white women. Powers has her usual bland, model's beauty (bland is positive in Hollywood); Shavers is loaded with unmistakable sex appeal (left over from *Desert Hearts* perhaps). Shortly into the chase, Shavers, against the wishes of Powers, traps and exultantly kills one of their pursuers: and again we know (if we hadn't recognized it as soon as we saw them) that we have just witnessed the signing of a death warrant. Like Vasquez, though with less sexual and more moral symbolism, Shavers has crossed a line that no female in dominant visual culture can cross without incurring punishment. The sexual order is not just a family order. It is also a moral order, and in the most frequently encountered version of that moral order, no matter how worthy the cause, female aggression (unauthorized by any male) is female transgression. This is not true of movies, explicitly marginal to the mainstream, about female kickboxers or gunfighters, in which the protagonist is a fetishized heroine (often a sexy cartoon figure) for male audiences, and there is no chance that anyone will mistake her for a "power feminist."[29] But the centrality of the mother/daughter dyad in *Survive the Night* tells us that we are in the much more rigidly bounded world of the conventional family. In the end, Powers and her daughter turn on their remaining pursuers and kill them, but this is clearly coded both as self-defense and as mother-child bonding (as with Ripley at the end of *Aliens*). Just as only Anne Archer can do the final killing in *Fatal Attraction,* only Powers can do it here.

Sometimes, as I've noted, simply being a lesbian signs one's death warrant: as in *Even Cowgirls Get the Blues,* in which, as soon as Uma Thurman finally tells Rain Phoenix "I love you," we can only wait impatiently for the latter to be killed. Of course this outcome is not inevitable, at least not any more. Given the expansionism of American pluralism, visual culture is constantly in process of change, as I suggested at the beginning of this chapter (see note 26).

In the 1995 movie *Wild Side,* a wealthy money launderer (Christopher Walken) falls in love with a high-priced call girl; meanwhile his bodyguard, an undercover FBI agent, rapes her as a means of coercing her to participate in a sting operation against Walken. By the end of the film, the agent is dead, Walken is under arrest, and the call girl has escaped with a good deal of his money *and* his wife. This narrative in its entirety was then almost instantly repeated in the 1996 instant "cult" hit *Bound,* as is its dénouement in the contemporaneous female action film (see Chapter 8) *Dangerous Prey.* Since, given the logistics of filmmaking, it's more likely than not that the makers of *Bound* and *Dangerous Prey* never saw *Wild Side,* 1996 viewers were presumably witnessing the beginnings of a shift of some kind in visual culture. If so, it was hardly an innocent shift: in these movies, enjoyable as they are in their iconoclasm, the association of deviant sex with violence not only remains, but is confirmed. "Insiders" and "outsiders" are still easy to identify.[30]

In any event, on the whole it is still very often the case, especially with gay men *(Philadelphia, Longtime Companion),* that the only good one is a dead one. More commonly, though, it's additionally the relationship of protagonists to children, and thus to the ideological ideal of family, that links character to destiny. Movies as diverse as *Aliens, The River Wild, The Big Chill, Dirty Harry,* and *Fatal Attraction* center virtually all moral judgment on the relationships among adult protagonists and children. A woman who deserts her children is a cold woman *(Kramer vs. Kramer, Ordinary People),* wholly defined by that one act. Conversely, women such as Diane Keaton *(Baby Boom)* and Christine Lahti *(Running on Empty)* redeem themselves and transform their onscreen effect by making a choice for child-centeredness. The caretakers of children never die (at least not without passing on their role to some other nurturer); and the most implausible plot twists are negotiated to save them, as in the rescue of Theresa Russell's golden-hearted and maternal *Whore* from the seemingly inescapable streets on which she has been trapped.

Heroes, similarly, are never cruel to or even dismissive of children without at some point repenting of their previous attitude. The changing role of Arnold Schwarzenegger from killer android to nurturant android in *Terminator* and *Terminator 2,* for example, is signaled by his relationship with the young boy who (in the latter movie) he is sent to save. In fact, his takeover of the caretaker role from Linda Hamilton in *Terminator 2* signals us that, despite her muscular heroics, *she* is not "the hero."[31] As the "mother," she can and must survive, but until the film's ending she is not shown as a *caring* mother, a role reserved for Schwarzenegger. Apparently, she can be a caring mother *or* an obsessed world-saver: but not both. Contrarily, in *Aliens* Sigourney Weaver is, finally, *only* a caring mother. If she saves the universe, that is incidental. Her obsession is to rescue young Newt, and *that* makes her the center of the narrative.

Of course this distinction between sexual and moral symbolism is artificial. In the dominant ideology, unconstrained female sexuality is aggression, but even in mainstream cinema or television unconstrained female aggression is also sexually supercharged. Hollywood always has it both ways (see Chapter 4). Ripley and Powers are the "straight" heroines, but at least for a while Shavers and Vasquez exist for male fetishists to admire (and perhaps gay women as well, though this is not an audience Hollywood has traditionally seemed to cater to). There is no question, though, as to what we are being told about the appropriate place of these women in the social order. We cannot possibly mistake the meaning of the fact that, as Carol Clover points out, the girls who are killed by the monster in horror movies are almost always sexually active girls, whereas the "final girl" who survives and defeats the monster is herself chaste.[32] To be sure, the meaning of "chastity" changes over time. In *The Desperate Trail*, for instance, Fiorentino does finally sleep with her partner, but she is suitably reluctant until that point.

Conversely, in the 1994 movie *Breaking Point* Darlanne Fluegel, playing a vengeful and tough cop with martial arts skills, seduces Gary Busey (who is estranged from his wife, Kim Cattrall), in order to get close to the investigation of the killer they're both hunting. On learning of her real motive he berates her furiously, and she replies unapologetically, "I gave you the best night of sex you've ever had." If that remark doesn't reunite him with Cattrall nothing will, and it will get Fluegel killed into the bargain. We could if we wished say that she has to die anyway, since in her vengefulness she's passed beyond the bounds of professionalism. But that never got Clint Eastwood killed. In any event, the point is that she's given the role of seductress *to emphasize* the rightness of her death. It's not just *whether* you sleep with a man, it's *why* you do it.

The "death warrant" is emblematic; ideological coding consists of many such elements. Coded affirmations of sexual hierarchy and conventionality can turn up in any genre, usually in the form of male activism and female passivity in the public sphere, female activism and male reluctance in the domestic sphere. Often this is described in a manner we might not notice at first glance. In most dance films, for example (see *The Turning Point, White Nights, Dancers*), "the emphasis is on the male dancer as athlete.... [c]ommercial cinema reinstates a powerful and dynamic image of the male dancer, relegating the female to passive accessory."[33] This is a situation quite different

from the contemporaneous turn in American dance signaled by the apotheosis of the ballerina-centered New York City Ballet under Balanchine, and even
more different from the movement in contemporary dance (e.g., Mark Morris, Trisha Brown) away from traditional male-female pairings.

In many classic Westerns, similarly, women exist only to symbolize what it
is that men are fighting about. That is why the greatest movie about the
"taming of the West" can be titled *My Darling Clementine,* even though
"Clementine" is a secondary character, and no one can remember the name of
the actress who played her. In these movies women function overtly as a sign
of exchange between men, signifying the terms in which moral winners and
losers will be defined (see, e.g., classic Westerns as diverse as *Along the Great
Divide, Shane, El Dorado, Decision at Sundown,* and *The Naked Spur*). But in
all genres, narrative development often hinges on the exchange of women: on
women as the currency that men pass around, compete for, fight over. Male
protagonists either get the woman they deserve, or fail to get the woman they
don't deserve. Woman's is therefore the purely ideological function of letting
us know who deserves what, of linking moral desert to outcome. *Only Angels
Have Wings, Casablanca, The Morning After, Working Girl, The Money Train,*
and *Reality Bites* are just a few among hundreds of examples. Perhaps the
most striking contemporary instance is the costume drama *Rob Roy,* a movie
about conflict over land, money, and debt in which, as Gina Rourke puts it,
"Jessica Lange's body is the terrain on which the battles are fought."

Television is different from cinema. In any comparison of the two, we have
to be aware that the extent to which a particular commodity is "ideological" is
determined partly by its content, but also, and more crucially, by the nature of
the genre to which it belongs. If, for example, we search out elements of
heterosexist ideology in three familiar modes of communication, we will find
it most unabashedly and perhaps most powerfully in classical ballet; somewhat more equivocally in classical dominant cinema; and least assertively of
all in the multiple viewpoints and fractured (often woman-centered) narratives of commercial television. However, if we ask which of these modes of
communication is the most ideological as such, our order of ranking will be
completely inverted. Television is almost entirely and ballet only minimally
ideological, with cinema falling somewhere in between. The reason for this
has to do with what is *left over:* with the extent and power of that which serves
no ideological (or even narrative) function at all, which as I have said is
what we mean by "imagination" and "beauty." It is completely absent from
commercial television, is intermittently but quite often present in dominant
cinema, and permeates the best of ballet even during the most outrageously

sexist pas de deux.[34] This distinction between levels of analysis has to be kept in mind during any comparison of cinema and television; else we shall make the mistake of thinking that television's sometimes promiscuous ideological pluralism makes it less of an absolutely ideological apparatus than it in fact is.

Most Hollywood-style films can be fitted into different genres, but genre functions primarily as a frame for storytelling and fantasy. Only the most perfunctory movies (e.g., Roy Rogers Westerns) can be reduced to their generic content. Episodic television, contrarily, is nothing but its genres, and as such programs are sold to advertisers, summarized in *TV Guide,* and described in reviews. Family dramas, sitcoms, and the like, are loci of endless repetition.

For example, all "teen" shows on television are about moral choices, either sexual ("do the right thing"), political (be tolerant); social (always take advantage of the equal opportunity structure, but never in such a way as to hurt one's parents); or ethical (don't cheat). Adjustment to normative institutions such as school, family, or the economy, is the goal of all the protagonists, no matter how much comedy or heartbreak may be encountered along the way. The identity and iconography of the youthful series regulars is also carefully calibrated. Shows such as *Family Ties* or *Family Matters* always feature a young male character who might be called "the nerd next door," whose role is to highlight genuine adolescent masculinity. Since powerful athletes are rarely the protagonists on these shows—who could identify with them?—the rather ordinary male teens who are usually at the center must be set off in such a way as to guarantee their masculinity. In the same way the promiscuous girl who drifts in and out of episodes (she is unlikely to be allowed to be a regular), by her negative example defines young womanhood in such a way that the other female leads can be chaste without being desexualized. Ads on these shows, meanwhile, are all about eating or looks, and normalize a sort of Norman Rockwell version of America in which nothing has changed except the availability of McDonald's.

Genre being everything, if we ask how, say, *Designing Women* or *Laverne and Shirley* or *Home Improvement* or *Coach* handles gender, we cannot expect any kind of detailed answer ("in one particular episode, Tim insists on trying to fix the plumbing despite Jill's skepticism"). Though I've said earlier that Americans habitually politicize sex, it might be more revealing, or at least as revealing, to say that we tribalize it.[35] The peculiarly American slogan that "men are from Mars, women are from Venus," could have been invented to describe sitcom-, soap-, and domestic drama-land. In one of these tribes, the members normally pursue public power; if they are corrupt it is because power corrupts, not because men are corrupt. The other's pursuit of public power is atypical and abnormal, and so every instance of it is a reflection on the entire gender. Because of this division of labor, the genders are necessarily antagonistic: an antagonism that does not contradict the ideology of family and community, but instead explores its necessary price.

Each television genre *as a whole* is therefore about its own configuration of antagonistic sex/gender relationships, and what makes a particular program interesting (if it *is* interesting) is how it fits into that configuration; what unexpected fillip, if any, it may add. Whether they take place in a household or partially outside it *(Designing Women)*, most sitcoms either take place around the site of domesticity or else transpose domesticity to the workplace. In Kate Ellis's words, "by making home the place of a woman's work, (they) also (make) the work place an extension of home."[36] Even when a woman is a man's boss (as on *Moonlighting* most famously), they are still mostly about the proposition that "a woman's place is in the home"; the most prominent source of tension is not the importance of work but the distractions of sex. And as every sitcom episode, just as every episode of every program on episodic television, ends with a pointed moral, that moral is almost *always* the virtue of the domestic environment, and the rightness of its conceptualization as a separate sphere, even when that sphere is transported to a seemingly nondomestic workplace. In the 1990s, again, shows such as *Roseanne, Grace under Fire,* and even *Home Improvement* have begun to challenge this coding, as the material crisis and its impact on married women hits home.[37] But they are still exceptions. By and large, men who do not accept this conclusion about the domestic environment are either figures of fun or sociopaths; women who do not accept it, villainesses (or worse); men and women who miss it, lonely and lost (e.g., *Can't Hurry Love*).

So we should not be overimpressed that a "strong woman" such as Jill on *Home Improvement* often has the last word, for her last word merely reemphasizes the social superiority of women when they are in "their" environment.[38] Nor is that environment simply describable as one in which houses are kept and children are reared; the sitcom and the domestic melodrama require neither of those premises, and some (*Seinfeld,* say) do without both. Rather, the environment of women is one in which *relationships* rather than accomplishments are primary, and establishing and maintaining those relationships is what women do best. Even on a series, *Empty Nest,* purporting to be about women in different social roles, the career woman and the housewife are indistinguishable in the attention they pay to broken relationships and private affairs; and the professionalism of the career woman, not atypically, seems to consist of attempting to seduce male colleagues. Alternatively, the career woman may be portrayed as one whose profession itself consists of preserving family relationships or righting family wrongs, even in an ostensibly court-room melodrama such as *John Grisham's The Client.*

Nor is women's primacy in the domestic environment in itself an unmixed ideological blessing. Tim Allen is only the latest in a long line of television husbands who score moral points by gently mocking themselves, undercutting the less gentle mockery of their partners and emphasizing, as in the case of *Home Improvement,* the unmistakable hard edges of the latter. What could be more endearing than rueful self-awareness?[39] So too, when Bob Saget plays the domestic female role on *Full House,* his ostentatious role-playing reinforces the normativity of traditional heterosexual union all the more. So do the recurring scenes on that sitcom (as also on, for example, *Step by Step*), in which wimpish men are shown how to be "masculine," by standing up to women, drinking beer, watching football games; or as does, in a slightly different manner, Paul Reiser's complete cluelessness in *Mad about You.* The same truth, that is, inheres in both the male and the female roles. It's a dirty job, but someone's got to do it. One way or another, either by affirmation or by negative critique of men, we usually learn that the domestic world is where women "really" belong.

What is most fascinating about the remark, quoted earlier, that the 1995 television season had adventure for men and sex for women, was not what it revealed but what it elided. Actually, there were also new dramas *(The Client)* and sitcoms *(The Home Court, Caroline in the City, The Naked Truth, Bless This House, Almost Perfect)* featuring female protagonists, as well as old shows with females replacing original male leads *(Chicago Hope).* But they were about the relationships as much as or more than, the professionalism of women, even including judges. Whether in drama or comedy, primary emphasis was placed on their difficulties in balancing dual roles, to the point where one female judge, after missing her daughter's school play, declared that "justice will be merciless today."[40] This is also likely to be the theme of any movie about a career woman with a family (as in, for example, the 1993 Lifetime movie *Other Women's Children,* a story about a pediatrician with a title that says everything). As the example of the merciless judge suggests, it is not the purpose of domestic melodramas to point up the obstacles in the way of professional fulfillment for women, but rather to suggest how professional fulfillment for women puts obstacles in the way of their womanhood.

So fully wrought is television's sense of the gender order that it carries over even to the relationship, or rather comparison, between black men and white women. In shows as diverse as *L.A. Law* and the more recent *Courthouse,* the work of black professional men is troubled by problems of race, but this has an understandable component for which the texts usually spend a lot of time apologizing. White women, though, are burdened by what are invariably presented as irrationalities of gender, and these are rarely explained as the reasonable outcome of impinging social or material circumstances.

On the face of it, sitcoms often seem in one respect to transgress against the gender code. Since only so much pleasure can be gleaned from the loveable antics of misbehaving children, domestic tensions occupy a prominent place on these shows. Role reversal, therefore, is one of the staples of sitcoms and family dramas, so that for every show on which "father knows best" *(Father Knows Best, Cosby)* there is another (more or less) in which father is a buffoon. There are mothers bringing up six children by themselves, fathers bringing up six children by themselves, women living with women, men living with men *(The Odd Couple),* women and men living chastely together *(Three's Company),* teenagers on their own *(Charles in Charge),* and so on. But all domestic sitcoms, without exception, are jokes built around the premise that this is the kind of work women are expected to be doing and the space in which they are expected to be doing it, and they are expected to be doing that work in this space as part of a nuclear family; and isn't it *funny* when a man does it instead, or a woman does it poorly, or there is no nuclear family but instead some other weird arrangement, and so forth. The comedy of role reversal is comic only because we need not take role reversal too literally but can (must) view it as an unexpected twist on what we know to be the "real" reality: the domesticated shrew who stands behind every untamed man. And in case anyone should miss the point that a joke is just a joke, the ads are there to remind us. The ads on television are what we are meant to take seriously, and sitcom ads are all, or mostly, about keeping house and keeping clean; there is little role reversal in them. For all of these reasons, even when the ideology of the family appears to be undergoing its most dangerous subversion (*All in the Family,* or *Roseanne*), it receives its most emphatic expression.[41]

Soap operas even more than sitcoms are the woman's genre par excellence. Unlike sitcoms, though, they are not premised on a joke, and role reversal is the last thing we expect from them. Their subject and their only subject is the pleasures and pains—mostly the pains—of the conventional sex/gender system. Television inundates us with day-and nighttime soap operas that are often, and uniquely, about nothing but female sexuality. Even the professional women on nighttime soap operas such as *Melrose Place* and *Central Park West* seem to use their offices mostly as occasions for sexual intrigue. Invariably, the more their sexuality is openly asserted the more it is finally punished (compare the superbitch Joan Collins with the good girl Linda Evans on *Dynasty*). Especially on daytime soap operas (for which women are the only audience) it often uncovers itself as long-hidden violations of the incest taboo, making out-of-control (female) sexuality the deadliest crime of all.

That the pains of conventional heterosexuality, and women's anger and frustration with it, are so prominently displayed on soaps—the only variant of visual culture scripted predominantly by women—has led some cultural theorists to conclude, again, that the genre is potentially, or even inherently, subversive.[42] This suggestion gains even more credence from the circumstance that soaps are not only endless but are endlessly open-ended, so that neither within a single episode nor at the end of any single soap in its entirety is there ever a simple example of narrative closure. Whatever the potential readings of female viewers, though, the manifest narratives of soap operas, daytime or nighttime, support a conventional view of sexual hierarchy without difficulty. In the first place, this appreciation of soaps suffers from the literal-minded assumption that the stories they tell are their essential content, although it would surely be much more faithful to the medium as both a formal system and a commercial institution to understand the *ads* as the most insistent and powerful narrative presented to the women who watch them.[43]

In any event, the angry power that women display on soaps is the disturbing or even destructive power of female sexuality. Women fighting with intimate male partners, or women fighting with women over men, is the repetitive image that most often drives their narratives.[44] But this is a realm of power that men have always gladly ceded to women, usually with the insistence of a grimly self-righteous gynephobia. This is what the separate spheres are all about: men's domination of the public sphere, women's "domination" of the private sphere. Or rather, men's total hegemony in the public sphere, women's occasional power within the private: the latter hardly disturbing the former. For women, only domesticity is unproblematic. Sitcoms often confront their male leads with nagging wives, who drive the men back into the public sphere (where, after all, they belong). But no television series to my knowledge has ever presented us with a *housewife* who is seen by men as "a ball-busting bitch." If we are looking for her, we had better go to the district attorney's office.

Moreover, if the perspectives expressed by the pluralistic focus of soap opera's cameras are usually those of women, these are women whose lives are defined by their desire for men. That men don't reciprocate that desire satisfactorily, that they are unreliable and occasionally evil, never makes them on soaps any the less desirable (even though often they are ridiculously young-looking for the jobs they allegedly hold). Nor, as the desired object of operatic passion, are these men cast in the same light as those women who are the object of man's quest in male-centered melodrama: these sex objects are desirable not for what they are but for what they do and what they have. The *woman* who makes things happen, rather than being made, is the "villainess," a character who is always in residence on any daytime or nighttime soap at any time.[45] Though women on soaps often work, they are rarely *shown* working for more than a few seconds at a time, except in hospitals: the one milieu above all in which Hollywood explicitly reproduces patriarchy. (Nor do housewives on sitcoms ever do housework; that apparently minor task is reserved for the ads, during which household dirt vanishes with the first application of Wisk or Joy). And as with sitcoms too, the ads on soaps tell us even more than the narratives. Serving a dual function, they are more than just a recognition of the audience. Diapers, tampons, baby food, diet programs, headache medications, detergents are also the explicit representation of that subject which soap opera narratives only display implicitly: the motherhood of womanhood.

As for sexuality, female sexual satisfaction, though not so rare as it used to be, remains at best, as in *Roseanne*, a sort of reward for making difficult moral decisions. Most of the time in television's world of sexual tease, men sublimate sex into power, but the metonymy is so familiar that their sexuality remains overt. Women sublimate sex into powerlessness or role confusion, and their sexuality is therefore concealed except as mere *appearance*. Again, villainesses are the exception; their sex is sublimated into power. But this is another exception that proves the rule, since their sexuality is clearly shown as predatory rather than merely self-defined. They are the women that women love to hate and men love to fear, the id that must be repressed but can be vicariously enjoyed when unleashed by others—as long as the others will eventually be suitably punished. I use the word "punished" loosely. What is the "punishment" of, say, Madchen Amick or Kylie Travis on *Central Park West*? It is never to be fulfilled for even a brief moment; never to have true male companionship, but only the obeisances of a manipulated puppet. With these women, making things *happen* in the world, as opposed to taking other women's men away from them, still remains a largely male prerogative.

Even during the 1990s, when economically active women have proliferated on television, in hospitals or law courts or mass communications enterprises, the institutions themselves remain bastions of unalloyed patriarchy, and as such go uncriticized by television. Hospitals are home to male surgeons (the tokens on *Chicago Hope* and *E.R.* aside) who right the body's wrongs; and who solve their patients' crises without any suggestion of their own domesticity (as is most definitely not true of Christine Lahti on *Chicago Hope*). In just the same way, although *L.A. Law* often satirized the legal profession—especially in the person of Corbin Bernsen's heartless divorce expert—it was the benevolent Richard Dysart who, as head of the firm, ultimately vouched for its integrity. The Good and the Male remain linked, not yet to be torn asunder.

Since television, with its ability to appeal to segmented audiences, recognizes the market value of upwardly mobile women much more readily than does the film industry, it gives them considerably more representation, even (as in *Sweet Justice* with Cecily Tyson and Melissa Gilbert, or the short-lived detective series *Leg Work*) creating scenarios of female partnership without male supervision. All in all, though, a large proportion of these new professional women spend an inordinate amount of time establishing, maintaining, overseeing, and fixing relationships: an activity "denied" to men. In the TV-movie *False Witness* (1989), typically, Phyllicia Rashad as an assistant D.A. must battle all the "old boys" in her own office and among the cops, who refuse to believe that a "respectable" surgeon could be a brutal rapist. Only another woman on her staff supports her against their opposition and even betrayal. The most treacherous offender, though, is her lover, and his betrayal is rendered as personal rather than professional.

Most important of all, since Hollywood never suggests that these hierarchical institutions might have to take on a new configuration in order to accommodate a central role for women, it cannot really criticize the old configuration. The ideology of liberal pluralism, according to which the fundamental institutional hierarchies, purged of all gross unfairnesses, are adaptable to needed change, stands firmly in the way of any acts of real social imagination. If Nancy Travis and Mike Ryan *(Almost Perfect)* can treat each other with respect and have a good time to boot (without any children to stand in the way, of course), then who could be so churlish as to recollect that the legal system and the mass communications industry are organized in ways that make them inhospitable to humane life?

The delicate approach of television to career women, and its clear delineation between what is normative and punishable in sexual behavior, is put into even sharper relief by the complaisant treatment of armed and violent men in films. When Arnold Schwarzenegger insisted that the ending of *The Running Man* be changed so that he not walk off into the sunset with a heroine who was a prostitute, he was only making explicit what is usually more subtle. Shooting any number of men is better than allowing yourself to be fucked by one unauthorized man: and it's men who do the authorizing. Again, not "whether" but "why" is the issue. At the conclusion of the 1995 movie *Jade*, we learn that Linda Fiorentino's descent into perverse (i.e., uncompensated) whoredom is going to be unrelentingly punished by her affronted (and philandering) husband, while all the men who have fucked her (except the one who turned her out and blackmailed the others) will walk away unscathed. Her punishment is clearly for having *enjoyed* what she was doing rather than apologizing for it or being coerced into it. Not the wrong kind of violent behavior but the wrong kind of sexual behavior is what triggers overt misogyny in the world of visual culture. Better to kill more than a dozen men in *The Desperate Trail* than to wind up as a whore without a heart of gold like Fiorentino, or a seductress like Fluegel.

In general then, Hollywood, whether in cinema or in television land, reinforces sex-role stereotypes and, if less forcefully than ever before, polices their boundaries—while flaunting occasional exceptions that themselves give a very mixed message. However, it would be misleading to "blame" this on Hollywood, on institutional misogyny, and so forth. Visual culture, though phantasmic and simplistic, is still only one expression of dominant culture in general. And because dominant culture is what it is—an ideologically normative core surrounded and interpenetrated by, but still distinct from, an aggregation of disturbing and threatening Others—its representations are never wholly innocent. Every representation of the Other stands in for the particular version of otherness as a whole, in a way that (nonethnic) white men never do. They stand for nothing but themselves, the free individuals of American mythology. The *problem* of the division of men and women into separate tribes is the problem of women; it raises the prospect of gynephobia, for which there is no female equivalent. Antifeminists have tried, with some success, to create an equivalent, which they call "man-hating." Certain feminist arguments (such as those of, say, Mary Daly) can be read as misanthropic. But that will only be the case if they are literally *read,* which is always by very few people. Gynephobia and misogyny, on the contrary, are part and parcel of the general, dominant ideology of family and community: a dominant ideology that, by virtue of the opposition its contradictions conjure up, is always under threat.

Whatever, according to a given representation, "women want" is too much, because *all* women are implicated in the depiction of any woman's desires. Stallone the killer makes no statement about men as killers; Linda Fiorentino the killer automatically makes a statement about women. Pro or con, women respond to Fiorentino, or Sharon Stone, ideologically, and so (if perhaps less reflectively) do men. But neither men nor women respond to Stallone ideologically as a man (though they may respond to him as an American, a representative of the working class, and so forth). He does not carry the sex wars (or tribalization) with him wherever he goes. So women in general—along with all people of color and of transgressive sexuality—remain culture's significant Other. Sexual women are sexuality incarnate, powerful women power incarnate, violent women violence incarnate. Put Tim's self-mockery in Jill's mouth and it becomes self-flagellation, a putdown of women. Omit it, and she becomes unpleasantly "hard." Moral linkage, though rarely avoided, is only contingent to narratives about males. It is necessary to any narrative about females, however briefly they may appear.

The heart of this coding persists. Sexually passive women suggest an endorsement of the traditional double standard, whereas sexually active women seem to be endorsing its repudiation. Troublemaking (that is, the politicization of sex) is always brought about by women. If they are corrupt, their corruption is sexual; when men are corrupt, their corruption is public. (David Lynch's television series *Wild Palms,* meant in some sense to be counterideological, was instead a perfect replication of these themes). The double standard still rules, if less obviously than in an earlier era.

From some standpoints our screens seem swamped with sex, but the moral rules remain different for men and women. Even in cinema, where discreet nudity is now *comme il faut,* the full frontal male, for no narratively compelling reason, remains relatively infrequent: it too evidently fails to appeal to the only form of prurience the double standard recognizes as legitimate. Try making a movie like *Showgirls* featuring men, and even an NC-17 rating would be hard to come by.[46] Sexuality is both pleasurable and questionable, and it is both of these at once because and only because it is coded as "female." The code reveals itself in what is absent as well as in what is present.

4 Recuperating the Sexual Order

Ideological justification can never be simple and straightforward. It is not just that the idyllic story of the family as patriarchal community may be a lie in the experience of many actual families. Even families that are based on mutual love and loyalty, and occasionally or often surmount patriarchalism, might also at the same time be repositories of external class and gender conflicts that condition them willy-nilly as sites of unadmitted hierarchy. And because material reality cannot remain hidden from those who live it for very long, ideological myths are not only partly spurious, they are also only partly successful. The production of symbolic goods is as hard to control as the production of material goods. The same printing presses that produce the Bible produce pornography (not literally the same, probably); the same arguments that justify the corporation as a fictitious "person" justify the human being as a real person. The liberal individualism that develops with and justifies capitalist accumulation also gradually grows apart from it. As Sacvan Bercovitch puts it: " 'America' is not an overarching synthesis, *e pluribus unum,* but a rhetorical battleground, a symbol that has been made to stand for diverse and sometimes mutually contradictory outlooks."[1]

As American liberalism both embeds itself and subjects itself to an autocritique, the long-term subordination of any group, as prescribed by the notion of separate spheres for women, or the notion of separate but equal education for blacks, becomes suspect and finally untenable. In the case of gender, at some point the *actual* subordination of women has gradually been displaced, by a conceptual sleight of hand, into the *ideological* realm of "the family": a spurious unity that looks enough like the real thing to be passed off as such. A subordinate productive institution, founded in part on unpaid human labor, is ideologically reconceptualized as an independent moral institution founded wholly on free human desire: the supposedly "free" and "natural" desire of women to be "in the home" rather than in the factory or the office. Gender and sexual relations in the home become not only materially but symbolically integral to labor relations in the workplace, and vice versa. (For example, only the proposition that male workers are working to support "their" families justifies the economic and resultant personal dependency of their wives.) Neither could function without the other, both in material practice and in ideological justification.

Because this ideology does describe how many of us have lived at one time or another, it works to some extent; that is, its justification of superordinate/ subordinate relations as in fact a moral unity comes to be believed by many men and women. However, because of the fragility of purely or partly symbolic resolutions, we shall always find elements of counterideology in dominant culture. Our critique will ultimately base itself on the grand affirmations of the early American Republic. It implicitly or explicitly deploys the buried (sometimes not so buried) rhetoric of a more radical Americanism—freedom and equality for all—in order to criticize the ideological triumphalism of order and subordination: for example, it can generate a critique of male domination in the name of "women," or of capitalism in the name of "workers," or of repressive community in the name of free individuals.

These critiques, though, are not equally salient. The United States, "born liberal" in Louis Hartz's phrase,[2] is of all modern capitalist societies the one in which class is most subdued as an acknowledged principle of social organization; it is, however, also the one in which gender relations are rendered most ambiguous by the unique force of liberal individualism. For any persons, the reconciliation between individual fulfillment and community membership is in principle more problematic for Americans than for most other people. So too then the reconciliation between individual and the isolated, fragile community of "the family."

In this perspective, the kinds of moral linkage discussed in Chapter 3 are too fragmentary, in and of themselves, to retrieve a social order threatened by the very success of its own public philosophy. Beyond such moral coding, it is the very structure of narrative itself (in the Hollywood style) that does the hard work of retrieving social hierarchies from the incipient critique of egalitarianism. What is this structure?

We have defined ideology as the substitution of a spurious unity for the reality of conflict. It follows that ideology reveals itself narratively by presenting a normative institution as threatened, but then recuperated, by a closure that disavows the threat, allays our fears, and justifies our original expectations. We are carried along to the *harmonious resolution* of an *initial opposition* that is finally *disavowed,* and the moral order rescued, because the conflict is revealed to have been *only apparent.* The most obvious illustration of this structure in cinematic fiction is also the most famous.[3] This is the basic narrative of Boy Meets Girl, Boy Loses Girl, Boy Gets Girl Again, and its endless variations: including even Girl Meets Girl, Girl Loses Girl, Girl Gets Girl *(Desert Hearts, Lianna);* and most recently Boy Meets Girl, Girl Steals Girl, Boy Steals Girl Back *(Personal Best, Three of Hearts).*

Ideologically, this formula works most powerfully when what originally seemed to be a *social problem* is resolved satisfactorily by the coming together of two individuals in heterosexual love. What is disavowed, that is, is the prospect of real incompatibility among sympathetic human beings. Whatever the occasions for our anxiety (class conflict, sex wars, mistaken identities) they have all been much ado about nothing, and the fundamental harmony of the social order is revealed with the reassurance that love (or, once in a while, patriotism) conquers all—even money. Most of the time, too, no hint of utopian nostalgia for a precapitalist social order (as in the work of the great Victorians such as Dickens or George Eliot) is allowed to disturb the ease of our acceptance. Here then ideological interpellation is accomplished not simply by linking character to destiny, but by the trajectory of the narrative as a whole; we are enfolded in a world that we recognize as "real," thus ourselves becoming real citizens of that world.[4]

The initial conflict, however, must be serious, or we have no reason to watch the rest of the movie (or television program). First, the appearance of apparently irretrievable conflict must be installed at the heart of a narrative; then, an ideologically acceptable ending must now somehow be retrieved. But this is not necessarily simple. Poorly made movies or television programs do not accomplish this goal at all, and surely do not succeed in interpellating their viewers into any role except superior viewer of mass culture. For most viewers at least the appearance of subtlety is required. So (in cinema) loners join the team *(Air Force)*; atheists wind up praying in foxholes *(Battleground)*; pacifists exist only to be converted to an endorsement of violence *(High Noon, Friendly Persuasion, Sergeant York)*; and films about divorced protagonists end in their reconciliation *(Seems Like Old Times, Overboard, Miracles)*. Most typically, a critique will be stated explicitly or implicitly, only to be subverted by its opposite: not to produce a resolution at a higher level of understanding, but simply to stroke every sensibility that might be watching. "Promiscuity" is visual culture's intellectual watchword. Most of us do have a divided consciousness about some, even many, aspects of our social existence. The ideological goal of most visual culture is to heal (or to appear to have healed) that division.[5]

Nonetheless, given the irreversible cultural revolution of feminism, the sexual tension that was once primarily a source of laughs (as in 1930s screwball comedies) no longer looks very funny to many people. If the Hollywood techniques of ideological recuperation had not already existed, they would have to have been developed for confronting the demands of feminism. Every night on television, every night in every movie theater, we encounter yet again the one clash between egalitarianism and hierarchy that is never off the agenda. Worse yet for the cultural status quo, the demands of uncloseted gay liberation, now clothed in the irresistible language of American individualism and civil rights, have escalated the general stakes of liberation as never before. If this last barrier is torn aside, what will protect "manhood" and "masculinity"—and to many, civilization itself—from complete collapse? The genuinely hysterical reaction of political and military leaders to an unsuspecting president's attempted abolition of the military's ban on gays, showed the limits of the Clinton entourage's notion that "It's the economy, Stupid." Up to a point, perhaps, "it" is the economy, but much more profoundly, *"it's* sex, Stupid." Contemporary visual culture cannot be understood outside this perspective. The transformation (or rather, the attempted transformation) of independent women into dependent family members, has become its staple subject matter.

In earlier Hollywood the family was occasionally a "problem," or rather was disturbed by a problem that needed explaining away, such as alcoholism or drug addiction *(The Country Girl, A Hatful of Rain)*. These explorations of disorder could be quarantined by the implication that they illustrated individual pathologies rather than general social distress. Now the family is almost always a problem. This change in emphasis can lead to the kind of confusion that is spread by the steady drumbeat of anti-Hollywood criticism from the Right. Here a little historical context is needed. Narrative suspense must always be contextualized to be compelling, and this means that over time the stakes of narrative suspense must escalate. In the period since World War II, capitalist enterprises and their advance men in advertising have overseen the transformative creation of a modern if not modernist consumer culture. For those who doubt its existence, a simple index of the extent of this transformation is the following: before the 1960s, *Lady Chatterley's Lover* was banned in most English-speaking jurisdictions, whereas it has now become the all-time best-seller of Penguin Books, logging close to five million copies sold by late 1993. Now only a naive nostalgia for "the way we never were" (in Stephanie Coontz's evocative phrase) can still separate old-fashioned "deviance" from everyday behavior.[6]

When mainstream movies, even directed by an alleged "conservative" like Clint Eastwood, treat adultery sympathetically, as an institutional difficulty rather than a moral disorder (Eastwood's *The Bridges of Madison County*, or *Four Weddings and a Funeral*, or the Arthurian *First Knight*), we understand that the line between the proscribed and the accepted has shifted drastically. The necessity to draw boundaries between the licit and the illicit is still there, though, constantly in motion, and Hollywood strives just as constantly to keep up with (or stay slightly ahead of) its forward progress. In what should properly be called the postliberation era, cultural spokesmen (and some women) have seen a need to recuperate established sex roles and hierarchies, while at the same time conceding to feminism ground that cannot realistically be reclaimed.[7] Although the sex war has always been a constant roiling undercurrent in American visual culture (compared, say, to England, where until recently it was virtually nonexistent), since the 1960s it has become an inescapable subtext of every film and television genre, and the manifest text of innumerable films and TV episodes.

That this text or subtext is often "seen through" by women (or audiences generally) should not, furthermore, lead us to mistake its general direction. For example, in her *Soap Opera and Women's Talk*, Mary Ellen Brown reports that women find "resistive pleasure" in talking together about soap operas.[8] Her interpretation of this "pleasure," however, is misconceived. If women who had watched a lot of Westerns or pro football games (with their husbands, say) came together to talk about that experience, their talk would also be "resistive." Since ideological accounts of unity are always partly spurious, and most people do not regularly suffer from false consciousness about this, one

of the operations of ideological discourse is always to call up resistance to itself
—and the more so the greater its pretensions to "realism" (which do reach a
kind of apogee in soaps). It would be a confusion, though, to think that this
makes the discourse itself any the less ideological; that is another question
altogether. The simple fact is that male independence and male solidarity are
never (well, hardly ever) stated and then disavowed.

In contrast, the need for disavowal of *female* independence and recuperation of the threatened sexual order is real, and manifested everywhere in visual
culture. It is no respecter of genre or aesthetic quality. On one episode of the
family sitcom *Happy Days,* for example, the comedy seems to be about
whether a housewife suffering from "empty nest syndrome" should take a job.
The narrative is cast as a debate between husband and wife, about which an
egalitarian might think that she gets all the best lines. However, the *laugh track*
features laughter at every one of her declamations, and none of his, and so
takes away what seems to have been given.[9] In a quite different genre, every
science-fiction series of the past twenty-five years has had at least one episode
in which a female-dominated planet is discovered by the main characters, and
eventually disavowed by its inhabitants, usually after one of them falls in love
with a visiting astronaut.

Most of these shows are cartoonish and, given time constraints, their narratives are cursory at best. Disavowal and recuperation need hardly be sophisticated, though, as the unintentionally hilarious ending of *The Vanishing*
(Hollywood version) attests. Even more striking, the entire metatext of Hollywood's sexual politics can be summed up in the ending of the seemingly more
substantial film *The River Wild.* Starring Hollywood's most "serious" actress,
this film is in an essay in recuperation so unabashed that it demands word-
for-word quotation.

The River Wild begins and proceeds as an extended contrast between the
macho superwoman Meryl Streep, and the ineffectual and alienated husband/
father David Strathairn (who gives new life to the epithet "four-eyes"
throughout the first part of the film). Less than halfway into the story, though,
another narrative begins to emerge. First we learn that his alienation is due to
the excessive demands placed upon him by his perfectionist, careerist wife, a
charge she does not deny.[10] Then, with his family (wife and son Roarke) under
siege by a pair of criminals who want Streep to take them through a whitewa-
ter passage ("The Gauntlet") that only she can master, he begins to fight back
(to shake off his original coding, we might say), and on several occasions
engages in fisticuffs with the main villain: a statement of self denied the
heretofore more physical Streep. Finally, escaping under seemingly impossible

circumstances through her unique skills and his conventional heroics, the family is united (and the villains dispatched). For anyone who is not certain how "narrative closure" and recuperation work, the movie now ends in this way:

> RANGER (*disbelievingly*): Did your mom take you down that river all by herself?
>
> YOUNG ROARKE (*proudly*): Yes.
>
> RANGER (*worriedly*): And what did your father do?
>
> (*Pause.* ROARKE *looks over at* STREEP *and* STRATHAIRN, *kissing.*)
>
> ROARKE: He saved our lives.

What is particularly interesting is the way in which the normative family is here recuperated twice, so to speak. In the first instance, the independent career woman is repudiated: she has been unwomanly. (Just so, on the woman-oriented series *The Client,* one 1996 episode had JoBeth Williams representing a young female gymnast who is being tyrannized by an abusive female coach: this in a world full of abusive male coaches, some of whom are internationally notorious). At the same time the woman, now retrieved, is returned to the newly heroized husband. Hollywood will go to any lengths to arrange this kind of reconciliation. We need only think, for example, of a more "serious" film such as *Class Action.* This trial drama descends to even greater depths of the ludicrous by unbelievably allowing father and daughter attorneys to oppose each other in a civil suit, so that the daughter can ultimately betray her client in order to reconcile with her estranged father (precisely, of course, why no judge would ever allow such an arrangement in the first place).

Hollywoodian recuperation is usually more subtle than that, but still unmistakable. Often, as in *The River Wild,* recuperation takes place through an unexpected reaffirmation of traditional gender roles. In a 1995 episode of *E.R.,* a nurse who's been trained as a doctor in Eastern Europe performs an illegal, life-saving operation. Called aside by one of the male surgeons, and fearful that she is about to lose her job or be arrested, she is instead told that in the United States "we" value individual initiative: the patriarchal order has inducted her into its ranks.

Much more famously (and conversely), but to the same effect, in *Aliens* the movie's emotional climax comes (as in all movies about the "outlaw hero") at the end of the movie's first phase, when, as I've noted earlier, Sigourney Weaver / Ripley seizes control of the marine troop carrier from the troop's ineffectual, paralyzed, commanding officer, in order to rescue the troop's trapped survivors.[11] At this moment most members of the audience will feel the same adrenaline surge that occurs when Humphrey Bogart / Rick Blaine turns to the band in Rick's Café and tells them to play the *Marseillaise;* or when Brando / Zapata says "Cut the wire!" and the revolution begins; or when Alan Ladd says, "Try me!" to one of the gunfighters who've been imported to terrorize the pacific ranchers of *Shane.* This is the moment of the birth of the mythic hero; at this point Ripley is the first truly universal hero (though still for white people primarily). Her heroic stature is emphasized even more when, later on, she slams the corporate lackey Burke / Paul Reiser up against a wall for attempting to smuggle an alien back to the home galaxy. At this point, the universal hero is saving not merely her comrades but, befittingly, the entire human universe.

All this occurs, however, concurrent with another text, in which Ripley is defined not by her heroism but by her commitment to the role of Holy Mother. The movie's final phase and narrative climax consists of her attempt to save neither her comrades nor the universe, but rather the little girl Newt, with whom she, as the lone clearly heterosexual woman in the film, has become uniquely bonded. In this way the centrality of female heroism is disavowed (as it almost always is in mainstream cinema) in favor of the woman's familial role, which is thereby recuperated.

A female protagonist's rejection of that possibility either signifies villainy (as in *Basic Instinct, The Last Seduction, Fatal Attraction*), or (as we have seen) functions as a death warrant for otherwise morally sympathetic characters: Vasquez in *Aliens,* Angelica Huston in *Crimes and Misdemeanors.* More generally (though certainly not in the case of *Aliens*), the threat to a normative institution such as the family may be quarantined by finding a scapegoat to represent an idiosyncratic, personalized source of moral derangement. Most often, this role has been filled by a woman, since in its sentimentalized version the family is held together by the woman. It can only be permanently destroyed by her subversion of femaleness (as in *Fatal Attraction*), or the emotional desertion *(Ordinary People, Kramer vs. Kramer)* or occupational desertion *(Presumed Innocent, Working Girl)* of her female role. Actually, in the contemporary era of sexual panic refracted through the prism of feminism, the domestic scapegoat is occasionally a man who abuses his wife or child: the reformist staple of "the movie of the week" on television during the 1980s and 1990s (from *The Burning Bed* in 1984 to *She Fought Alone* in 1995).[12] Typically, though, these movies are considerably less than oppositional, in that they ask us to reflect on shortcomings in law enforcement or personal failures rather than to ask any more profound questions about the institution of the family itself.

The kind of 180° turnaround that distinguishes *The River Wild* is actually a rarity in Hollywood. It works best in the action/adventure genre, but will usually be jarring in more reflective contexts such as the family drama. The most frequent means of recuperation found in Hollywood culture is instead a kind of fence-straddling, or what can best be called, "Having it both ways," which ensures that uncomfortable readings are answered, or otherwise safely disposed of, before the closure of a narrative.[13] To be sure, "ensures" is too strong a word. Social change is not something that can simply be boxed in, like raisins or computer paper. A 1980s episode from the sitcom *Three's Company,* for example, illuminates the thin line between ideological disavowal and ideological disaster. In this episode the wimpish John Ritter unsuccessfully tries to protect Priscilla Barnes from a masher; she knocks the offender out with a single karate punch. (Later, underlining the event, she opens a jar that Ritter can't get open). In an ensuing scene Ritter accidentally knocks out (from the rear) a cop who has intervened, and is arrested for the offense. The other cons in the holding pen are cowed by his new persona. He finds himself lionized for his accomplishment, and is forced to invent a suitable past. This includes his having been a boxing champion in the navy, and concludes with a fantasized reenactment of his greatest victory, which is "shown" to and "seen" by both his cellmates and us the audience. All this is a fiction, of course. Within the fiction the wimpish Ritter is the reality and the tough guy Ritter the fantasy, except that the two scenes of him losing and winning receive equal *visual* weight. Is anyone fooled by this sleight-of-hand into thinking that somewhere underneath the ostensible story we're being shown there's still a traditional role for traditional men? Hardly likely: that there is an unrecuperated dilemma lying barely below the surface is suggested by the fact that this same plot line, with similarly unsuccessful resolution, has since resurfaced on (at a minimum) *Happy Days, Family Ties, Married with Children,* and *Step by Step.*

Here, apparently, social being is so divided, if perhaps primarily at a subconscious level, that the division can't be healed. Even among the desperate recuperative efforts of *The River Wild* it is quite possible—even likely—that what finally stays with audiences, or at least some audiences, is the fetishized but also "power feminist" vision of Meryl Streep, rather than the less diegetically credible reinvention of David Strathairn. This film's narrative may well be seen by viewers as placing it in the female action genre (described in Chapter 8): a genre in which male power is on the whole *not* recuperated.

Most of the time, though, movies and television are more successful at subduing the cultural threat whose invocation they rely on for generating narrative interest and suspense. Even the most contemptuous misogyny can be recuperated from such narratives. In a 1995 episode of *The Single Guy*, Jonathan dates a woman who demolishes him in one athletic contest after another. In the midst of a round of golf, she tells him how much she likes him because he's a "great loser." He then proceeds to eke out a victory, at which point she dissolves into imprecatory shrieks and furious sobs, and stalks off with an ex-boyfriend. Virtually the same narrative, in a slightly different format, took place at roughly the same time on the African American-oriented show, *In the House*, produced by and starring one of the leading creator of such shows in recent years, Debbie Allen.[14] On this episode, her free-spirited biker sister, a world-traveling photojournalist, travels with the family and two muscular male models to a photoshoot in Mexico. In midflight the pilot deserts the plane (sitcom plots must not be interrogated too closely) and the sister has to crash-land it. Having done so successfully, she faints into the arms of one of the men. Recuperation is not yet done, though. Now she reveals that all her stories about her worldly success are lies designed to prop up her ego, because unlike Debbie Allen she doesn't have a family to give her life value. Again and again, the repellent independent woman (Sigourney Weaver in *Working Girl*, Glenn Close in *Fatal Attraction*) is brought to book.

The repressed can never be definitively prevented from returning, but it can be and usually is represented in such a way that we encounter it detached from its truly serious implications. So the one time that Hollywood has directly confronted the issue of homelessness, in the 1989 TV-movie *No Place Like Home*, the trials of the carefully conceived nuclear family that is the collective protagonist are caused by a fire—no homeless persons of other than impeccable work-ethic credentials need apply. We can have both our compassion and our social self-satisfaction at once: even more so, in that the final family reunion is brought about by the heroics of the father.[15]

In this sense, "having it both ways" most prominently means, among other possibilities, that we can "have" our feminism or our women's liberation as entertainment without having it as a persistent politics; that remains absent. On *Caroline in the City*, a 1995 series, Caroline's Wisconsin aunt, visiting her in the big city after recently separating from her husband, plays the dual role of both the elderly woman now hungry for sex *and* the stereotypical relative pressuring the single woman into marriage. Get married, have good sex: the old welded together with the new.

"Having it both ways" is usually not just a joke, and can be much more complex than that. The long-running "feminist" series *Cagney and Lacey* offers a perfect example of this technique at work. From one standpoint, I should not have scare quotes around the ideological signifier in the previous

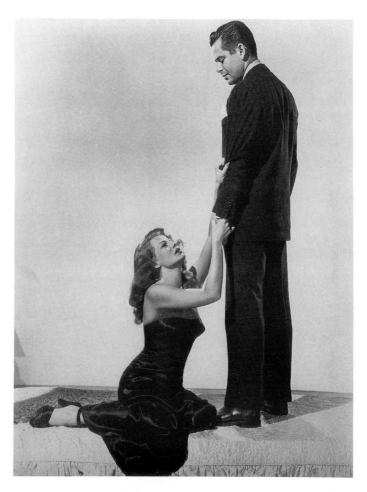

Rita Hayworth and Glenn Ford in *Gilda:* Which one is the underdog hero? Imprisoned by a vengeful Johnnie for her supposedly wanton infidelities, Gilda begs to be released. (Courtesy, Museum of Modern Art)

The Family Recuperated: from superwoman to good wife, the two Meryl
Streeps. Meryl Streep and David
Strathairn in *The River Wild*. (Courtesy, Museum of Modern Art)

Universal hero—and mother: Sigourney Weaver as Ripley in *Aliens*. (Courtesy Museum of Modern Art)

In *Cagney and Lacey*, Sharon Gless and Tyne Daley as New York City detectives Christine Cagney and Mary Beth Lacey—something for everyone. (Courtesy, Photofest)

Helen Mirren as Detective-Inspector Jane Tennyson in *Prime Suspect*—without glamour, without compromise. (Courtesy, Photofest)

Unreconciled and on the run, Melvin Van Peebles as Sweetback in *Sweet Sweetback's Baadasssss Song* turns his back on Whitey. (Courtesy, Photofest)

What the male gaze sees: women warriors. Linda Hamilton in *Terminator 2* (courtesy, Museum of Modern Art); Jenette Goldstein in *Aliens* (courtesy, Museum of Modern Art); Cynthia Rothrock in *Tiger Claws* (courtesy, Photofest).

As Thana, the Angel of Death, Zoe Tamerlis prepares for another victim in *Ms. 45*. (Courtesy, Photofest)

"What are you going to do, charge me with smoking?" Sharon Stone revises "Gilda" in *Basic Instinct*. (Courtesy, Photofest)

sentence. Certainly the creators of *Cagney and Lacey* intended it to offer a different kind of representation of women on television, and they were successful enough that in our household, at least, it was the only television series we watched regularly and faithfully while it was on the tube. On the other hand, we were never unaware of what was also going on in the guise of cultural innovation. "Having it both ways" meant that to a certain extent we were being had. In what manner becomes clear when we consider the iconography of this series.

Lacey the family woman, played by Tyne Daly in a frumpish mode, is also the liberal feminist. Cagney the single woman, played by Sharon Gless looking and dressing as though she'd just dropped in from the Miss Universe contest next door, is the hard-nosed upholder of "law and order," and derider of constitutional rights for accused persons. She is also the victim of gender discrimination, and has (at times) a Jewish boyfriend from the American Civil Liberties Union. There is something for everyone here; correlatively, this means that we cannot make consistent sense of these women politically. Familialism is split away from conservatism, "liberated" sexuality from liberalism, and the cross-everything affair between Gless and Steve Macht tells us that politics is not important enough to interfere with sex. (Obviously sometimes it isn't. But often it is—and this narrative choice makes an ideological choice. It's not as though Steve Macht and Sharon Gless have an unslakable mutual passion: they're just characters in a fiction.) Any viewer who could detect her own political stance amid this deliberate confusion must have wanted to do so very badly. In the end, "feminism" attached to an uncritical conception of the law and the police, and detached from any critique of the nuclear family, is barely feminism at all. Here, to say that the show has it both ways is to say that it both has and does not have its putative feminism.

Quite differently, "having it both ways" can mean that a particular narrative simply embraces a social contradiction, so that we are satisfied whatever side of the contradiction we approach it from. On an episode of *Evening Shade,* a pregnant young girl keeps her baby even though she is a poor, single mother —but at her new boyfriend's urging gets a job working in an ice-cream parlor, as well as an offer from him to get her into the local college. At the end of the episode a dream voice, addressing the audience, explains that "miracles really do happen." We have been told by the show's male protagonist and the boyfriend's father (Burt Reynolds) that hard work and desire always pay off, but this was in the context of a parodic pep talk to an incompetent football team. Hard work, miracle, or both: you can take your pick, but one way or the other, traditional morality will work out after all. Sitcom and family drama's

young women never have abortions, but they never suffer from the consequences of not having them either.

In a related sense, a narrative can recuperate traditionalist viewpoints, even
bigoted ones, by reversing our initial expectations about the Other who is its
object: again, "having it both ways." Television sitcoms that engage in the
mockery of men (see my earlier comment about *Home Improvement*) often
turn on this narrative trope. The 1990s sitcom *Coach* is a particularly insistent
repository of this approach. In one episode of *Coach*, for example, Coach
makes fun of a male seamster ("ya have ta wonder about a guy who makes
dresses for a living"). Since Coach is obviously always the buffoon on this
sitcom, his homophobia is made to make him look ignorant at the same time
that it is, after all, normalized. At the end of the episode, however, it's revealed
that the seamster is a "real man," once a general in the British Army, and
Coach realizes his "mistake." His bigotry has been disavowed at the same time
that its object has been sanitized, so that we are given to think that what's
wrong with prejudice is not its expression, but merely that it's been directed
against the wrong persons. This is a very common means of presenting,
disavowing, and excusing homophobia on television generally: the same trope
being used, for example, in episodes of both the intensely dramatic *Homicide*
and the satirical sitcom *The Single Guy* at roughly the same time. Just as with
many liberal defenses of accused "Communists" in the McCarthy era, the
accusatory stance turns out to be not a violation of moral principle but an
empirical error. In addition, as Coach is always made fun of for his working-
class demeanor and behavior, this episode manages to put him down not so
much for being homophobic but for being, compared to "the General," a
lower-class idiot. In the end, all hierarchies return to their normal state.[16]

Conversely, just when we were beginning to feel uneasy with ourselves, the
Other can turn out to *deserve* our hostility. Another episode of *Coach* is far
from unique in the way it recuperates misogyny. Dragooned into giving an
ignominious lecture in a history class by the new female president of his
college, Coach makes misogynistic fun of her. Initially, as always, he is being
made fun of himself. But then we discover that she had, in fact, slept with him
several years earlier, and is now angry at him only because he had thereafter
sexually rejected her. Indeed, she has devoted her entire career toward getting
herself into a position where she could humiliate him. The independent
woman is independent only to secure sexual revenge for a mere slight. Compared to her, the ignorant coach and his dimwitted football players are harmless and perhaps even lovable. (Here, intellectual scapegoating and misogyny
are brought together beautifully in a mere half-hour).[17] This kind of reversal

of fortune also appears in movies about witchcraft such as *Black Magic* or *Spellbinder,* which begin by first foregrounding and then quickly disavowing what looks like paranoid misogyny—only to recuperate it at the end by establishing that there really are witches after all!

Similarly, a narrative can recuperate an institution that appears to be disavowed by finally treating it as normal and natural. On an "Amazon Planet" episode of *Star Trek: The Next Generation* (see above) the women are bigger, stronger, more violent and sexually domineering than the men. In the end, prodded by the "egalitarians" from Earth, the matriarchal Ruler (no democracy among women!) begins to compromise and offers freedom (in a kind of Siberia) for rebellious men. We can read this as a satirical critique of unalloyed patriarchy, and the text, full of double entendres that seem to mock Earth as well as high heaven, explicitly encourages this reading. But the female ruler is literally the phallic woman, and her rulership conceived of only as an inverted phallocracy. The logic of domination is naturalized as a mere extension of size and strength, and any possibility that women as such might produce a more egalitarian version of rulership is carefully negated. Only the men of Earth (Captain Ryker) can bring that about (where have they been all our lives?).

This ideological fence-straddling can define the trajectory of a superficial TV episode, as in the examples above; it can also occupy the entire narrative of a much more complex and lengthy film. In the film *The Music Box,* Jessica Lange discovers that her apparently upright father, whom she is defending against war-crimes charges, *is* in truth an ex-Nazi, and is guilty of the acts with which he's been charged. In the course of events, though, a witness at his trial testifies that the KGB has forged dossiers to convict innocent men in other such trials—an unsustained accusation made during the John Demanjuk hearings. That testimony in effect rewrites the entire movie that we thought we'd been watching. It remains to assuage the feelings of those who prefer German war criminals to Communists.

One scene judiciously placed can accomplish the same end. In *A Few Good Men* Demi Moore, whom we (with Tom Cruise) expect to be a liberal feminist lawyer, suddenly breaks into a speech borrowed from the liberal Jewish lawyer Barney Greenglass in *The Caine Mutiny* (the literary and cinematic prototype for recuperation by working against type). Marines like Jack Nicholson, she says angrily in a clear address to the audience (à la Sharon Gless), protected "us"; if we were to be threatened by invasion, it "would not be on their watch." On the witness stand later Nicholson, before breaking down (again like Captain Queeg in *The Caine Mutiny*), uses almost exactly the same words to justify the fatal persecution of one of his enlisted men. Had we not been alerted by Moore, we might think this was the nonsense of a criminal lunatic (invasion from Cuba? the Dominican Republic? Mars?). In a very subtle touch, though, patriotism and militarism have been recuperated for us, so to speak, *avant la lettre,* while being safely separated from Nicholson's obsessive behavior. At their most creative, Hollywood's ideological fence-straddlers can accomplish this kind of result even in a single phrase, as in the reference, in *Under Suspicion,* to someone as a "victim's rights do-gooder": a phrase that boxes the law and order / civil liberties compass so perfectly that the viewer cannot even begin to deconstruct it.

More generally, Hollywood comedies often recuperate sexual hierarchy by following the classical trajectory of *The Taming of the Shrew,* in which a strong woman causes much hilarity by disrupting social convention, only to be put in her place at the end. The most unabashed example of this convention in recent years is the movie *Blind Date,* in which Kim Basinger throws Bruce Willis's smug bourgeois life into anarchic chaos until the very end, at which point she settles for a lovey-dovey reconciliation in the midst of a society wedding that we had thought was being satirically subverted. From Hepburn in *Adam's Rib,* through Doris Day in *Teacher's Pet,* to Barbra Streisand in *What's Up, Doc?* this has been a favorite trajectory of Hollywood's domestic comedies: films about strong, independent women (Hepburn, Joan Crawford, Bette Davis) who finally wind up in the arms of a man after all.[18]

Similarly, from *Christopher Strong* (1933) through *Mildred Pierce* and the original *Cape Fear* to *Little Man Tate, Lorenzo's Oil, City Slickers, Rain Man,* or the *Cape Fear* remake, the family has been placed under siege in film after film, only to survive in the end stronger than ever—even if completely im-plausible plot turns are required to turn this trick. That in 1993 the remake of *Cape Fear* could not quite bring off the family's recuperation is an index not so much of any counterideological tendencies at work, as of the difficulty, at century's end, for simple naïveté to do the job it used to be able to do forty or fifty years ago. Still, the ideology of the family is remarkably resilient; it turns up in the most unexpected contexts. As Marina Warner says of *Jurassic Park:*

> The story can be reduced to a naked confrontation between nature coded female [the velociraptors] with culture coded male. Velociraptors collaborate on the kill . . . and want nothing more than to snack on human flesh. It's not incidental that the final confrontation takes place between a picture-perfect nuclear family—mom, dad, boy, girl—and the two velociraptors on the rampage, and that the outcome of the feeble romantic interest is that the surviving paleontologist decides to accept his role as a man and even become the father of a family.[19]

The ideology of the family is also sometimes about much more than "family." Together with the "classless" ideology of community it describes as well the way we organize our productive institutions. We can see this clearly by considering briefly a recent and superficially dissident movie genre: movies about gay men. Neither on cinema screens nor on television has Hollywood given us any movies or series about gay men's lives, such as the British-made *Tales of the City* or *The Buddha of Suburbia*. Instead it purveys (not very often, of course) such positive movies about gay men as *Longtime Companion* or *Making Love* or *Philadelphia* (whose producers, Tri-Star, actually did everything possible to deny its subject matter in their pre-release campaign). These movies, unlike their British counterparts, recuperate "family values" by begging to be incorporated into an expanded and liberalized notion of "the family" (as in the funeral service at the end of *Philadelphia*); while at the same time avoiding any suspicion of celebrating (or, in the era of AIDS, nostalgically mourning) the libertine side of gay male sexuality. And they recuperate community values by resolutely restricting their subject matter to successfully employed gay men, as though to reassure us that these are *not* men who have deserted their masculine role in the social order, even if they may have deserted their proper sexuality. *Making Love,* indeed, manages the feat of ending with *two* happy (and well-off) families where we had begun, in effect, with none.[20]

In contrast, we might call the typical Hollywood treatment of lesbianism, "the rescue": Scott Glenn rescuing Mariel Hemingway from lesbianism in *Personal Best;* William Baldwin doing the same for Sherilyn Fenn a decade later in *Three of Hearts,* after being hired by Kelly Lynch to retrieve her fickle companion. Retrieval is what Hollywood does best with lesbians. Or desperate end runs, as in the case of Ellen de Generes *(Ellen)*, surely the most openly closeted gay person in history: being frantically set up by her scriptwriters with one futile blind date after another, while knowing members of her audience slapped their thighs and waited for the "next season," promised year after year, when she would finally be released from purgatory.

It's impossible to imagine such a plot the other way around, at least in a movie made by men. Partly the difference is one of sexual ideology: many men really believe that lesbianism on the part of what they otherwise see as a desirable woman is simply a momentary error. But the ideological difference goes beyond that. Men who maintain the rest of their bourgeois social status but desert their sexual identities can occasionally be forgiven (especially if they come to an appropriately sad end); just as men have always been forgiven for, say, premarital sexuality that can still (in some circles) earn a woman the reputation of "damaged goods." (Here *Torch Song Trilogy,* Harvey Feierstein's personal testimony to the sexuality of drag, comes closest to being a truly subversive mainstream "gay" film.) But women who leave men for other women (like "loose women" generally) are destroying the fabric of society.

The essence of the sex / gender order, *ideologically*, is that men's function is economic, women's function is biological.[21] The latter's sexual treason is therefore much harder to recuperate, in the same way as is a man's refusal to work for wages (his economic treason) compared to a woman's. In Hollywood a man doing housework is comic or sad, and usually has to be rescued from his fate by some helpmeet who reestablishes the family as a functional unit even without being part of it in the traditional sense (as in television's *The Nanny*). But a woman with a career and no male partner is threatening: a man without visible means of support, and a woman whose enjoyment of sexuality has no visible social anchor, are both beyond the pale. In straight Hollywood as in straight life, there is no such thing as a male slut, and no such thing as a female idler (unless she is on "welfare"; i.e., stigmatized as receiving other people's tax money). It is difficult, though certainly no longer impossible, to explore lesbianism as a way of life (rather than as the focus of a movie-of-the-week social "problem"), because the question that will insistently arise is, "who is the *woman?*" In 1995 sitcoms began to show lesbian weddings—but not a social life thereafter.

A world of men without women is familiar and to many audiences even preferable. It is the world of action, of doing. A world of women without men *(Come Back to the Five and Dime, Jimmy Dean, Jimmy Dean; Steel Magnolias; Boys on the Side)*, though it appears much less frequently and has only a segmented audience appeal, is still acceptable: it's the world of frustrated romance. But a world of women without "women" is off the charts. What we mean by recuperation of the family here is that (as in *Aliens* or *Survive the Night*) in any narrative with female protagonists, at least one of them must be recuperated for womanhood. This requirement is no respecter of genres, either. *Wonder Woman* almost always ended with its mythical heroine delivering social work homilies (clearly coded as female in American culture) about their appropriate social roles to men or women she'd rescued from villains but also from themselves. Similarly, although the syndicated pseudo-epic *Xena: Warrior Princess*, generally presents us with as unrecuperated a female hero as Hollywood has ever imagined, its introductory episode (a spinoff of the very successful series *Hercules*) delivers Xena from villainy to heroism by having her preventing her murderous warrior band from killing a child. In the next episode, now on her own, she reconciles with her mother and bonds not only with a female follower but also with every child in sight: Sigourney Weaver revisited. "Her courage changed the world" (so the prologue intones), just as Ripley's saved the universe. But the additional mission of these female world-savers partially disavows what seems at first (this is especially so in Xena's case) to be a stark contrast to conventional womanhood.[22]

Beyond all of these examples, which could be multiplied forever (as there are several new ones every night on television), there is a recurrent master theme: the absence of recognizable *politics* from the presentation and ultimate disavowal of opposition, dissidence, or disturbance. The examples I've given are mostly oblique, but Hollywood is also quite direct when need be. On an episode of *Empty Nest* that seems at first to be escaping the carefully guarded boundaries of *Cagney and Lacey,* feminine caring is opposed to a conception of tough law and order (clearly coded as masculine): a snobbish professional woman hires an ex-convict in an attempt to "rehabilitate" him by molding him to her design. She of course fails as he wins the battle of wits between them by playing on her liberal guilt. So the cynicism of "law and order" is vindicated, and opposition is made to seem inauthentic.

In the name of comedy this kind of disavowal can be carried to astonishing heights. One 1992 episode of *Fresh Prince of Bel Air* manages to delegitimize antiwar protest (by turning a judge who was once a radical into a buffoonish, cynical, sexist pig); to turn feminism into an egoistic con game (the Fresh Prince's girlfriend, far from protesting his use of her for his own status purposes, has been doing exactly the same thing to him); and to depoliticize black protest by turning it into consumerism, as the Fresh Prince happily observes that he "can be righteous and stylish at the same time." On *General Hospital* (1995), a bartender and a businesswoman worry only about their sexual relationships. Their exchange is capped by a scene in which the businesswoman says to a boyfriend who's been talking sympathetically about "sisterhood": "when you started rattling on about the feminine mystique all I could think of was the male mystique"—at which point they kiss. Not only are the pleasures of sex shown as clearly opposed and superior to the dubious pleasures of feminism, but the latter are put, as inauthentically as possible, in the mouth of a man.[23]

Conversely, opposition can be deauthenticated by depriving it of its real object of concern: as in the episode of *Murphy Brown* in which the idea of liberal tolerance gets extended to short, bald, and fat men, and lawyers and dermatologists, amid many jokes about "political incorrectness"—but never to the real people for whom tolerance is often a matter of life and death.

The disappearance of political speech is also often structured (in genres as disparate as comedy and action drama) as the disappearance of coherent opposition. In comedy, laughs can be garnered by putting politically incompatible characters together to discover their mutual lovability, as Rush Limbaugh and Markie Post on 1994's *Hearts Afire* (another production of that Clintonian "liberal" Linda Bloodworth-Thomason). However, Limbaugh appears as a cuddly and jokey teddy bear with virtually no angry political views at all. There is also the 1995 series *Ned and Stacey* in which, in *TV Guide's* apt but misleading description, a "Left-Wing reporter" manages to get along quite well with a roommate of the opposite sex who is a "self-centered ad-agency hotshot." However "Ned" might be described, Alexander Cockburn he is not. Of course, given the front-page romance between Republican Mary Matalin and Democrat James Carville, this could be viewed as just another case of art imitating (slavishly) life—except that what in real life represents the degeneration of American party politics is the only politics television knows.

This absence of politics appears more often than not as the repudiation of politicized *women* (it is no particular political conviction that leads Julia Roberts in *The Pelican Brief* to set out to discover the assassins of the murdered justices). Most pointed in this respect is *Running on Empty.* Although professional radical is not the typical American career, this is in the end another Hollywood film (and directed by one of Hollywood's most "leftist" directors) about the "problem" posed by the woman who puts "career" ahead of "family." In this movie, typically, it is the father not the mother who is first willing to compromise "for the sake of the children" (or child, in this case). When Christine Lahti decides to surrender to the authorities so their son can have his own school career, the audience (except for unrepentant activists among us) heaves a collective sigh of relief, and there is hardly a dry eye in the house. Again, ideology as the spurious reconciliation of opposites has triumphed.

Similarly, women rarely right wrongs against women directly on TV. In the television series *Street Justice,* one episode "dealt with" the problem of battering, but the narrative's battered woman (the only one to be met) was rescued by the series' two male protagonists, with help from their female sidekick (a plotline later duplicated in a Lifetime made-for-TV movie). No one in the course of the story ever mentioned the existence of shelters, which are run by women for women, without any participation at all from men. Several years later a similar narrative development, even more subtle in its implications, could be observed on the series *Hearts Afire,* in which Markie Post confronts the sons of a wife-beater, but not the man himself. The sons will presumably straighten him out—no women from the battered women's movement need apply. Meanwhile in cinema, at any time during the mid-1990s there were more films available about men who are framed for sexual harassment *(Oleanna, Disclosure)* than about men who actually commit it.

All these examples suggest two things. First, there is a perceived need in visual culture to rein in women who appear as independent moral actors. Second, and even more profound, it is not so much the denial of politics that is at stake as the denial of the possibility of meaningful political alliances. This is only necessary, of course, if we are expecting them: not on *Homicide*, for example, but very definitely on *Cagney and Lacey*, whose producers had always to work for an appeal to other than feminists. In general, this denial of a common politics is such a commonplace on television that it has become almost a reflex, to have rapists defended by women, accused blacks prosecuted by blacks, and so on. (See also the movie *The Color of Night*). In particular, whenever there is a socially sensitive trial, casting is carefully arranged so that white men are not seen to be oppressing women or minorities, in the role of judge or district attorney: an astonishing number of whom, in the Age of Reagan, therefore turn out to be black, Latino, female, and so forth. On the one hand this could be viewed as a laudable effort to overcome stereotyping, but its latent function is quite different, in that on shows such as *L.A. Law*, and *Law and Order*, lectures about "law and order" are seen being given by the very people who are actually the object of its oppressiveness.[24]

One can be sure that if a woman claiming justifiable homicide is suspected to be misusing the battered women's defense, she will be prosecuted or judged by a woman. The one outcome that is not to be permitted is the appearance of political solidarity among the victims.[25] Only *The Glass Shield* (see above) permits an exception, as two rookie officers, a black man and a Jewish woman, come together to break the code of silence that is protecting a murderously racist conspiracy in a thinly disguised LAPD.[26] This kind of disavowal perhaps reached its height in *Serving in Silence*, a TV-film about Marguerite Cammermeyer, the first field-grade officer to be court-martialed for being a lesbian, who faces a board headed by a black colonel (did anyone watching believe that this really happened?); or in an episode of the seemingly hard-hitting series *China Beach*, in which a working-class black soldier who has confronted a middle-class black woman with her class privilege, leaves her at the end of the episode with the remark, "Free love, baby, that's what the movement is all about"; or above all, in the 1994 TV-movie *Shadow of Obsession*, in which a female judge, mimicking many male judges in both Britain and the United States, but not to my knowledge a single female judge in real life, frees an accused attacker because his victim had been dressed "provocatively."

In cinema, *Philadelphia* takes this technique to a ludicrous height, as the law firm being sued by a dying Tom Hanks is represented not merely by a white woman but by a black man as well. In a perfect example of "having it both ways," Mary Steenburgen (the defense attorney) whispers to her vis-à-vis (but not too loudly), "I hate this case." Having lost it, she offers what seem to be heartfelt congratulations to the victorious attorney (played by Denzel Washington as a stereotypical black homophobe), and a few seconds later is planning her client's appeal. There could hardly be anyone so churlish as to complain that her character has not done what they think any lawyer should have done, but along the way the notion that there might be a community of interest among women, gays, and blacks has been hinted at, and then elided. And when, in contrast, solidarity among outsiders is occasionally fore-grounded, it is only by being carefully defined against an alien Other: "Arabs" in *Courage under Fire,* or more literal aliens in *Independence Day.* Solidarity, with its suggestion of resistance, is replaced by "integration," with its underly-ing theme of ultimate satisfaction.[27]

Again, in an episode of the notoriously "liberal" *Murphy Brown,* the techni-cians at Murphy's station go on strike. Many reporters and writers cross the picket line without any apparent qualms. Tensions are high, especially when the station's owners use managerial personnel to replace the strikers. How will the ideologically cheerful world of sitcom handle this apparently irreconcil-able conflict? With no great difficulty. The replacement workers foul up every-thing they touch and management is desperate for a solution. Meanwhile Murphy, who has carefully taken no side beyond her own refusal to cross the picket line, invites representatives of both sides to her house, bakes them a cake, and makes them sit there eating it until they've achieved an agreement. (It's not clear whether subjection to Murphy's culinary skills is the "punish-ment" they both must undergo.) The agreement's content, of course, is never spelled out for those of us in the audience who might have mistakenly thought the issues were serious. The techs go back to work, the managers back to managing, Murphy back to reporting, and everyone is happy: everything is for the best in this best of all possible worlds.[28]

The ultimate absence from the dominant ideology, in other words, is the absence of solidarity: not just as an ideal, but even as a possibility. This absence is most noticeable of all, I think, in what look like Hollywood's most "political" films, where we badly want to find it and yet cannot. *Country* and *Norma Rae,* for example, while purporting to be stories of collective struggle, are actually *hommages* to individual female heroism. In visual memory, the farmers' protest in *Country* is the apotheosis of Jessica Lange, the leader and inspiration of an otherwise faceless and anonymous horde, a horde that is also replicated in frequent scenes of apolitical religious observance. Men in *Country* are useless, the two leading male characters being a drunk and a suicide, and the villainous bankers being identified as (Eastern) "college boys" in a characterization that recuperates the mythically virtuous, classless "people" as well. But this sexual opposition serves primarily to depoliticize the narrative: women stand for home, community, and religion, whereas the oppressive institutions are bastions of absentee maleness rather than of corporate capitalism.

From *Norma Rae,* similarly, the one truly indelible image is of Sally Field standing on her worktable, Oscar-winning sweat staining her armpits, looking defiant, determined, and yet still winsome, the perfect image of the regendered reluctant hero; as one by one the machines, tended by other women of whom we have no memory at all, grind to a halt. We can compare these scenes with similar moments in *Salt of the Earth* and also in *Viva Zapata!* (perhaps the only film of collective struggle ever made in Hollywood). In *Salt,* even though the film is narrated by one woman, Esperanza, its transformative moment comes when the miners' wives, whose husbands have been enjoined from picketing, form a picket line around the mine, not as faceless women but as a group who remain in our memory as a united circle. That Esperanza decides to join them is a private (though emblematic) epiphany for her, rather than a necessary inspiration to the others. *Zapata!* is necessarily about the mythic hero, yet again its most unforgettable visual sequence is of the revolutionary people: Zapata dragged down the road by a troop of Federalistas, while the village women sound an alarm of clicking stones, and the peasants, armed only with machetes, scramble down the hillside in groups of three and four (in tableaus from the great murals of Orozco), to form a protective screen around their not-yet leader; until finally we see the patrol engulfed by peasants and Zapata standing smiling in the middle of the Revolution, as the dramatic musical score rises to its climax.

Even more strikingly than *Country* and *Norma Rae, The Big Chill* introduces us to an attractive ensemble of—we are given to believe—ex-radicals, who are now, after the suicide of the most unrepentant among them, trying to come to terms with their "radical" pasts, as well as a conformist future. However, aside from one vague reference to a generic long-ago protest, we never hear about anything that the remaining members of this group actually did or protested. Their politics hovers at the edge of, and finally plunges into, a cloud of historic invisibility. The suggested contrast between the familial, "personal" politics of the present and the communal politics of the past is therefore not a contrast, but only a celebration of the former, measured against nothing but the failed life of one suicidal bachelor. Like *Running on Empty, The Big Chill* purveys a fake nostalgia for the "radical" past: a past we never in fact see, so that our only real images of the allegedly political protagonists are images of their repentance, the politics of domesticity in each case replacing the politics of public action. Family 7, democratic politics 0, is the final score of this ballgame.[29]

In sum, the method of disavowal and recuperation allows us to feel as though we have been attending to a real social critique. The military is corrupt and out of control *(A Few Good Men);* Nazism was the real enemy of Americanism in World War II *(The Music Box);* better that the guilty should go unpunished if that's what respect for due process entails *(L.A. Law);* management is oppressive and union-busting *(Murphy Brown);* women may be better off living without men *(Star Trek*—or, "A woman needs a man the way a fish needs a bicycle");* independent women can be heroes just like independent men *(Aliens, Survive the Night),* and so forth. In every case however—and these are only a handful of examples of an ubiquitous phenomenon—the original critique is disavowed, and social reintegration is achieved around a rediscovered harmony. The military is necessary for national security, and as a whole its members are morally upright; Communism is also the enemy of Americanism, and the Good Middle rejects both Right and Left; the law must be fair, but justice also require that the guilty be punished by whatever means necessary; management is finally reasonable and unions need have no fear for their survival; women without men are oppressive and unfulfilled; a woman's ultimate heroism lies in being a good mother; and so forth. Taking Hollywood's entire cultural product as a complex metatext that over time elaborates a consistent (if uneasily cohering) message, we see that what is recuperated here is not just this or that institution or ideal, but the dominant ideology of national, communal, and sexual unity as a whole. As Judith Williamson says of *Blind Date,* "films like this shake up a social order only to let it re-settle more securely."[30]

To understand what is going on in these films and television programs, it is useful to look at a work of visual art that is truly political without disavowal. The non-Hollywood film *A World Apart* explores the politics of a woman without in the end reassuring us that she can be domesticated, and tells us, without ever lecturing or preaching at us, that some opposites are in truth irreconcilable. The story of Ruth First, a South African Communist and anti-apartheid activist who was eventually assassinated by South African Intelligence, it was scripted as a labor of both loving *and* unforgiving memory by her own daughter, Sean Slovo. Showing First's unyielding dedication as well as her daughter's unbearable pain, the movie reminds us that there is such a thing as true tragedy. The Good is real, not a fiction created out of our own self-interest, and it may be unachievable as such because its requirements are in self-contradiction. As Antigone's honor required her destructively to turn her back on the Law and the City that nurtured her, so First's honor makes her turn her back not only on her own society but, figuratively, on her own daughter (at least as the latter sees it). In making this tragic choice she is both right and wrong, wrong and right. Her daughter knows this, and we know it if we didn't before. Even among people pursuing a better world, the obligations of love and the obligations of civic duty cannot be happily brought together. Not only are black and white a world apart, so too are the Good and the possible. In this movie, the separation with which ideological narratives always begin in order eventually to recuperate it, cannot finally be recuperated. In the name of love, mother and daughter have both lost, but in the name of truth, which cannot repair that separation, they have both won. As Hollywood perhaps can never understand, a film about a woman's loss can also be a film about her indelible triumph: not in self-sacrificial love, but in the world that she has helped to change. Hollywood cannot understand this, because in Hollywood there are no worlds apart.

5 Media Structures and Dominant Ideas

Why can Hollywood never show us a world apart? The comments I have made so far seem to imply that what we get from television and movies can be explained by paying attention to real social relationships and psychological needs. That is true, but it is not the whole truth; or rather, it is often only true to the extent that those relationships and needs appear to us in an ideological, that is, a distorted, form. What we want from our cultural consumption is derived from and related to, but not reducible to, how we organize and consume our material lives. The products of visual culture especially are conceived by their makers, and if successful by us their consumers, as day-dreams constructed around what people can reasonably hope for, or reason-ably dream of, *in the given circumstances*. Marx's pronouncement on religion is for many people even truer for visual culture; it is "a haven in a heartless world; it is the opiate of the masses." The production of cultural commodities is therefore parasitic on the production and reproduction of the material world in general, and fundamental changes in the former must await fundamental changes in the latter: "The arm of criticism must be replaced by the criticism of arms." Since we cannot dream our way out of the fallen world, better to redefine it as though it were not fallen after all.

In this respect we seem to consent to being manipulated, even when we are aware of what is going on (as anyone must be, for example, at the conclusion of *The River Wild*). Our apparent or partial consent has to be explained; to say that it has been "manufactured" may accurately describe the manipulative process, but still does not explain the outcome.[1] The search for an explanation can begin nowhere better then with another look at Marx's formulation of the problem:

> The ideas of the ruling class are in every epoch the ruling ideas: i.e., the class which is the ruling *material* force of society, is at the same time its ruling *intellectual* force. The class which has the means of material production at its disposal, has control at the same time over the means of mental production, so that thereby, generally speaking, the ideas of those who lack the means of mental production are subject to it. The ruling ideas are nothing more than the ideal expression of the dominant material relationships, the dominant material relationships grasped as ideas; hence of the relationships which make the one class the ruling one, therefore, the ideas of its dominance. The individuals composing the ruling class possess among other things consciousness, and therefore think. Insofar, therefore, as they rule as a class and determine the extent and compass of an epoch, it is self-evident that they do this in its whole range, hence among other things rule also as thinkers, as producers of ideas, and regulate the production and distribution of the ideas of their age: thus their ideas are the ruling ideas of the epoch.[2]

What could it mean, to refer to the phantasmic worldview of Hollywood as "the ideal expression of the dominant material relationships?" Why are unabashedly fantastic film genres (e.g., horror films) so popular? Why even, when social reality is made to intrude, as in occasional films about the business world, the typical picture of cold-eyed monopolists versus charming old geezers who run corner drugstores and the like, or of dashing con men who look like James Garner, or those evil conspirators against the national interest whom Andrew Duggan made a career of playing, is what we enjoy so completely at odds with the daily reality of a society whose business is simply business?

What is precisely the case is that, as Marx would expect from an industry so inextricably entwined in the global world of monopoly capital, these genres do express an ideal version of that world: as though we did not really live in the midst of a mundane social order that has a ruling class, a communications elite, and is structured around relationships of gendered and racial domination and subordination. There are many possible ways in which these conditions can be expressed artistically, and we can never deduce that any particular cultural commodity *must* have taken the exact shape that it did take. But the general shape that *all* our cultural commodities take is what it is because we are what we are, and a large part of what we are is persons who are imbued with, respond to, and express or oppose the ideological constellation that upholds this kind of social order.[3]

At the same time, the general sociological truth that representations of an ideological ideal may be preferable to more truthful accounts of the social order, is false for many people, among them minorities of various kinds, and also adult women (and some but fewer adult men) dissatisfied with their conventional cultural representations. But for structural reasons, the producers of commercial visual culture cannot afford to become too immersed in any subcultural nuances that can't be quantified as part of the audience for their product.

By way of comparison, we might consider the field of American book publishing, which has not yet been totally overtaken by oligopolization, although it is tending more and more in that direction. The founders of Naiad Press, for example, without intending to do anything but meet a collective need that mainstream publishing was ignoring, began publishing fiction for lesbians and discovered that they had tapped into—or, in a sense, created—a million-dollar market. The Naiad list, apparently without saturating the market, grows steadily year after year and now numbers in the hundreds, despite the fact that few nonlesbians (i.e., "average" readers in the mass media sense) would ever want to search out the works of Anne Bannon or Katherine V. Forrest. Though not with such astounding results, the Women's Press has similarly found a niche publishing feminist works in fiction and nonfiction, just as Humanities Press and Henry Regnery have in publishing left-wing and right-wing social analysis respectively. Even Burning Deck Press, which virtually no readers of this sentence will have heard of, makes an adequate living publishing nothing but obscure fiction and poetry that would be untouchable by the mainstream. The number of similarly viable small presses (not to mention the world of academic publishing), though individually they come and go like all small businesses, is uncountable. It would be hard to find any subcultural group in the United States that does not have its own institutions for the dissemination of both fictional and nonfictional representations of itself.[4] These representations are formally indistinguishable from the products of mainstream literature and propaganda. From various critical perspectives Jane Rule's *This Is Not for You* may be "better than" or "not as good as" *The Bridges of Madison County* or *Madame Bovary,* but no reader can have the faintest doubt that it belongs to the same genre—the novel—as they do.

The equivalent is not true in the world of visual culture. The costs of production are so high, the channels of distribution so few and so monopolized, that it is extremely difficult to produce and distribute feature-length films, or television series with normal production values, that deviate from what this expensive—and expensively rigged—marketplace has made familiar.[5] Although Maria Maggenti's *The Incredibly True Adventures of Two Girls in Love* was made for $60,000, and even before its release to video had already earned upward of $2 million from its theatrical release, this astonishing rate of profit might in absolute terms be useless to a major Hollywood studio trying desperately to recoup eight-figure losses from some previous, misguided blockbuster. Bigness feeds on itself, and finally becomes recognizable as natural and normal to a mass audience that is only rarely exposed to anything else.

In other words, wholly aside from questions of familiarity, the aesthetics of expensive production values, and other determinants of visual pleasure, there is a material explanation of why we do not see what we do not see. But this is not to say that what we *do* see makes no sense to most if not all of us; in fact it does, as we can appreciate when looking at some of the basic Hollywood genres of film and television.

For example, the male cop as hero represents individualism in action from what seems to be a working-class (and thus "democratic") standpoint. Although individualism itself is an important part of the dominant ideology, in actuality the dominant material relationships of late capitalism are primarily bureaucratic and conformist.[6] There are great films, such as Satjyajit Ray's *Company Limited,* or Ernano Olmi's *The Sound of Trumpets (Il Posto),* that are about that slow rise of individuals through bureaucratic hierarchies—the true story of capitalist "success" for most persons who achieve it. But although the dominant ideology has different streams to interpellate us into different social roles, only one of those—heroic individualism in the mode of the nineteenth century's great entrepeneurs—is meant to be the stuff of our *dreams.* It is also meant to be specifically the stuff of *men's* dreams, thus limiting the scope of the dreams women can have, let alone express as commodities of visual culture. Such men still do exist, but hardly in numbers great enough to justify an entire genre based on their exploits—or to sustain, under the pressures of narrative credibility, the ideological claim that their behavior typifies individual heroism *and* generates social progress. So the most successful depictions of American business, such as *Dallas* and *Dynasty*, are not really about business at all, and they are mostly meant to be the stuff of *women's* dreams: the sexual and occasionally criminal exploits of rich people (especially rich *women*) and their idiosyncratic deployment of their riches. Any actual entrepeneurial accomplishments that have given these people their wealth have mostly occurred offscreen.

If the kind of allegedly heroic accomplishment undergirding capitalist self-justification is not an acceptable component of visual culture, some substitute must be found that will credibly link individual accomplishment to the social order. War movies have sometimes filled this role, but less easily than we might assume. Except under conditions of total mobilization, as during World War II, they are always out-of-date, and disillusionment or loss of interest have usually set in by the time they are made. The most historically satisfactory substitute myth, the Western, has become anachronistic; the cop story, along with the martial arts film, is what remains. If producer, writer, and audience look for an arena in which their joint hunger for the ideal—heroic individual action—can be realized, the portrayal of public, authorized violence is where they are most likely to find it.[7]

Because the problem of domestic law and order is perennial, the law-and-order film (or television series) serves a twofold purpose. For the dominant classes, "crime" substitutes for structural domination and subordination as a self-serving explanation of the widespread violence inevitably caused by authorized child abuse, oppression, poverty, and exclusion from an otherwise affluent social order. For the mass audience, crime genuinely does appear as oppression, since most crime is committed by the powerless against the powerless, and no one seems able to do anything about it. The cop quite logically appears both as protector and, more crucially, as the idealized heroic self that fights for "justice" in its only visible form, with an effectuality unavailable to most men and women.

Seen in this perspective, the supposedly fundamental link between visceral action and some putative aesthetic requirement particular to the cinematic medium is revealed as being completely superficial.[8] What non-Hollywood films most certainly fail to provide, however, is acceptable images of the bourgeois ideal: individual heroism. They also, of course, fail to provide violent action. This in turn appears in such profusion in visual culture not because it is particularly "cinematic," and not out of some "liberal" conspiracy against average Americans (as fantasized by such conservative demagogues as Michael Medved, who understand neither the central position of Hollywood in social reproduction, nor the nature of art and creative artists compelled to do their work in a market society). Rather, the cinema of violence does appeal, for various reasons having mostly to do with phases in the life cycle, to those teenaged males who in recent years have made up such a large part of the audience for movies; it has a real historical determinant in addition to its other determinations.[9] As Patricia Holland puts it (in a discussion of censorship), films and television programs are "the result of a multitude of pressures and prohibitions"; the question that then has to be answered is "Why *these* were the films [or television programs] that got made." The answer in this case, clearly, is that "when the commercial imperatives that bind film-makers to those audiences with a taste for pain, blood and violation are set free, routine violence can drive out other forms."[10] Finally, given Hollywood's domination of world markets for commodities of visual culture, what begins as a comprehensible but limited aesthetic standard gradually becomes a general expectation.

The police story and its variants, then, when constructed with a skillfulness that makes them credible, satisfy the kinesthetic demands of part of the audience *and* resolve the individual/community paradox both symbolically and materially. At one level they place the fantasy figure of the hero in a recognizable social milieu. Symbolically, they resolve the "woman question" by finding a secondary role for women—now an active partner rather than a helpmate—that is more or less logically deducible from the physically heroic role available to very few men in reality, but granted to the hero in almost every movie or television drama. And symbolically as well, they show that the hero, whether reintegrated into the social order *(Casablanca, Aliens)* or remaining apart from it *(High Noon, Dirty Harry* and its successors, *Shane)* can shoulder the burden of pursuing justice. The "dominant material relationships" make that pursuit chimerical, but the utopian longing for its success is emotionally necessary, even if we can only imagine it, like religion, as an "ideal expression." As I have earlier noted, the structuring of many such movies around the exchange of women replicates the historical "deal" (in Wendy Brown's word) by which "the state guarantees each man exclusive rights to his woman . . . [and] agrees not to interfere in a man's family (de facto, a woman's life) as long as he is presiding over it (de facto, her)."[11] This deal is wearing thin, on both sides, but no new structure has replaced that one, in film or television, because none has in reality.

As well, the glittering and glamorous surfaces of Hollywood movies and television, produced easily and even inevitabily by the same techniques that aestheticize violence, are also part of this ideological fit with material reality. The American ideal is a peculiar one, perhaps having more "reality" than Marx would have credited. From the standpoint of the affluent, American riches are a material phenomenon; from the standpoint of the poor and excluded everywhere in the world, a tantalizing affirmation of the ideal as a possibility. In the absence of credible alternatives, the criticism of everyday life looks all too much like a criticism of one's own life. Better to join a religious community that preaches accommodation to this world in the name of salvation in the next one; better yet, watch American television. Some people, even many people, do find the exposure of national myths satisfying. Hollywood, however, lives not by an appeal to many (let alone some), but by its appeal to the broadest possible mass of people, for most of whom ideological fairy tales, *even while we understand that they are nothing but fairy tales,* represent the best "material reality" on offer.

Similarly, in social fantasies such as *Rocky, Breaking Away, Saturday Night Fever,* and *Flashdance,* the working class is a milieu from which one escapes *as an individual;* it is not a site of solidarity, or organization, or communal struggle.[12] This absence of any collectivist ideology in Hollywood productions corresponds to reality: not so much the absence of working-class solidarity as of its relative weakness in the face of superior power. So on network television's most class-conscious production, *Roseanne,* working-class anger is finally locked into the domestic arena rather than being opened out into a milieu of class conflict.[13]

The alternative dream of socialism was based on the Marxian notion that human liberation could be achieved via the collective, communal appropriation of productive labor. In a different way, this was also true of the later dream of women's liberation. But as the twentieth century nears its end it is no longer clear that collective power over work, or collective satisfaction through work, however work might be redefined, is the most promising alternative to the domination/subordination relationships of work under patriarchalist capitalism. Perhaps productive labor, whether in the factory or the home, can never be better than a burden. Perhaps, as Marx during other of his contradictory moments suggested, the path to human liberation lies not through the communal appropriation of labor but in its longed-for abolition. Better, in the end, to be a boxer, or a bicycle racer, or a dancer—or to marry a rich man. That way the dream of community *and* independence remains alive. Though an ideological dream, it may be, short of a massive and credibly progressive social upheaval, the most accessible one we have to live by. Certainly, at any rate, there are enough material reasons for people to "consent" to the ideological promise of individualist escape; we do not need to attribute that consent either to their own pristine ideals, or to the machinations of the media. Both those ideals and those machinations are congruent with the material realities of our time; both address the divided consciousness that those material realities ineluctably produce.

In their treatment of ideologies of the family and sexuality directly, dominant cinema and network television follow the same pattern of framing impossible ideals against a social backdrop that makes them the only credible reality: at least for white people, who are usually the only audience these shows care to address. Fairy tales and fantasies need not be *persuasive* to be credible, they need only be *responsive* to the audience's needs. For example, it would be easy to think, at first glance, that the delirious nighttime soaps (e.g., *Dallas, Dynasty, Melrose Place*) offer nothing but exploitative sex, and that their popularity testifies to the mindless prurience of their audience. On the contrary, in these shows the two halves of the real world's sexual equation come together in perfect balance.

The adventuresses, "career women," and resident villainesses of Hollywood productions imitate the aggressive individualism of men. For the rest, the Hollywood dream (and perhaps realistically the genuine dream as well) is not to match but to complement men's dreams. Here women arrange their bodies for the delectation of the Father (John Forsythe, Larry Hagman) for whom they compete. The voyeuristic and fetishistic men in the audience watch them doing it. Meanwhile the women, the basic audience for these shows, identify with their unrepressed display of the only desire women are unequivocally allowed to have, while enjoying the fashion show. Nor, if some of these programs appear to highlight the manipulative power of women and the flabby character of men, does that make them really oppositional or counter-ideological. The sexual sphere is the one sphere in which many men will happily concede an inversion of normal hierarchy (up to a point): not just because the illusion of being dominated is as capable of being pleasurable as the illusion of dominance, but also because in this sphere the ultimate sources of men's social power are not at stake. No wonder this was for so long the most popular television genre of all.[14]

For similar reasons, a movie such as *Pretty Woman* could be a smash hit, and make Julia Roberts a star, whereas *Sleeping with the Enemy* could only be a career detour for her. Why should an absurd and insipid fiction about a reformed prostitute who snares a rich man be so successful, while a grimly topical story about an abused wife should have only moderate box-office appeal? The answer lies precisely in the former's fairy-tale absurdity. Women watching *Pretty Woman* can dream of trading their bodies (the only commodity that many women securely possess) for money *and* love. Men can dream of going to bed with an uninhibited lover and waking up with a wife: two fantasies for the price of one. In a sense, too, the fairy tale is bound to be a *better* movie; it does not need to mingle sense with nonsense, as the more "realistic" movie does. Within the confines of the existing social formation there is no permanent solution to the "problem" of violence against women. If movies about that "problem" are to be at all optimistic without being revolutionary they must ignore the economic dependence of women, and end in either implausible counterviolence, or in their own heterosexual solution of the "hair of the dog that bit you" variety. So a movie like *Sleeping with the Enemy*, which embraces each of these evasions without missing a beat, lacks aesthetic integrity when compared to an uncompromisingly inane film that, like *Pretty Woman* (or, say, *Indecent Proposal*), requires only the consistency of its convictions without any courage.

In the same way, the absence of battered women's shelters from *Street Justice* (see Chaper 4 above) is understandable. They could be represented in a one-time made-for-television movie or documentary, but to intrude their presence into a series such as *Street Justice* would cast its whole enterprise of male heroism into doubt. It is not that we don't really all doubt that enterprise, nor that it shouldn't be doubted. The difficulty is that without it there is nothing; the women's anti-violence movement by itself does not present the realistic possibility of an alternative sexual regime or family structure. To see it in that light, we would have to kick over the traces of the hegemonic ideology altogether to focus our attention on that movement as a collective movement of revolutionary women. Simpler, of course, to adopt the reformist position and go on hoping (without too much hope) that the embedded institutions might suddenly start to work.

Ideological interpellation is a complex affair. When we say that ideology "works" by interpellating us into familiar social roles, we have to realize that those roles and that familiarity may quite possibly themselves be phantasmic. We do not want to fall into the functionalist trap (as Althusser sometimes does) of assuming that society itself "works," that institutions and actors effectively accomplish what the needs of social stability require them to accomplish. Often, especially when depicting social relations that are in a state of flux (such as contemporary gender relations), ideological fictions do not so much describe a social order as they reveal a society's lack of order. The ideological fantasy tells us what is absent, not what is present, and it appeals as much for the one reason as for the other. Its lack of fit with social reality increases rather than diminishes its strength. "The social transformation we are currently witnessing," again in Wendy Brown's words, "is one in which, on the one hand, for increasing numbers of women, [their] dependence is on the state rather than individual men; on the other hand, the state and economy, rather than individual men, are accorded the service work of women." [15]

To the extent that there is a replacement for the earlier "deal," this is it; we see its instant effects in the demonization of "welfare mothers" and "single mothers." But none of this appears in visual culture. Its fairy tales elide the new form of social (and racial) polarization, and see only those women who are male-dependent in the old-fashioned sense, or who function as independent laborers in the manner once reserved for men. As the intrusive state does begin to appear in visual culture (as it must, given the drastic rightward turn of the polity), we can be sure that its functionaries will be scapegoated as such, rather than revealed as doing the dirty work of a broken-down system of gender relationships. On the one side fairy godmothers and godfathers, on the other side wicked witches and perverse tyrants, substitute for a cold-eyed, systemic gaze at the social order that is not within the dominant frame.[16]

Just the same, the mass media cannot help being disciplined by their own (and their audience's) reality check. An extraordinary proportion of contemporary Hollywood productions in cinema or televison are actually about sexual disarray, but often so indirectly that we might completely miss their significance.[17] This is true, to take an apparently unlikely example, of martial arts movies. Unlike classical Westerns, these are not about the end of a romantic, precivilized life with the coming of "The Law," but are really about the absence of any socially meaningful way for a man to be "strong"; they are about a felt loss of privilege. The view of society they present, therefore (and again their social surfaces are completely "realistic"), is idealist in the worst sense. But the point isn't that we could not possibly find such "real men" in real life; it's that at least we can find one on a film set. Men have to settle for an image they can't possibly fulfill; women (though not nearly so many watch these movies) for a fantasized protector against violence in general rather than the particular men, not to mention "faceless bureaucrats" and legislators, who are the most real threat to their well-being.

These considerations enable us to look once more at what is probably the most decisive distinction in cinematic culture. This is the distinction between "women's films," in which reflection, talk, and the revelation of emotional states are visually central, and voyeuristic appeal to men is minimal; and "men's films," in which action and especially violent action is the core visual component, and women appear primarily as objects of the male voyeur's gaze.[18] How does this difference work itself out in the marketplace? To begin with, a corollary of the Hollywood truism that its basic audience consists of heterosexual couples, among whom men (or boys) make most of the decisions as to what to do for entertainment, is the associated truism that although women will more or less cheerfully go to films by, about, and for men, men will not return the compliment.[19] Rarely in recent years has there been more than one actress among the top ten money-makers in Hollywood; and rarely does what is known as a "woman's film" reach the multimillion-dollar heights of profitability that are today essential to economic survival. But what accounts for this male resistance, if not any differential in aesthetic quality or ideological acceptability?

To answer this question, we must return to Mulvey's discussion of the "triple male gaze," for at its most critical point she fails to make explicit an essential connection between the three gazes: namely, that *the voyeuristic gaze of the camera and of the male audience are socially unacceptable unless mediated by the gaze of a male character within the diegesis.* The male voyeur, "caught looking" without the plausible intervention of his fictional counterpart, is engaging in what is effectively a forbidden act. Often, men will not even admit that they are going to see socially proscribed films by themselves, or in the company of other men (unless the event can be passed off as some kind of lark, or semicomic male rite). It's no accident that the only serious book written about hard-core films has been written by a woman, for it would take a very exceptional man to admit in public that he had seen all the hard-core films that Linda Williams has seen: no one on earth would believe that he had done it in the name of "scholarship."[20]

What this means from a marketing standpoint is that mass-market movies designed to appeal to men sexually must have a male protagonist, *and* seem to be about something other than sex. Aside from productions for the specialized markets of soft-core porn or female action/adventure (see Chapter 8), mainstream films starring women must either be aimed at women, or else (see Chapter 2) appeal to men on some basis other than or in addition to the sexual. But what can that be? The answer to that question is the most plausible explanation for the unnerving connection between sex and violence in so many mainstream Hollywood films, especially the new films noirs: violence makes sex acceptable by disguising its prominence. In contrast, and contrary to Meese Commission and feminist antiporn propaganda, most hard-core films (as canvassed by Linda Williams) are devoid of violence. The hard-core actress who said in an interview that she did not want to "move up" to "legitimate" R-rated movies because she was opposed to the association of sex with violence knew what she was talking about. Hard-core doesn't usually make that association because it doesn't need to; it is the only genre that represents the male voyeurs longed-for power in an unmediated sexual form.[21]

What is left over, after violence and graphic sex and male protagonists have been removed, are known as "women's movies" (or television programs) and the industry's received wisdom is that most men will not voluntarily watch them. Why not? The answer is that on the whole, in our culture, it is not desirable for them to do so. Maleness, and the male version of individuality, is normative in our civilization. For women to identify with men in their struggles may be socially upsetting on occasion, but it is not demeaning of women. Furthermore, women have something to gain by being complicit with male voyeurism; they refamiliarize themselves with the dominant culture's version of what it is men are looking for in them. For many men, though, to identify with women—and especially for adolescent or postadolescent males, still insecure in their masculine sexuality, to identify with women—is to be demeaned, or worse yet, unsexed. To them it represents the worst form of downward social mobility. The market for the commodities of visual culture, in sum, does not respond to men's and women's *pleasures* equally, because in the first instance and above all else it must avoid triggering off the more volatile and dangerous *fears* of men. To use the language of Bentham's utilitarianism, avoiding pain takes precedence over the positive search for pleasure in most people's "pursuit of happiness."

In a similar way (though with a different psychodynamic), just as women will watch films with male protagonists but men will not nearly so often watch films (again the specialized genres excepted) with female protagonists, so adults will watch films made for youths, but the latter will not watch films made for adults. Young people (especially young men) have little sense of the motivations, needs, problems, or desires of older people. Mature women and even men will watch movies made for mature women, and sometimes make them unexpected hits (e.g., *Terms of Endearment*), but they are not so reliable a part of the audience as are young people. The latter have more free time and in a sense often have more disposable income than their elders, since many of them have no responsibilities or financial obligations and themselves may be the recipients of most of their parents' (especially their mother's) disposable income. The structure of the consumer market, but nothing about "popular taste," therefore dictates that a majority of movies will be made for a very unrepresentative population of viewers.

On television this imbalance is somewhat redressed, but in a very peculiar manner, which needs to be understood in its own distinctive way. American television is a market-driven industry par excellence. But more precisely, it is an oligopoly, in which a handful of producers dominate the bulk of the market and compete with each other for profit. In fact, profit (as is the case for most oligopolies) is guaranteed: owning the right to monopolize a particular band of the airwaves is like a license to print money, since this is an exclusive franchise to sell one of the most valuable commodities in the modern world. From a narrow point of view, network costs may outpace revenues in a particular year, but the worth of the basic asset—the network franchise—is beyond price. Monopolizing a group of channels is not what it once was, now that the UHF band on cable television is almost indefinitely extensible. But other producers, even the pay-per-view movie channels, are mere satellites within this system; the networks are the planets.

Any given network, however, must reproduce and expand its value, because the oligopoly is competitive. There is no fixed source of income: theoretically, every program produced by NBC or CBS or ABC or TNT or Fox could not only lose money, but could fail to return a single dollar, if every viewer absolutely preferred a competing program on some other network. Advertisers would go on strike, shareholders would disinvest, the price of the network's stock would collapse, and hundreds of corporate raiders would be competing to buy control and throw the existing ownership and management out on its collective ear. Though profit-seeking is only comparative, it is as desperate and ruthless as if it were absolute. Market share within the oligopoly must be roughly maintained, if for no other reason than to guarantee the power and wealth of its ruling class—and what reason could be more compelling? The ratings game, which measures market share, is no game but a life-and-death matter. Millions of advertising dollars (and more important, dozens or even hundreds of well-paying jobs) can be lost on a single ratings point.

The key to the operation of this system is that, as has often been said, networks do not sell programs to audiences, but rather sell audiences to advertisers. Not only are the advertisers the only actual purchasers of commercial television time: they have only a notionally accurate guess, based on the ratings, of who is watching their programs, and not even the faintest notion, most of the time, as to whether a sponsored program is really selling their product. However, all the major advertisers on commercial television are in exactly the same position as the networks. That is, they are competitors in an oligopoly, trying to maintain or improve market share. What they do know is that if the other oligopolists advertise and they don't, their product will fade from sight. If, less dramatically, their programs are even only marginally less popular than those of their oligopolistic competitors, that may or may not be bad for their sales, but for certain it cannot possibly be good: once again, heads will roll. Innovation or originality are therefore, and for good reason, fundamentally suspect.[22]

In order to understand the way this system of oligopolistic competition determines the production of cultural commodities, we have to rid ourselves of the fantasies about "free markets" that are propagated by their ideologues. The Market Democracy Paradigm describes a system in which producers respond to every varying demand of the market, and the implication we are supposed to draw is that cultural production thereby shares the most important features of political democracy, consumer choice being a close analogy to voter choice. This much is true, in the sense, and only in the sense, that political parties are also oligopolists, and that political party competition is ologopolistic competition. In the well-known analysis of rational choice theory, competitive parties organized for the winning of elections therefore tend to deliver *similarity rather than diversity*.[23]

A simple thought experiment will show why this must be so. Let us imagine three companies—A, B, and C—that dominate a particular consumer market and whose products are largely indistinguishable: the condition under which oligopolies arise in the first place.[24] Suppose Company A decided to market a *distinguishable* product; that is, one catering to a part of the market not yet actually satisfied by the oligopoly. This would require a major diversion of resources, but at great and pointless risk. Since similar types of products cannot meaningfully be patented or copyrighted, B and C would immediately copy A if A's innovation were successful, and A's brief lead in marketing a new product would disappear (after one season, if we are thinking of television shows). On the other hand, if the innovation were a failure, A would have wasted precious resources and lost some portion of market share by being, in effect, a guinea pig for the rest of the industry. The game is not worth the candle: little to be gained and much to be lost.

Free market oligopoly cannot produce diversity. It cannot cater to minority or exceptional tastes unless these can be isolated as an identifiable group of potential consumers. This is especially true of television, where the traditional product is so familiar, the costs of production so high, and the risks of failure so great. Network television caters to the *average viewer,* and only the average viewer. The average viewer may be different at different times of day, and for different television genres: children for Saturday morning cartoons, women for daytime television and soap operas, men for professional sports, adult families for primetime television, but adult men for cop shows. Whatever the genre or time, though, only the mass audience—of women, of families, of men, of children—is the advertiser's target. More specifically, only the mass audience of likely *consumers* is the target.

Television is specifically intended to be addictive, like heroin or crack or any other addictive substance; the main goal of any commercial television program is *not to be switched off.* The best analog to television in visual culture is pornography, and only moral and sexual panic about the latter prevents us from seeing their virtual identity. Like pornography, television has a narrative line (a charitable description of all pornography and most television) that is intended to hook the viewer, carrying her (or him in the case of pornography) from one segment of the action to the next, and promising a sense of completion—which never is, and never can be, delivered.[25] Just as the core purpose of pornography is to get its audience to watch more pornography (or else the industry would go out of business), so the core purpose of any TV episode is to get the viewer to watch more television: the next segment, leading to the next set of ads; the next program, leading to four new sets of ads; and the same program(s) next week, leading to a repetitive seeing of the same ads.

This being the case, we can no more imagine commercial television producers consciously trying to insert into the middle of this schedule a sense of holy terror, or unbearable anxiety, or Brechtian cynicism, or profound outrage at injustice, than we can imagine the producer of a pornographic film inserting one of Bergman's endless husband/wife dialogues in between two scenes of orgiastic coupling. "Get on with it!" is their common motto. This is not to say that intellectual thoughtfulness will never be found in fictional presentations on commercial television, but only that it must be kept in its place, bracketed off from the rest of the schedule and at the same time reintegrated into it by a major publicity campaign, so that it will not lead us to want to do something other than watch television. It's not just that only the average viewer is addressed by this system, but that the average viewer is offered only average aesthetic experiences: nothing that would turn the attention elsewhere or inward, distract us from television watching itself, throw us into a state of real emotion or real intellection. In T. S. Eliot's prescient phrase, we are "distracted from distraction by distraction."

With very few exceptions, therefore, most television series fit into genres that are sexually (and also nowadays racially) coded to find a particular primary audience, an audience that can instantly be deduced simply by watching the ads. Because of this fragmented pluralism, television is much less centered on the erotics of male desire than is film. The endless frantic couplings of almost everybody, regardless of class, color, or, finally even sexual orientation, in a series like *Courthouse* or *Melrose Place*, is not intended to have the same effect as cinematic voyeurism, especially as women are the largest audience for most such shows. In this respect, perhaps, more than filmmakers the producers of television can say that they produce "what the public wants." But with the exception of only the most successful "crossover" programs (e.g., *The Cosby Show, L.A. Law*), they accomplish this only by the newly discovered technique of "narrowcasting"; that is, quite deliberately structuring and *then* appealing to a fractured public.

This public cannot help recognizing its re-presentation as ghettoized. That is, when a white woman watches a program for white women she knows that that is what she is watching (if somehow she managed to miss this point, it would be brought forcibly to her attention at the first commercial break). In this way television's simulacrum of pluralism affirms the divisions of the sexual and racial order while seeming to appeal to particular subject positions within it. And no matter what genre we are watching, television's stylistic naturalism is even more decisive than cinema's; it always seems to suggest that we are just eavesdropping on reality. The separate spheres—women "good" but powerless, men less good but more powerful—are television's major contribution to our understanding of ourselves.

For television the effects of market structure on the consumer side are matched by the effects of market structure on the producer side. Exceptions stay firmly within the bounds of humanistic naturalism, do not stray far ideologically, and refuse any possibility of formal innovation such as might confuse viewers who understand television as a site of relaxation and passive enjoyment. (Steve Bochco's early version of *N.Y.P.D. Blue*, which imitated the British *Pennies from Heaven* by adopting a Greek Chorus approach of occasional musical interruptions, was quickly shot down by its network). The caustic wit of *Roseanne*, the quirky multiculturalism of *Northern Exposure*, the sometime feminism of *Cagney and Lacey*, the racial consciousness of *Frank's Place* or *A Different World*, the counterideological "movie of the week" productions of Robert Greenwald and his successors, have stretched TV's boundaries slightly.[26] But nothing on network television can equal, or could possibly equal, the visual terrorism of *Psycho*, the nightmarish nihilism of *Jacob's Ladder*, the elegiac look and tone of *Unforgiven*, the unrepentant vengefulness of *I Spit on Your Grave* or even *Thelma and Louise*, or the sexual transgressiveness of *Basic Instinct*.

As for those independent but still recognizably narrative films that trail in Hollywood's wake, such as the movies of Hal Hartley *(Trust)*, Julie Dash

(Daughters of the Dust), or Cynthia Scott *(Strangers in Good Company)*, there is no equivalent anywhere within the television system, no matter how many channels cable has added to it.[27] What commercial television reveals, even more decisively than cinema, is Hollywood's own ideology. It is a particular version of the ideology of "community," according to which people share a (partly spurious) gender unity as members of families and a (partly spurious) class equality as consumers; knowledge of significant social differences among them is suppressed; and any developmental needs they have that can't be expressed as patterns of material consumption might as well not exist. As Marx's analysis would suggest, this picture of our world, as false as it is, bears enough resemblance to what many of us would like to believe is its reality, to require no further explanation of its appeal.

PART II Cracks in the Pedestal

6 Resistance and Opposition

How resistant to existing constellations of power can commercial culture be? In thinking about that question, we must not be misled by, for example, the plethora of TV-movies that recycle what their makers seem to think is courageous opposition to wife-beating or incest, or by the fact that what can be called "liberal" or "populist" or "anti-authority" films are often made (and even, on occasion, television programs).[1] Liberalism and populism and an anti-authoritarian individualism are integrally part of the complex amalgam that makes up the dominant ideology of Americanism; only because this is so can crude and methodologically inept demonstrations of "liberal bias" in Hollywood take on some semblance of reality. Even such "antiwar" movies as *Salvador* or *Under Fire* or *Full Metal Jacket*, by presenting the controversial adventures of Americans abroad, can be seen at worst as taking sides in a "foreign policy" debate without in any way doubting the coherence and goodness of the nation as such. The producers of mass culture can freely explore the political universe only when specific policy options, as opposed to fundamental values or taboos, are being contested—or when, as in the relationship between individual and community, the exact nature of fundamental values themselves is in question.

However, films that seem to repudiate one or more American ideological conventions are produced from time to time, even in Hollywood, and more so in the wake of the feminist revolution than at any time since the 1930s, with its proliferation of vaguely anti-capitalist (or at least anti-"money") movies. But it would be a great mistake if we were to conclude that an ideology hunt through Hollywood, like a bug hunt on an alien planet, will say all that needs to be said about dominant visual culture. Given the instability of our relations to ourselves and to the social order in which we're embedded, ideology is always the historical result of a process of contestation. Therefore it is always being contested. At the present historical conjuncture the contest has become explosive in many arenas, and the sex/gender system is at the forefront of the struggle. It would be astonishing if Hollywood did not register such a fundamental conflict: if visual culture uncontroversially transmitted, without serious exception, the kind of transparent ideological closure, within the dominant frame of family/community/nation, that is the core of the Hollywood style. In fact, although the struggle is one-sided, Hollywood is a battleground, where more than just harmless war games are being fought out.

Nonetheless, the struggle rarely results in outright resistance or opposition. The terms themselves suggest a problem. Ideological discourse is what we become inured to in visual culture, and its impact is strongest in its apparent absence, its invisibility. In contrast, it's difficult for resistance and opposition to be implicit. Counterideological implication is likely simply to go unnoticed. Once stated overtly, however, it's more likely to be received by opinion-makers as "propaganda," as a didactic lecture about oppressed peoples instead of as art. As is always the case with social criticism, it will be said to be "shrill" or "strident," whereas films that can more easily rely on what is generally accepted and therefore unsaid will be praised as "thoughtful" or "complex." Thus *Dead Man Walking*, made by committed opponents of capital punishment (Tim Robbins and Susan Sarandon), ends by overwhelming Sister Helen Prejean's experience of the execution of Matthew Poncelet with horrific images of the antecedent crime that, visually at least, may now be seen as justifying it. The social order is partially recuperated. So the movie was received by mainstream reviewers as "thoughtful," "provocative," and so forth *despite* its commitment. This was possible only because the latter tended to disappear. In contrast, cops, district attorneys, and victims' relatives can make casual remarks about "letting a killer free to kill again," "not caring about the victims," and the like, and be seen not as mouthpieces for an ideology, not as propagandists, but simply as "real people." [2]

This conflation, however, between opposition and propaganda is mistaken. What is at stake in visual culture is not what audiences are told to think but how they are positioned, or interpellated. A brief comparison from the different world of information/propaganda can make this distinction clearer. If we think of programs such as *Sixty Minutes* or *Nightline*, we shall instantly recognize that whatever else happens on the occasions when their reporters "expose" some putative social wrongdoing, the programs unabashedly flatter their viewers. *We* can tell the difference between right and wrong. We may be somnolent—no other posture is possible in front of a television set—but we can be briefly awakened. This kind of audience positioning can be compared with that implicit in a French made-for-television series called *Prostitute*, carried by Britain's Channel 4 in the fall of 1993, as partial fulfillment of its legislative mandate to "represent minority viewpoints." The first program in the series consisted primarily of interviews with a forty-five-year-old transsexual prostitute who, with surprisingly philosophical reflection, described his life as a total outsider: cast out by family, rejected by friends, dismissed by employers, brutalized by the lawless forces of law and order, with little to look forward to but the companionship of his dog and (as he did not say but is clear to viewers) an early death.

How this film positions its audience could not be in sharper contrast to what American audiences have come to expect. It gradually becomes clear that not just bigots and brutal cops but *we*, the collective viewers of good conscience, compassion, and tolerance, are "Simone's" mortal enemies. It is *our* sexual fears, our acceptance of conventional law and order, the entire sex/ gender/class system into which most of us unprotestingly fit ourselves, that condemn "him" (the failure of the personal pronoun here is indicative) to the lower depths. *We* are going to kill him; nobody else. You and I (or our French equivalents), not the cops. There is nothing to be done by the compassionate, nothing that "democracy" can achieve; the invocation of that word would be obscene. To ask "our" legislators or police or judges to render "justice" to Simone would be like asking wolves to administer an Act for the Protection of Sheep. Finally it's difficult to face him, and impossible to watch the ads that follow (Channel 4 is a "commercial" channel that does not interrupt "serious" programs). *Prostitute* forces us to look at the frightful core of our social being; our somnolence is destroyed. We might not emerge from watching it any different, as political persons, than we would from watching *Sixty Minutes*. But at the very least we will have been made slightly more aware of a moral standard according to which, among other things, the entire institution of network television as we know it stands condemned as evil, and becomes a little less watchable than it was before.

Propaganda of the network news sort, in other words, emanates from the false consciousness of the powerful, who link themselves and us their viewers in a united front against some scapegoated Other who helps us define our own innocence—and willy-nilly that of the newsgivers, who might otherwise be seen as integral to a class, race, and gender hierarchy that itself helps to create "otherness." Propagandistic inserts that, in law-and-order films or television programs, distinguish "real" justice from the constitutional legal process, similarly interpellate viewers as allies of the powerful and monied persons who control the production processes of dominant visual culture. Because they are not diegetically present, however, this is not seen to be done. Because there is no forthright debate about law and justice but merely a series of unspoken assumptions, the most ideological film-making seems happily free of any didactic content.

Conversely, when years of intense dissemination of propaganda and ideology have succeeded in narrowing the permissible bounds of moral discourse, counterideological filmmaking suffers from *seeming* to be "propaganda," merely because it does not take the given for granted. Since to be taken seriously a movie must avoid the appearance of being mere propaganda, the effect of this kind of issue-framing is to limit the choices filmmakers (or television producers) can make and still hope for commercial success. This effect can be seen, again, in the making of *Dead Man Walking*, which, since it is consciously participating in a debate, must present its opponents in the strongest possible light, or else be perceived as setting up straw men. So Robbins and Sarandon must evince a state of divided consciousness to interpellate a skeptical audience as sympathizers with Sister Helen.

This creates the appearance of intellectual and even narrative complexity, as "having it both ways" always does. But this is only the appearance of complexity, and only if we accept the fundamental ground rule of Hollywood style, that the given is normal and need not be interrogated. Perhaps there are some things about which we ought *not* to have a divided consciousness. It would be equally "complex," and no more "ideological" (and possibly more courageous) for a film knowingly and openly to flout the beliefs of its audience (or some large part thereof), as does *Prostitute*. A film that made the simple statement that capital punishment is barbarous, and that those who commit it might be worse barbarians than those they execute, would have to take the chance of not interpellating many of its viewers as anyone at all, leaving them outside its frame. But it would not be propaganda, for it would still be telling a story like any other narrative film: a story that by virtue of the narrative form can not pass itself off as the authoritative "truth," and does not flatter its audience into a make-believe alliance against a scapegoated Other.

This direct confrontation with what is unappeasable, not recuperable, marks what I call "resistance" or "opposition." It is harder to achieve in fictional narrative, but certainly not impossible. Fortunately, a clear-cut contrast between what we might mean by "ideology" and by "resistance" or "opposition" (or counterideology) is easily available from the world of narrative fictions. In a wonderful moment of serendipity, the same storyline appeared on two very different television networks on one night in 1988. On ABC-TV's *L.A. Law,* Kluzak defended an accused rapist by attempting to show that the victim's conduct could reasonably have led the accused to believe that "she wanted it." Three thousand miles away, on British television's *Blind Justice,* its female protagonist was doing the very same thing. In each episode as well, the defense attorney apologized to the victim at the end of the trial, and was told by her to go to hell. There, however, the similarities end; the differences tell us about the contrast between ideology and resistance.

The American episode concludes, after the accused's conviction, with a confrontation between Kluzak and ex-prosecutor (also ex-womanfriend) Van Owen. Although she begins by chastising him for the pain he has caused the victim, their discussion soon devolves into the familiar subideological conflict between order and Constitutional liberty, "putting a rapist back on the streets" versus "even a rapist deserves the best defense he can get." "Why," snaps Kluzak with the last word, "don't you just shoot the bastard and not bother with a trial?" In an excellent example of ideological promiscuity, civil liberties wins the argument, but the rights of an innocent victim win our emotions. Having it both ways wins the day, as one way or the other narrative dissonance is recuperated for anyone who might happen to be watching. Even Kluzak, during the course of this "debate," celebrates a liberal version of the American nation, in which civil liberties are protected and "we" can be proud not to be like "them" (the police states).

Blind Justice moves in another direction entirely. Assigned by her firm to defend the accused man, Catherine Hughes demurs with the uncompromising statement, *"I don't do consent rapes."* Here she, unlike Kluzak, has already established a crucial asymmetry within the accepted standards of "fair trial" and "due process of law." A "consent" defense to a rape charge actually *requires* that the character of the victim be blackened, in order to show that the defendant could reasonably have expected *this* woman to be "consenting," despite the possibility that in her own mind she had no intention at all of so doing. Mocked by her associates as a hypocrite, since she has been quite willing to blacken the characters of policemen accused of brutality, she is too disdainful even to argue the inappositeness of the analogy. However, forced by circumstances into finally handling the case, she does what she has said she won't do—"just doing her job," as she must—and secures the accused's acquittal. This is the most likely outcome of all such cases, but one that *L.A. Law* has carefully hidden from us. There are no conclusive reflections about "putting a rapist back on the streets" after this story, though, because for the creators of *Blind Justice* the issue is not one strand of mainstream ideology versus another. Instead, Catherine resigns from the firm to join a radical law collective that she had previously scorned for its marginality; a collective whose members presumably will understand why she doesn't do "consent rapes."[3]

Unlike *L.A. Law, Blind Justice* recognizes that the law of rape, as Catharine MacKinnon and Carole Pateman have shown us, is in many ways still the law of a patriarchy. "Consent" is inferred only on the basis of what a man *as a man* might "reasonably" have thought a woman "wanted," even though force has admittedly been used. This doctrine of "consent" wipes out a woman's perception of her own nonconsent as though it did not exist, and thus the law's pretense of neutrality and equality is belied in practice.[4] For a lawyer who takes the rights of women seriously, then, the larger question is how she can do her job in an unjust society. It's not that this question couldn't be answered on American television, but that it could never be raised. Catherine's only possible response, in her own view, is to opt for a life not of accommodation but of *opposition:* she must change her life.

There are of course various paths that resistance may take, and complete overthrow of the established order is only one of them. However, just as we may not recognize the Hollywood style unless we immerse ourselves in its opposite, so we may not recognize that we are in the presence of something less than full-scale resistance or opposition unless we have been seriously exposed to it. And it's harder to find than European "art" films.

Hollywood recently has made small (better, microscopic) steps in the direction of female-centered interpellation in the form of movies about lesbian couples: for example, *Desert Hearts,* and several TV-movies about lesbians trying to adopt children, or keep their own. These movies are only problematically oppositional, though. In the first place, as Mulvey would probably remind us, films involving lesbian sex cannot escape the overall male-oriented framework of fetishistic voyeurism: many men are more turned on by sexuality between women than they are by the heterosexual variety. Furthermore, definitions of sexual normalcy and gender hierarchy are deeply embedded in our culture. That being the case, to tell a gripping, humanistic story about *any* kind of sex is, all else aside, to reaffirm its central organizing role in what remains a sexually hierarchical social order—in which "marginality" is admitted but only to play a supporting role.

Full-scale escape from the reach of the sex/gender system is possible in two ways. The first is through repudiation of the culture's conventional aesthetic forms. At its most elementary, this kind of ideological resistance takes the form of a refusal to interpellate the spectator either as a man or as, in the style of "women's movies," a woman trying to get a man. This is an accurate description of such diverse films as Sally Potter's *Orlando;* or the woman-centered films of Jacques Rivette *(Celine and Julie Go Boating, Duelle, Nor'Est),* in which dominant actresses essentially write their own scripts. These, obviously, are not Hollywood films. Escape from aesthetic and social convention is also possible via the route of making "boring," virtually non-narrative films such as *Clair of the Moon* and *I've Heard the Mermaids Singing.* This too is a difficult task to accomplish, for obvious reasons. Even the refreshingly different love story of *The Incredibly True Adventures of Two Girls in Love* can be read, as by some gay viewers, as nothing more than "a John Hughes movie with dykes," recuperated for acceptable humanistic narrative conventions by all but the most homophobic.

Something much more recognizably political happens when a film overtly rejects conventional myths of unity without allowing them to be recuperated, resists interpellation by refusing to ingratiate itself, and allows spectators no sense of moral familiarity when confronting its structure: unless they inhabit the standpoint of some *counterideology.* That is, it is possible for a film to repudiate the ideology of the aesthetic, to strive for (and perhaps achieve) the Brechtian effect of alienating the audience from the easy relaxations of pleasure in order to subvert our passivity. With the single exception of Melvin Van Peebles's *Sweet Sweetback's Badasss Song* (which finally did not find a Hollywood distributor), it is hard to think of any Hollywood movie that has ever resolutely carried out this program of disturbance through displeasure to its bitter end. For example, though *Malcolm X* gives voice to a rare, radical critique of the American social order, Malcolm is still a standard figure in humanistic ideology: the prodigal son returned, the outlaw redeemed as hero, Wyatt Earp briefly settling down in Tombstone. Dominant cinema, even the fringe of it colonized by Spike Lee, could not give us a figure like Sweetback.

In *Sweetback* we see black men sitting on the toilet, treating women as sex objects, engaging in brutal violence, killing a policeman. Sweetback himself, his life and fortunes wrapped up solely in his sexual prowess, is the very caricature of a white audience's view of the degraded Other; Malcolm, and even Spike Lee in *Do the Right Thing,* are easy to take by comparison.[5] What *Sweetback* says to the (white) audience is, you can all go to hell, I can be anything I want and will be and *still* I am and must be treated as the equal of you. Sweetback will not return except behind the barrel of a gun, he is unredeemable, and he can never be anywhere but on the run until Whitey's power is totally overthrown. This position cannot be recuperated; this outlaw cannot be reconciled. All thoughts of ideological unity disappear at the moment he kills a white cop and still remains, unequivocally, the only protagonist this film is ever going to show us.

Hollywood, in contrast, always tries to avoid *counterideological* closure. Whenever this kind of ending threatens, Hollywood retreats to what I have called promiscuity, the fence-straddling position of having it both ways; or else to genre conventions that have no particular political meaning. For a commercially oriented cinema, counterideological films are a hard sell.[6] This is not because most people accept the dominant ideology unquestioningly.[7] The dominant ideology, however, *is* the only available "common sense"; its discourse is "natural" and "normal." In the absence of a consciously adherent mass constituency, counterideology aimed at a general audience *will* seem to be necessarily didactic: it must not only tell a story but teach a lesson. Alternatively, counterideological narratives must seek out a more selective, initially sympathetic audience, thereby limiting potential returns on the investment that has gone into them. Thus *Sweet Sweetback* . . . interpellates black men as victims, sexual surrogates, and revolutionaries; black women as objectified sexuality (though it can be argued, probably incorrectly, that this is meant to be seen as the standpoint of white society, not as the moviemaker's own view of black women); and whites as brutal oppressors who must be smashed. There is no middle ground. Van Peebles, veering from scatology to political defiance, deliberately set out to alienate the white audience.

To hegemonic common sense, individual guilt and innocence matter, casual display of bodily functions is degrading, and violence is always wrong unless morally justified in a specific situation. Given this set of beliefs, and only given this set of beliefs, can "law and order" be upheld. In this perspective, unforgiving rejection of *all* whites, and contemptuous flouting of common behavioral standards, is at best "irrational," at worst morally and socially pernicious. To make a morality out of what seems, cinematically, to be two hours of shouting "fuck you" at one's audience requires the kind of systematic argument that visual culture can never really provide. The gaps have to be filled in, and the viewer has to want to fill them in. Many white viewers in my own teaching experience are initially repelled by *Sweet Sweetback . . .*, and only come to see it more positively (though that is not quite the right word either) on a second viewing, or after class discussion. These, however, are Smith College students who share a profound desire to be "antiracist" (if not being themselves nonwhite, as many are). For the ordinary audience, such a film can only be marginal.

To find this kind of opposition in cinema or television we either have to go out of Hollywood, for example, Nancy Savoca's first (independent) film *True Love*, Lizzie Borden's *Born in Flames* and *Working Girls*, Julie Dash's *Daughters of the Dust*, Cynthia Scott's *Strangers in Good Company;* or abroad, as in the films of Sally Potter *(Orlando, Thriller)*, and Marlene Gorris *(A Question of Silence, Broken Mirrors).*[8] *True Love*, for example, offers a devastating picture of preparations for what in Hollywood is invariably rhapsodized as the comical buildup to some subcultural version of the wedding ceremony: ethnic versions of *Father of the Bride*, in which the profusion of pratfalls does not obscure the basic joyousness of what is taking place. In *True Love*, by comparison, the Italian-American version of masculinity is finally unacceptable to the would-be bride, nothing about it can be recuperated, and our heroine can only walk away from the sacred rite in rage and resignation. Not even a countercultural recuperation of a more "sensitive" heterosexual masculinity, as in the ending of *The Graduate*, is allowed to brighten this picture. Similarly, Lizzie Borden's *Working Girls* provides a useful contrast to the "whore with a heart of gold" theme of which men are so fond, and which reaches its apex in *Pretty Woman*. Borden's "working girls" (like those portrayed by Marlene Gorris in *Broken Mirrors*) have nothing but contempt for their clients, none of whom is a repressed millionaire in disguise. Her protagonist's heart, as much despairing as golden, is reserved for her (fatherless) young child.

It's the films of Gorris, most notably, that take us into an unfamiliar world. This is a world, as in *A Question of Silence*, where three ordinary women cold-bloodedly beat a harmless salesman to death in front of three other approving women.[9] The salesman's only "crime" is that he has caught one of the women shoplifting and intends to report her. He is, in other words, enforcing the law of the patriarchy, of which they have all, in quite different ways, been victims. Only that, and nothing about his personality, is what justifies his murder. In the narrative core of the film, their action is then declared "rational" by a female psychiatrist who has been appointed by the court with the express mandate of declaring them insane. In a courtroom dénouement that mocks the entire (male-dominated) legal system, a hysterical prosecutor shouts at her that it would be no different if three men had killed a woman: and all the women in the courtroom burst into laughter. These women can kill an "innocent" man in solidarity with each other and feel no guilt about it, in other words, precisely because they know that individualism and its morality is for them a fraudulent myth, and "justice" a chimera.

Gorris's films achieve the status of all-out opposition because they are not only about love or sex or solidarity between women. They are also about the rightfulness or necessity of repudiating or even destroying men. They are *not* recuperable in any way by dominant culture. The fetishistic man who goes to *The Hunger* to see Catherine Deneuve and Susan Sarandon making love, or the masochistic man who revels in being vicariously dominated by Sharon Stone or Linda Fiorentino, can find psychosexual satisfaction in those visual fictions. But even those men will not be able to find any such satisfaction in *A Question of Silence*. The only intimate emotion that it evokes is the emotion of angry (but until the very end, silent) female solidarity. Its only larger social resonance is with the desire for a complete social and sexual revolution, and that is the only ground on which it can appeal (if its creator wanted to do so) to the hearts of men. It is not so much that *Sweet Sweetback ...* and *A Question of Silence* totally resist interpellation, for of course this is not the case. Rather, they defiantly interpellate only a selective band of their potential audience: black men in the former case, feminist women in the latter. The rest can go hang.[10]

From one standpoint, only this kind of utter rejection of the social given is what we mean by opposition. That is, it's possible to argue that no repudiation of the given less uncompromising than this amounts to anything. This of course is the critique that radical feminism generally makes of liberal feminism, and that radical socialism has always made of social democracy.[11] From the standpoint of radical critique, there is no middle ground between revolution and hegemony. Reformism is not a way station between the two, but simply a facade for the latter. And it is certainly true that, unlike *A Question of Silence* or *Sweet Sweetback's Badass Song*, cultural commodities from either Hollywood or its fringes offer no suggestion of real revolution. There are, however, two serious difficulties with the critique of reformism.

In the first place, the ideology of Americanism—that is, the belief in "liberty," "equality," and "democracy"—already contains within itself the terms of any possible critique. What else can rebels be rebelling on behalf of except some realized version of those abstractions? They are defined differently than in the hegemonic presentation, no doubt, but still they are inescapably the same words, the same ideas, and have the same ideological saliency as that against which critique is attempting to express itself. Opposition must therefore appear to be connected. There is nothing on behalf of which it can mobilize itself that is not capable of being reinterpreted on behalf of the status quo by proponents of the conventional wisdom. This requirement necessarily limits the field of discourse for any opposition not intent on dooming itself to irrelevance.

In the second place, many cultural critics equally fail to understand that politically this disagreement over reform versus revolution is purely a matter of strategic judgment, about which history offers no grounds to be dogmatic. There is nothing inherent in the notion of ideological hegemony to suggest that the historical settlement on which it rests is necessarily impervious to all incremental challenge. The implication that reform never changes anything essential in people's lives, at the moment or in the future, has nothing to do with any ordinary definition of "change," but everything to do with one's ideas about what is "essential." Ask any group of prostitutes, say, whether they would rather support a program of producing full sexual equality and abolishing prostitution, or legalizing prostitution and according its practitioners full legal protection, and the variability of that word ("essential") will instantly make itself manifest.[12]

Suppose, then, we start from a critical position in which the dominant ideology is seen as hegemonic, but also as neither monolithic nor monopolistic; reformism, if not privileged, is at least seen as a viable option; and compassion for the powerless and a willingness to question the given system count as oppositional. That is to say, by "opposition" or "counterideology" or "resistance," we might mean not principled, all-out rejection of the core beliefs of the dominant ideology, but rather adherence to one of several competing strands within it. From that position, Mulvey's cynicism about "narrative pleasure," even men's narrative pleasure, is more compelling as a psychoanalysis of audiences than as a statement about sexual politics. In part this is because the revolutionary "gender trouble" of which her analysis (as I've remarked earlier) was an early expression, has now noticeably begun to disturb and alter the institutions even of dominant cinema (much as the "class trouble" of which Marx's *Capital* was an expression began to disturb and alter the institutions of classical, laissez-faire capitalism).

From this less demanding perspective real ideological resistance, although rare to the point of extinction, does occur in Hollywood. Both the limitations and the possibilities of resistance as compassion can be seen, for example, in the relatively uncompromising *Stop at Nothing,* a made-for-Lifetime ("The Women's Channel") movie, which is now available in video stores and often shown on other channels. In *Stop at Nothing,* a husband whose apparently hysterical wife has accused him of child molestation is given custody of the child. Suspecting his wife's intentions, he hires a bodyguard for the child: "the best in the business," who turns out to be a woman (Lindsay Frost). He tells her that his wife is disturbed and vindictive, and she believes him. At the same time the wife's lawyer, also a woman, puts her in touch with the leader (Veronica Hamel) of an underground network that kidnaps children given by the courts to the custody of molesting fathers.[13] (It is a very nice touch that Frost is glamorous in an icy way, as in a sense befits her job; whereas the sometime glamorous Hamel, whom we gradually come to see as the real hero, wears baggy clothes and looks morally earnest throughout, providing no purchase to the imagination of even the most avid voyeur). The film then becomes a relentless duel between the two women (as few mainstream films have ever been), until the revelatory moment when the bodyguard sees the mother give herself up to the police to allow kidnapper and child to escape. She turns to the lawyer to find out what she now suspects to be the truth, and from then on, risking her career, she joins in the effort to spirit away mother and child: all the women united against the law of the patriarch.

Stop at Nothing has the obvious limitations of its genre frame and of prime-time television, even Lifetime: including, in its original showing, the ads that reassure us that whatever is going on we need not take it too seriously, compared to the real business of commercial television. Underneath everything, we might think, this is a private eye or "outlaw hero" movie in which, typically, the protagonist outwits the FBI, the local police, the state police, and any other law-enforcement authorities who happen to be in the vicinity (except that she does not). It also has, for "average viewer" reassurance, a heterosexual subtext so gratuitous that its constant recurrence is like a series of slaps in the face of the actual viewer, who must also endure the equally gratuitous (and incredible) inclusion of a man in the underground women's network that Hamel leads. Moreover, merely by virtue of appearing on commercial television, as part of the metatext, a seemingly oppositional statement takes on an exegetical weight that contradicts or limits its force. Shortly after making *Stop at Nothing,* Veronica Hamel starred in *The Baby Snatcher,* also made for Lifetime, in which she plays a pathological woman in the title role. See the films in succession, and the heroic woman-for-women disappears from view, or at least blurs at the edges. Of course that's the life of an actress; we can hardly complain. But that is also the meaning of the commercial metatext: it has no meaning, and swallows up any attempts at fashioning a discrete political stance.

Still, we have to recognize what *Stop at Nothing* does accomplish as a single statement within the metatext. Instead of setting the individual moral principles of the hero (Gary Cooper, Clint Eastwood) against the law, it suggests as a higher value the collective solidarity of women. It is hardly revolutionary; this is a rebellion in the name of conventional moral standards and notions of the family. The father of the piece is a *villain* (in a badly misjudged scene we are shown his villainy from a spectatorial standpoint that is attached to none of the characters, merely in order to reassure us that we're on the "right" side), and therefore these women are *good*. Unlike the audiences of the truly revolutionary *A Question of Silence*, we are not meant to identify with these protagonists because they are women, but because of their moral rightness. Their crime is not really a crime, whereas the murder committed by the women in the Dutch movie is inexcusable by any conventional moral standard. Yet the murder is meant to be not only excused, but endorsed, and finally a source of rage transmuted into laughter. But *Stop at Nothing*, with its invocation of the solidarity of women, remains a more radical statement than we ordinarily see on network television, or in dominant cinema.[14]

Just how far can dominant visual culture go? Another comparison of an original and a remake is useful here, in that remakes (such as that of *The Vanishing*) often illustrate the timidity of Hollywood, when it comes to resisting ideological resolutions or grounding them firmly in opposition or counterideology. In the Australian movie *Shame* (1987) a martial arts-trained, leather-clad lawyer rides into a small, outback town on her Suzuki and finds herself taking on almost the entire male population of either rapists or their accomplices. Reviewed in the United States as just another "exploitation" movie, a trashy remake of Brando's *The Wild One*, it disappeared from sight: only to return, like *Salt of the Earth*, to college campuses everywhere, where female viewers have no difficulty understanding its subversive intentions, even when they are less than fully realized.

In its narrative line and especially in its mise-en-scène, *Shame* actually belongs to the genre of the "lonely town," a genre that followed in the wake of the 1956 film *Bad Day at Black Rock*. In all such films (or television episodes) the protagonist finds himself isolated in a small town where a terrible crime has apparently been committed, and is now being covered up. For a period of about fifteen years, from the mid-1960s to the beginning of the Reagan era, clones of this basic story made it perhaps the most recurrent plotline on all non-sitcom television. *The Fugitive, Run for Your Life, Harry O,*

The Rockford Files, Bonanza, Burke's Law—these and many other series not only had their bad day at Black Rock, but had it every year for as long as they ran, so that any viewer "collecting" the story of the lonely town would have had dozens of examples of it by the end of that era.[15]

The story was always the same. Somewhere in the Far West or Southwest (never in the Deep South or New England), the protagonist arrives in a small town, a town so depopulated that it is almost a ghost town.[16] He is looking for someone who has disappeared, but no one will talk to him. Everyone wants him out of town, and when he is attacked the police appear to be on the side of his attackers. His only assistance, if any, comes from either the town rummy, or hooker, or the dead man's widow, or a teenager; that is, from someone who is comparatively unsocialized within the closed universe of the town. Eventually, when he finds the truth, it turns out that (as in the cinematic original), there has been murder done and a cover-up instituted. It is not merely the murder that is being concealed, though, but the invariant motive: a theft of land from the missing victim, a theft upon which the well-being of the entire town now depends.

The ostensible meaning of this story is ambiguous to the point of disappearance, but on repeated viewing one possible interpretation finally becomes unavoidable. In the prototypical *Bad Day at Black Rock* the missing man was a Nisei, returned from the internment camps after the war, and the land was his land—until as it turned out valuable minerals had been discovered on it. It is, in other words, not just a movie about racism, but about riches being amassed through racial oppression. In one way or another this is true of almost all its dozens of successors. If it is nothing else, this story is a variant of Marx's description of original accumulation, in which Capital comes into existence "dripping from head to foot, from every pore, with blood and dirt."[17] It tells us that a representative American town and—since these are highly symbolic narratives—by extension the American West itself, was founded on a primal crime: the crime of dispossession, and extermination, of the indigenous inhabitants.

Nonetheless, whether as a term of critique or as a rallying cry, neither the word "socialism" nor the name, "Marx," ever appeared or ever could have appeared on mainstream television: not even at the height of 1960s politicization. "Racism" could be depicted (though hardly ever named), but not any general interests that might lie behind it. In this entire period, the Lonely Town was virtually the only evidence of radical social thought to be found in visual culture—not, however, evidence of the visible, but evidence only of the invisible, the unspoken, and the unthinkable. The ostensible mystery is solved, as in all examples of genre; it is the genre's relationship to political consciousness that remains truly mysterious.

Within this context it's especially instructive to compare the Australian *Shame* with its American television remake, which premiered, again on the Lifetime network, a few years later, in 1992. Lifetime, as we've seen, sometimes carries movies that are critical about women's treatment by men. But although the line between cautionary tales of danger and oppositional tales of resistance is a thin one, Hollywood rarely crosses it, *Stop at Nothing* to the contrary.

The story of *Shame*'s two lives makes clear how the line is maintained. The pervasive difference between the movies begins where ideology always begins in dominant cinema, with the visual mise-en-scène, and the iconography of the lead players themselves. As to the former, that *Shame*, even though Australian, is essentially a *Western* (the lonely town always being in "the West") and has the feel of a Western, heightens the aura of loneliness and threat that emanates from the screen. This aura corresponds to what women feel walking down any street alone at night, and makes the look of the film seem an objective correlative for male violence. The remake's more ordinarily contemporary American small-town atmosphere deprives it of this quality and makes it seem, instead, more the personalized story of one girl's ordeal.

The other major difference is even more critical. Amanda Donohoe, the lead in the American TV version, though slightly taller than average for a woman is otherwise conventionally female in Hollywood's terms. As a miscast English actress playing an American lawyer in small-town Oregon, she has clearly been chosen for no other reason than to call on viewer familiarity with her persona as one of the partners in *L.A. Law*.[18] Since her character in *L.A. Law* was flamboyantly bisexual, this automatically makes her sexuality in the remake ambiguous, though the screenplay tries to establish that she is heterosexual. From any standpoint, however, she is very much the kind of actress Hollywood relies on to appeal to male voyeurism. In contrast, the Australian lead, Deborra-Lee Furness ("Esta" in the film), is not only taller than many of the males (or, at any rate, all the teenage boys) in the Australian film but also, in her outerwear, appears to be a large woman in every dimension, so that (as photographed, at least) she often seems to loom over the almost allegorical landscape like a threatening figure.

Of course, staying within the dominant cinematic mode of appealing to a mass audience, *Shame* can hardly free itself of the requirement to offer something for everybody. As in most rape-revenge movies its heroine's persona is not resistant to the fetishistic gaze of the male masochist. Because the director's intention was to reach the consciousness of teenage males (whose dates, he optimistically and probably erroneously presumed, would drag them along to it), concessions were obviously made to realize this goal.[19] Still, to the extent that an appeal to male masochism is implicit in *Shame,* it is much more politically ambiguous than voyeurism (see Chapter 9), as well as decidedly more open to a female audience. Although the gaze of the audience at Esta is potentially that of the (masochistic) male voyeur, the diegetic gaze within the filmic narrative, the gaze that defines and confirms the truth and value of what "we" see, is the gaze of Esta herself.[20] In any event, the murky meanings of leather fetishism aside, the sexual politics of *Shame* are unconventional.

Shame was criticized by a reviewer in the British journal *Spare Rib* for its allegedly unbelievable and therefore cowardly declaration of the heroine's heterosexuality (in the form of an absent "fiancé"). As in many such scenes in contemporary visual culture, this one feels as though it was parachuted onto the film set by a relief flight from the Sexual Preference Office.[21] We would have to feel sorry, the reviewer then scornfully declared, for any man foolish enough to take up with this Amazon. But that criticism surrenders to the standard polarization of sex and gender that the film rejects, and misses its crucial point. In one of the Australian movie's key scenes, Esta bathes in a pond with the young rape victim, Lizzie. As they talk about sex, Lizzie asks, "Would you let a gentleman kiss you *there?*" and Esta replies (quite clearly leaving her alleged "fiancé" in limbo), "If I were ever to meet a *gentle man,* he could kiss me anywhere he wants."

Her sexual choice is not about physical preference: it is political. She will not sleep with the enemy, but any man who knows how to dissociate himself from the enemy need not stay away. She is looking for what Joan Cocks calls a "sexual rebel," a good man who's hard to find, but whose goodness is defined through a feminist optic.[22] Donohoe offers a more instantly recognizable sexual ambiguity, but it is exegetical to the movie, remaining at the level of the actress's reputation. Furness/Esta's sexual *dissent* is intrinsic to the diegesis. Of course *Spare Rib* is right, in a sense: the epigram I've quoted would be more telling if it came from some dedicatedly Hollywoodized female such as Julia Roberts or Michelle Pfeiffer.[23] But then Hollywood will allow no such thoughts, and the American version omits Esta's remark.

This basic fault line determines the ideological divergence that follows. What is most striking, or even shocking, about *Shame* is that the hero *does not succeed.* Unlike the standard teenage bullies, voracious landowners, or wealthy murderers who dominate life in the lonely-town genre, the avatars of male supremacy can't just be unmasked, arrested, and put in jail by the law. They are the law. Though the American version also ends tragically, the resemblance is only superficial. In the original, after the hero's intervention has led to a tragic conclusion, the ineffectual (and complicitous) male sheriff nastily asks her, "Are you satisfied now?" But another woman replies, "No, we're not, mate, not by a long shot," and the women, who have finally come together as a social force, collectively stare into the camera, at the audience.[24] The Australian movie's ostensible narrative of gang rape and its aftermath actually underpins an oppositional story of the development of female solidarity; the final scene I've described is immediately preceded by one in which a young girl rejects a boyfriend who has been part of the cover-up. Both these scenes disappear from the American version, in which two separate rapes (from the original) are also conflated into one, and a brutal attack on the young girl's grandmother is eliminated as well.

The Australian original itself goes only so far. Esta's maternal bonding with Lizzie puts her squarely in the Ripley tradition of recuperating the strong woman for femininity (though she is considerably more reluctant than Ripley). So, too, the coming of solidarity to this population of women is belated; until the very end, what we have seen is the education of an almost primitive people by the sophisticated professional from the big city elites. Unlike *A Question of Silence*, in which the psychiatrist/protagonist is taught the truth by the three accused women whose sanity she is supposedly investigating, this movie never interrogates its own relationship to its audience: who teaches whom remains totally within conventional bounds. Who, in the words of the Third Thesis on Feuerbach, shall educate the educators? Still and all, its intentions are clearly counterideological.

In the remake, however, the net effect of all the changes to the star's persona and the narrative thrust, is to soften a potentially oppositional film into a conventional family melodrama, with a compassionate individual hero—a female Spencer Tracy—who sets out to the rescue of the oppressed. Precisely because of its crudity (every man in this Australian town is either ineffectual or a rapist), the original stands as a critique of hegemonic sexual ideology, and practice. The remake, remaining in the limited tradition of the lonely town and with the limited perspective of mere compassion, never passes beyond the bounds of implication. It is actually more like a remake of Samuel Fuller's *The Naked Kiss* (1964), in which ex-prostitute Constance Towers, in the face of angry disbelief on every side, brings to justice a child molester who is the son of the most powerful man in town—and then, like Alan Ladd or Randolph Scott, rides off into the sunset (on a bus) while the townspeople celebrate their reborn community.

Not so in *Shame*. At the beginning of the American version, a female voice-over informs us that this is a story about America, about rape: "It could happen in any town." If you're not careful at night, that is, and don't have a good lawyer (or a tough woman) looking out for you. But no one needs this voice-over. Furness herself said, after a speaking tour of the United States, that everywhere she went women came up to her and said, "It's just like that here." The Australian film, with no voice-over, makes it perfectly clear that this could happen, and probably has, anywhere there are men. It names the system. Despite its crudities, it is only "just another biker movie" if biker movies are subversive revelations of sexual hierarchy and violence.

The hero indeed rides *into* town alone. And, as in all the classic versions of this genre (and like Ripley in *Aliens*), she is a reluctant hero. So far the story is faithful to this classical American narrative convention. As one description puts it: "A community in a harmonious paradise is threatened by evil; normal institutions fail to contend this threat: a selfless superhero emerges to renounce temptations and carry out the redemptive task; aided by fate, his decisive victory restores the community to its paradisal condition: the superhero then recedes into obscurity."[25] But in this movie, paradise neither exists nor can it be restored. The oppression of women is constitutive of the social order, not an exogenous evil. And so the hero does not ride out of the lonely town alone.

Even though the word "feminism" is never uttered in *Shame*, the moment at which the women collectively face the camera and voice their resistance, makes its counterideological stance clear. *Shame* is not by this token a better movie than *Bad Day at Black Rock*; well-intentioned crudity can only take us so far. But by revising the Western and lonely-town genres, it brings to light an underpinning of "Western" civilization that they, even at their most progressive, repress. It is worth contemplating how different visual culture would look if enemies routinely named each other, instead of hiding behind the abstractions of genre.

It is certainly possible to make more, and potentially better, such films (not, I think, episodic TV series, though 1996's *Dangerous Minds* begins to move in this direction). Films can attempt to interpellate viewers into an underdog but not marginalized position, mustering the resources of conventional cinema to present an easily identifiable counterideological standpoint to spectators. We might wonder, for example, why there are not more films about labor organizing, such as *Matewan* or *Norma Rae* or *Salt of the Earth* ("such as" may be a euphemism here, since I cannot think of another instance). They offer a perfect frame for Hollywood's favorite trajectory of narrative tension, together with the opportunity to highlight individual heroism in the midst of collective struggle; and there are certainly more workers than bosses in any potential audience. On the other hand, such films are institutionally very dangerous, as Hollywood itself is in one aspect primarily an employer of potentially rebellious labor. John Sayles, the director of *Matewan*, is really outside Hollywood rather than of it; Martin Ritt, the director of *Norma Rae*, has for decades been Hollywood's only recognizably "Old Left" director.[26] When Hollywood produces a film about labor, it's as likely to be anti-union as anything else (e.g., *F.I.S.T.*, or the seemingly sympathetic *Blue Collar*).

Even nationalistic "race movies" such as *Do the Right Thing* or *Malcolm X* are probably easier to produce. On the one hand, black nationalism or revolutionism stand in implicit opposition to the American racial settlement and the American liberal tendency to make that settlement fair: to make ourselves live up to the presumably more fundamental elements—democratic and egalitarian—of "Americanism."[27] But given the facts of America's racial history, to call all ideals of accommodation or integration into serious question must be seen by many white Americans as simply an unavoidable eruption of the real into what would otherwise be a dedicatedly ideological discourse. These films can reach a racially mixed audience, and their rebellious or revolutionary message can potentially be quarantined. Such movies do not so much ask us to overturn the social order as to change a type of behavior—and most whites who are sympathetic to their message would deny that we are consciously engaging in such behavior anyhow.

In contrast, whatever the contours of patriarchalism and sexual oppression, white women are integrated with white men to a much greater extent in the United States than are blacks with whites generally. Therefore no Hollywood product, on either the movie or the television screen, has ever confronted sexual hierarchy with the manifest bitterness of *Sweet Sweetback* or Spike Lee's movies. Whether in the rape-revenge cycle that culminates in *Thelma and Louise*, the plethora of television films about battered wives, or the protofeminist confrontations of Hepburn with Tracy, Hollywood's portrayals of angry women remain at one level firmly ensconced within the ideology of the nuclear family (about which the worst that can be said is that it so often fails to live up to its advertising). To an "innocent" viewer, Hollywood's rapists, batterers, and male chauvinists are invariably presented as failures rather than avatars of manhood; a distinction not to be found in Lee's movies. Happy marriages (as between Hepburn and Tracy) and consensual sex await the "good" man and the woman who affiliates with him. In most of these movies in fact (though not the Hepburn-Tracy cycle) it is a certain kind of *man* who is stereotyped as "other," most usually a "redneck" *(Thelma and Louise)* or a borderline psychopath (*Sleeping with the Enemy* and most "battering" films). And whereas *A Question of Silence* utterly disrupts the humanistic pleasures of morally realistic fiction by apparently justifying the cold-blooded murder of an "innocent" man, Hollywood's rape-revenge movies do not go this far, since most if not all of the victims in these films really are rapists or would-be rapists.[28]

Despite the collapse of traditional norms governing relations between men and women—a truly world-historical event of which everyone is conscious—there are only limited possibilities even for as skillfully and commercially made a reflection of that event as *Thelma and Louise.* That film, despite its fairy-tale warmth and despite being immensely successful, provoked a cautionary outrage that is striking when we consider, for example, the relative lack of furor occasioned by Clint Eastwood's *Sudden Impact,* in which a cold-blooded, mass murderess of rapists is finally allowed to walk away unpunished. The difference is that *Sudden Impact* uncritically appropriates the acceptable American male notion of vigilantism (e.g., *Dirty Harry* or Charles Bronson's series of *Death Wish* movies). Its female vigilantism is validated by Eastwood, a male authority figure both onscreen and off. In no way does that film contemplate, as does *Thelma and Louise* (if only momentarily and fragmentarily), the possibility that women may not need men to define the moral universe for them.[29] That is about as far as mainstream Hollywood can go toward a direct confrontation with the unsayable.

Beyond that limit, I can think only of the more recent movie *Double Exposure* (directed by a woman, Claudia Hoover, and written also by a woman), in which the entire plot—a series of mistaken identities resulting in murder—revolves around a husband's assumption that his wife's secret lover is a man, when it is actually another woman. As audience, we are privy to his fantasies (in black and white rather than the color of the rest of the film), which show her sleeping with a man. Only after the dénouement do we realize that we have been gulled with perfect legitimacy: we accepted his assumption when we had no reason to do so, and several clues led in the other direction. This critique of the mainstream *audience* as well as of conventional plotting is unique, and the movie has been received with complete silence. Opposition in Hollywood apparently can't be recognized even when it really does occur. And that means, of course, that it becomes even less likely to occur.

7 "Put the Blame on Mame, Boys . . .": Ambivalence and Ambiguity

Works of art can also achieve some of the effects of ideological resistance by leaving themselves open to interpretation and courting ideological ambiguity. By this, though, I mean something other than, and different from, "having it both ways": hinting at a critique in order only to disavow it later. Cultural commodities that have it both ways do so to free their producers from the burden of divided consciousness; to make themselves whole for either emotional satisfaction or commercial success (or both). It is possible, though, to express a divided consciousness without disavowal, so that a normative social institution appears rather as the contradiction it really embodies. From the standpoint of radical critique this kind of ambivalence may appear as evasion, as disavowal of something that has never really been avowed. However, from the standpoint of dominant visual culture, the interpetative ambiguity it courts allows critique, or the suspicion of critique, to insinuate itself into the consciousness of a viewing public that has been trained to be suspicious, if not scornful, of overt politics.

Though we can mean many things by "ambiguity," what we are least likely to see in commercial culture is the ambiguity that ensues when a work of art is genuinely open to interpretation. The films briefly described in the introduction may be characterized in this way. They are neither overtly ideological nor counterideological narratives, not stories in search of a statement to make. To let us make up our own minds about moral truth or error, right or wrong, is difficult. As Stanley Kubrick has remarked, "It's easy knowing what you want to say in a movie; the hard part is covering it up." Again, a few comparisons may be useful.

Again serendipitously, in one week of December 1993 it was possible, on British television, to see episodes of two police drama series, *Prime Suspect 3* and *Between the Lines* (as well as various quite conventional examples of the genre), virtually in sequence with a highly praised, Emmy-winning two-part episode of the American *Homicide: Life on the Street*. At first glance there was a superficial resemblance, in that all three concluded with failure. Most strikingly, *Prime Suspect 3* and *Homicide* both featured a detailed, grippingly portrayed, but ultimately unsuccessful interrogation of a "prime suspect," who walked away unscathed at the end. There the resemblance ended, however, and it is the fundamental difference that was so striking, a difference that could not be more decisive even though *Prime Suspect* was produced for British commercial television by Carlton TV, the most notoriously Hollywoodian (British critics would say "trashy") of British commercial production companies.

Put simply, *Homicide* was a paean to "law and order," and to the efforts of those who try, on behalf of the rest of us, to make it a reality. They do not always succeed, as in this case, but there'll be another chance. As one of the detectives remarked, "the great thing about being in Homicide is that there's always more of them." The failure of the police here symbolized their humanity, for nobody is perfect, especially when forced to endure the hazards and brutalities of "life on the street." This is the strange, inverted version of Hollywood naturalism, beautifully realized in its gritty urban surfaces, but totally unlike the naturalism of Zola or Dreiser or Norris. Here, except on a handful of *Homicide*'s episodes during which American apartheid is (as from time to time it must be) confronted, the good guys are us, on this side of the interrogation table; and the bad guys are them, on the other.[1]

In contrast, *Prime Suspect 3* and *Between the Lines* are not about the defense of law and order, rendered somewhat more "realistic" by occasional depictions of failure. Rather, they are about the frightening ambiguity of police work, or of the very concept of the "police," who as any picketer or community activist could testify do not exist only to protect citizens from crime. A state with police is to some extent a police state: this is the painful truth that most of us try to avoid because it would be too costly to confront it. The police exist also to aggrandize their own powers as an interest group and a closed fraternity, and above all *to protect the state,* and the elites that staff and run it, from having to undergo full democratic accountability for their own often illicit behaviors. The murderer in *Prime Suspect 3* does not walk away simply because Detective Chief Inspector Jane Tennison (who inter alia has sex with the wrong men, can't stop smoking, is having an abortion to advance her career, and is unglamorous even though played by an actress famous for taking off her clothes) is unable to break his alibi, as in *Homicide.* Rather, he walks because the police hierarchy and powerful political forces have combined to make it impossible for her to pursue her case properly in the first instance.

This is also the constant theme of *Between the Lines,* a series about a mythical "Complaints Investigation Bureau" that investigates not "police brutality" but alleged (and often real) police crimes. Its ambiguity runs even deeper than that of *Prime Suspect;* the narrative and symbolic manipulations by which ideological narratives lead us to their unique conclusions are absent. There is systematic injustice, and there is police work that ineluctably leads to it, yet seems necessary in its own right. What exactly are we to think?

Beyond this openness to its audience, the equivocal and ambiguous nature of *Between the Lines*'s moral stance is an even more crucial difference. It's not merely that *Between the Lines* emphasizes the reality of systematic injustice more than the humanity of its characters, or that its "hero" himself engages in cover-ups to "protect the honor of the force," but that even the humanization of its protagonists is equivocal. The male lead Tony Clark (played by a good-looking and sexually attractive actor) is a philanderer who in one of the series systematically betrays both women in his life: an ironic commentary on his assigned task of rooting out the same kind of work-related behavior among his colleagues. Dominant American visual culture always politicizes sex, but without ever extending its insights to the public political realm. We learn nothing about law and order from the sexual bickering between, say, Kuzak and Van Owen. Watching *Between the Lines,* on the contrary, we are confronted with the real meaning of the slogan, "the personal is political," without ever engaging in a discussion about it, or seeming to encounter the idea overtly.

By extension, that Tony Clark betrays his wife and his mistress (herself a policewoman immersed in a cover-up!), while compromising two of his own cases in the process, does not by itself reveal anything about the alleged politics of personal life to us. What's truly political is the revelation of how thoroughgoing, how all-enveloping, is the life of secrecy, betrayal, and antisocial solidarity that policemen are forced to lead. A man whose job it is to root out lies is himself constantly telling lies, and does not even notice the contradiction. Watching him negotiating his sex life we wonder not about male philandering, which would be a trivializing response, but about policing as an organized activity: whether "law and corruption" might not be a more accurate epithet than "law and order"; and how it is that a good policeman may be not quite a good man. Like *Blind Justice*, these British shows do what cannot be done on American commercial television: they interrogate and challenge the ideology of "law and order" itself.[2] They do not simply repudiate it, thus generating their own simplistic counterideology. The case for the police is stated with unequivocal tough-mindedness in all these series. But it remains an argument, rather than a conclusion all the more decisive for being implicit.

In comparison to this, Hollywood narratives without the semblance at least of recuperation are almost unthinkable. What use is the natural and normal world if its very essence is alien to our moral intuitions? Beyond this structural agreement, though, television and cinema are quite distinct, and a symmetrical discussion of their responses to almost three decades of feminist resistance and counterideology is not possible.

It's not that television as a medium must always be less provocative, less challenging, and less oriented to minority interests than cinema. The contrary is more likely to be the case, in that by virtue of Hollywood's distribution system all movies in theory aspire to a general mass appeal, whereas television is capable of constructing specific audiences for specific products. Television's movies-of-the-week, especially, which construct their own (usually female) audiences with the help of advertising, *TV Guide,* and the other instruments of hype, have often been more apparently critical of the treatment of women or counterideological than anything mainstream cinema has to offer.[3] This can even be true of weekly series. In cinema the equivalent of a program such as *Northern Exposure,* with its post-hippie multicultural outlook, would be possible only as an independent production. The costs of a full-length, major studio venture would be considered too great to be recouped by such a narrowly targetted audience. Similarly soap operas, luxuriating in a mass female audience that watches them faithfully every day while only rarely going out to movies, can play with themes of sexual identity, familial dislocation, and the like that dominant cinema only touches in order to create spectacles of violence. In general, network television offers many more programs aimed at women—and also, especially, at African American women—than one will ever find in movieland.

What commercial television's weekly series almost always are, however, whether imaginative or mindless, is ideologically unambiguous and without irony. Peculiarly enough, though narrative closure is impossible in episodic television (Will Maddie and David make it? Once we know the answer the suspense is over), ideological closure is absolutely necessary: if not for every episode, certainly for every plot segment. Episodic television often elaborates multiple protagonist viewpoints, both in order to give every possible viewer someone to identify with and, more important, to make what may turn out to be the equivalent of watching a fifty-hour movie bearable. Any particular episode of a dramatic series may end in a temporary ideological standoff. The point, though, is that we *know* the standoff will eventually be resolved. A version of the right or the good will triumph or perhaps even lose, as in sadistic soap operas (e.g., *Melrose Place*) that deliberately terrorize their female audience. But we will still be in no doubt that the good was the good. And if two goods are hopelessly in conflict, one of them will usually turn out to have been not what it originally seemed. From, say, *L.A. Law* to *Designing Women*, the ideological holdout (e.g., Blair Underwood, the almost-angry black man; Delta Burke, the political reactionary) almost always compromises in the end.

In the absence of ideological closure, one inference might be that life itself, what we call "civilization" or "our society," is meaningless or absurd. Much more crucial from a structural standpoint, the more immediate inference would surely be that this particular show is meaningless or absurd, that it is not going to be one thing or another: it is pure self-reflexivity passed off as entertainment. A film can permit this inference without destroying its own raison d'être, since (except in the rare case of a super-blockbuster on which some studio has staked its existence) its producers and distributors will have no desire that viewers go on watching it again and again—let alone every week.[4] Two hours of purely meaningless entertainment is bearable, where fifty hours are not. Commercial television, though its narratives are often predicated on a never-ending tease, must still give the kind of satisfaction, if not actual catharsis, that maintains interest in a given program as a series of meaningful outcomes.

Certain ambiguities are possible on commercial television, so long as they are, so to speak, *political* ambiguities. That is, where there are two recognized "sides" to a question, a narrative may actually take neither, but rather leave the moral choice between them indeterminate. *L.A. Law* was a repository of such indeterminacy, and a viewer could exit one of its episodes thinking that justice either had or hadn't been done. Some episodes of *Homicide* have also entertained discussions among the show's protagonists that acknowledged— but who could possibly deny it?—that the intersection of race and class may present an insoluble "American dilemma." In any event, the frequent didactic exchanges between Kluzak and Van Owen, or Roseanne and Dan, cannot only be contained by commercial television but are sometimes even required by it, as a substitute for the sustained narrative suspense its fractured segments never permit to develop. These exchanges may be and often are confused, but they are rarely ambiguous, because coherence, or its semblance, is what carries us from one episode of a series to another. This is much less, though, than any questioning of our basic suppositions. It is also much less than the kind of cinematic ambiguity that is possible even within the confines of the Hollywood style: not simple, clear-cut disagreement about what policy we ought to adopt on this or that issue, but conflict internal to the narrative structure of the medium, in the sense that the very story being told is at war with itself and we don't know who we are supposed to be.

In this sense, the content of commercial feature films is potentially, and often even necessarily, ambiguous. Unlike television, which is designed to be as affectless as possible—who wants raging passion in their living room?— many films in all the genres of dominant cinema are deliberately designed to stir up our deepest fantasies. For this reason, we often cannot presume anything about the ideological content of a given film. Television's occasional fence-straddling is pro forma and schematic, since its ad-to-ad and week-to-week trajectory must not be interrupted by any moral or psychic disturbances. In contrast, filmmakers (and sometimes, more important, their sources of finance) aspire to capture our attention at a deeper level. Therefore the effort to "have it both ways" requires treating each way with emotional (rarely moral or intellectual) seriousness. This is not to say that the dominant ideology in public political culture is not also the dominant ideology in the make-believe world of cinema, but rather that in the latter, as in the former, it can only be dominant, not monopolistic. Television's dominant ideology may, as conservative critics charge, be out of touch with some important currents in American political life, but the conditions of oligopolistic competition ensure that it remains, if not monolithic, at least clear-cut. Furthermore, on network television official control over the finished product is absolute and direct (except to the unhelpful extent that it may also be shared with commercial sponsors). So ideological ambiguities of race, class, and gender do occur and reoccur, because the social order itself is immersed in them to a perhaps historically unprecedented degree. But they are always brought under control in the end (if only via the extreme sanction of cancellation).

Cinema is, or at least ought to be, different in all these respects. Even the condition of oligopolistic competition it shares with television lacks (perhaps only for reasons of tradition) any equivalent firmness of control. Still, commercial pressures are strong enough that when ideological ambiguity does occur in mainstream cinema, it is not as the result of a conscious desire to leave open the possibilities of interpretation. It is instead usually unintentional, being the result of conflicting agendas among the creative talents at work on a project, or even within individual psyches of scriptwriter or director (or occasionally, star). At such times cultural commodities may manifest an uneasy ambivalence, at various levels of depth and more or less open to ideological recuperation. And whereas once the most fundamental ambivalence in Hollywood storytelling was the clash between *male* self-realization and social order, in the wake of the feminist intellectual and cultural (if not yet political) revolution, uncertainties about gender structure and even sexual identity have come to the fore. Given the changes adverted to in Chapter 1, there are possibilities that must be repressed if the given order is to be maintained (for it is never simply given). But we are too aware of them for their continued repression to be a simple matter.

Under the circumstances, what's surprising is how little ambiguity does escape the limits of cultural commodification, of disavowal and recuperation.[5] For this kind of ambiguity—that is, uncertainty about what we are finally supposed to think—always threatens to break through even in dominant visual culture; the major accomplishment of what I've called the Hollywood style is to suppress it. Because the social unity that ideology imagines is spurious but the reality of social conflict it represses is real, the triumph of even a hegemonic ideology can never be complete. To cope with the obvious messiness of reality requires a patchwork of ad hoc inventions to solve unsolvable problems. These cannot be hidden for long, as there is always someone with an interest in exposing them, and so the patchwork becomes ever more frayed. The development of outright resistance may require a chance conjunction of social forces and historical events, but slippages in the confidence of hegemonic elites, and in the certainties it attempts to purvey, are always on view. In visual culture, these slippages are revealed, every now and again, sometimes in one genre or sometimes in another, in some ways in one historical period and in different ways in another, as cultural commodites at war with themselves. What we see when viewing these commodities is not resistance or opposition, but inconsistency within what seems to be intended as a basic framework of compliance.

Hollywood, for example, has a long institutional history of revealing but concealing, or refusing openly to avow (even to be disavowed later), the attractions of male or female homosexuality.[6] What exactly *was* the subject matter of *Rebel without a Cause, The Strange One, Tea and Sympathy, Cat on a Hot Tin Roof,* or *Suddenly Last Summer?* What is the despair that could not be spoken out loud, the horror (as in *Suddenly Last Summer*) that cannot be defined? Viewing these movies when they first came out, we were left in a state of not ease but unease. In the midst of all this concealment, the films were revealing the rickety construction of what was otherwise being portrayed to us as a salvageable social order.

We must be careful, however, to distinguish this kind of genuine ambivalence from a manipulativeness that looks like it but is in fact its opposite. To see the difference, we can look at two recent movies about cross-dressing men with hearts of gold, *Tootsie* and *Mrs. Doubtfire.* These movies are designed to appeal to women, in that they begin with the assumption of women's moral superiority; and to men in that they can be read at the same time as denying the moral inferiority of men. These are in the genre of other films about the "new (postfeminist) man": *Kramer vs. Kramer, The Good Father.* Dustin Hoffman especially is the Barney Greengrass of the men's movement: how can anyone doubt that this liberal Jew who exudes both his liberalism and his Jewishness, really is a *good* man? Either of the two responses to those films is therefore defensible, depending on who the viewer is and what he or she wants out of the film. This is *promiscuity,* or "having it both ways": something for everyone, contriving the story so no potential audience feels left out. Artistic promiscuity deliberately appeals to anyone's consciousness at all—as long as that anyone can pay the tariff.

To see, in contrast, how repression—the failure of this apparent openmindedness—can in its ambivalence reveal what is really at stake, we can look at a contemporaneous film, *Dead Poets Society.* Harry Keating (Robin Williams), a recently hired English teacher at (and ex-student of) an exclusive and snobbishly conformist boy's prep school in the 1950s, founds a rebellious secret society with some of the boys in his English literature class. Meeting together with him in a hidden cave, the boys read the romantic poets (especially Whitman), call their teacher "Captain" (as in "Oh Captain, my Captain"), trash the required syllabus (eschewing all "realist" poets and actually tearing the philistinish introductory essay from their textbook), and discuss the large issues of life and ambition. One of the boys (Neil), encouraged by Keating to pursue his ambition of being an actor but forbidden to do so by his tyrannical father, commits suicide. The frightened boys tell on Keating, and he is dismissed in midsemester. In the film's last scene, the disgraced teacher comes to collect his "personals" as the headmaster conducts his class (in the most philistinish possible way). As he is about to walk out the door for the last time, another one of the boys, who has been both cast and played (by Ethan Hawke) as an unsurpassable representative of adolescent male sensitivity and beauty, leaps onto his desk and cries out "Captain, my Captain." As the headmaster admonishes and threatens, one by one the other members of the Dead Poets Society (quite a few of whom could also be described as "beautiful") do the same, each in turn looking at Keating/Williams with the fondest of tender smiles, as he does at them. "Thank you, boys," he says, "thank you." The music swells to a crescendo.

A long line of movies, from *The Strange One* to *Taps*, have peered into the psychosexual abyss of male boarding schools and blinked. In foregrounding the relationship between teacher and students rather than among the boys themselves, this film takes an additional step that is even harder for its producers to spell out. Ideological discourse, I have argued, is usually recognizable by its repression of underlying but unpleasant realities of conflict and contradiction, and one could easily offer such a characterization of *Dead Poets Society*. Sometimes, however, repression reveals as much as or more than it hides. That is especially so when a film's ostensible subject simply cannot carry the weight assigned to it by the narrative. Whatever moral stance they might prefer, most viewers will *know* the reason why boys like Neil commit suicide, and being denied a theatrical career isn't it. Once that realization intrudes, we must actively resist the text to avoid seeing its residues. The hidden cave, the torn textbook, Whitman, the Captain, the tyrannical patriarch(s), the opposition of the romantic and the philistine, the "personals," the desire to be an impersonator, the beautiful boys, the teacher's injunction to "suck the marrow out of life"—the symbolism is so heavy-handed it finally is not even symbolism. This movie is the closet, or better The Closet, brought to life. Its attempts to lead us in some other, nostalgic, less threatening direction, are self-evident red herrings.

Some of the overt films about gay men I have referred to earlier—*Making Love, Philadelphia, Longtime Companion*—want to be liberatory but are still hopelessly ideological. Not what Marcuse called "The Great Refusal," but rather peaceful resolution, is what they desire. What they repress is the full scope of the closet and its pain, and the brutality of those who inflict it on them. Terrified of spelling this out—for we are still within the realm of dominant visual culture—*Dead Poets Society* reveals it all the more. Ideological texts achieve their effect by avoiding or papering over conflict, and so they produce a satisfying facade of social accommodation. But the conflict between what is being said and what cannot be said, or can only be said in another guise, produces not satisfactory accommodation but narrative uncertainty. Real ambivalence produces real textual ambiguity.[7] The line between the conscious desire to manipulate us, and the unconscious inability to say what is actually being said, *is* uncertain; but it *is* there.

Artistic ambivalence, that is, exhibits (or more commonly, as in *Dead Poets Society,* conceals) the divided consciousness of its creators, and leaves us in a state of real *ambiguity.* We are not certain what it is we are being shown. Rather than being cheerfully satisfied with either of the interpretations that is being made available to us (as in *Tootsie* or *Mrs. Doubtfire*), we are unable to accept the most readily available interpretation on offer.[8] It's easy enough to identify with the romantics against the philistines, but as what kind of *men* are we (those of us in the audience who are male) being interpellated? Ostensibly we are watching an early attempt at overthrowing the patriarchy, but if the relationship between Harry and the boys is not patriarchal then what is it? It is certainly not egalitarian. Why, years after the abolition of the Production Code, and two decades after the open revelations of *Cabaret* and *The Boys in the Band,* is *Dead Poets Society* still talking in whispers? The question, once we ask it, answers itself. *This* movie is about the love that still dare not speak its name, and thus shouts it all the louder.

Again, to take perhaps the most famous example of ambivalence and uncertainty, and one very much worth a re-viewing for what it tells us about the possibilities of resistance within a framework of compliance, the 1946 movie *Gilda* promises me as a man identification with a misunderstood hero (Glenn Ford) who will eventually be vindicated and will obtain his heart's desire. This is a satisfying and enduring version of man's heroism throughout the ages, and my own, as many men's, favorite plotline. The problem, though, is that this movie has two incompatible texts. The ostensible text, narrated by Ford ("Johnny Farrell") tells the story of two men betrayed by a faithless woman. Only very late in a screenplay full of self-contradictions does Johnny discover that his boss is a villain and Gilda was not faithless after all. To accept this text as *the* text, though, we first have to accept Johnny as a reliable narrator. And this is difficult, not only because his initial view of his employer (George Macready) is so obviously misguided (not to mention overtly homoerotic) but because his view of Gilda encounters immediate subversion from the star who plays her: Rita Hayworth.

As the kind of man to whom Hollywood aims its appeal, I am instantly in love with Rita Hayworth, who is phantasmically my heart's desire as well as she is diegetically Glenn Ford's. As I watch the movie, furthermore, I quickly realize that she too may be a misunderstood hero, or heroine. That is because Hayworth's status as noble victim is confirmed by her constant disdain, all raised eyebrow, curled lip, and mocking delivery, of the more obvious femme fatale role offered her by the script. In the course of the film Ford's misreading of Hayworth (finally underlined by her delivery of "Put the Blame on Mame") is so gross that he has lost all authorial credibility and thus his status as trustworthy narrator. His every word is so neatly undercut by Hayworth's mockery that even his own sexuality has become suspect. Worse yet for any hope of a simple and satisfying resolution of the conflict between them, the condition of her strength as a beautiful woman who is also an independent woman is quite clearly and quite rightly that she is not willing to be "obtained" by anyone: including me in my guise as the potential ego for whom Glenn Ford is the alter.

Now we see the meaning of divided consciousness. Although I want to position myself as a man (which is how Hollywood wants me to position myself), I also want to position myself as the underdog, as the truly misunderstood hero. But it gradually appears, with more and more certainty, that *that* person is Hayworth/Gilda. Realizing that they had a tiger by the tail, the filmmakers (scriptwriter, producer, and director, two women and a man respectively, the producer a close friend of Hayworth's) lunged desperately at a standard happy ending: Ford walks away with Hayworth after all. But films noirs aren't intended to end happily, and this ending has always seemed ludicrous to most of its viewers. I don't believe it for a second. Despite her gender, my identification with *Hayworth* (not just my longing for her) has been too close.

Also, many male viewers who are drawn to sexual libertinism will simply reject the idea that the free spirit Gilda/Hayworth could ever be tied down to a bourgeois marriage. As I've remarked earlier, the ideological stance of familial heterosexualism is preserved by having sexually aggressive women come to bad ends, and the treatment given to this theme in *Gilda* seems to be a perfect exemplification of this tendency. In order to make this mostly grim and bitter film noir come out "happily," it therefore has to be revealed at the end that Gilda has not in fact been sexually active: it was all a pose, to punish her ex-lover Johnny for having deserted her. This is the ostensible narrative conclusion of *Gilda*. However, Hayworth, taking unashamed delight (uniquely for that period) in her own sexuality, managed to repudiate completely both the conventional film noir role of "bad girl" *and* the reconstructed role of "really a 'good' (i.e., sexually inactive) girl." A contemporary audience (whatever audiences in less sexually revelatory times may have thought) can neither accept her as a "bad" girl *nor* believe for one moment that she had really been sexually inactive. And since *she* is our hero, we just don't care. "Resistance through charisma," one commentator has called this—and therefore as well, ambiguity through resistance.[9]

Gilda is capable of creating sexual unease in its viewers (if they are men), because for at least a moment they have been unsure who they are; Ford/ Johnny's bottomless capacity for self-flagellation is unnerving and disorienting. As for women's responses, when *Gilda* is shown to college classes, female students with little understanding of American popular culture are often enraged by scenes of Hayworth's humiliation, and never get over the hatred for the movie that these engender in them. However, since Gilda certainly is a victim, and the narrative makes every attempt to persuade us that Johnny is also, male viewers are potentially subjects of a *double* victimization. That women fail to recognize this possibility (this is also true of the more recent *Fatal Attraction*) is perhaps due to too much immersion in a particular kind of psychoanalytically founded feminist cultural theory. This kind of theorizing has the severe drawback that its practitioners rarely think to ask *men* how they are seeing whatever film is under discussion—perhaps under the mistaken impression that a generalized psychoanalytic theory can answer this question.

On the other hand, more culturally sophisticated female students are often so proud of "seeing through" the mystifications of the film's overt narrative, of not being fooled by Ford/Johnny, that they actually come to think there is a secret film hidden beneath the apparent one, to which only they as women are privy: a "real" story that the film itself is trying to conceal from them.[10] Whether Gilda (and by extension themselves) is victim or victor then becomes a question to which there is no answer, but which is capable of producing intense argument and being resurrected again and again. In any case, there is no easy ideological message to be drawn from *Gilda*. Its sexual uncertainty is real uncertainty, not just an easy matter of momentary role reversal. Like other films of the postwar period, it superficially confirms the lack of any social role for an independent woman. But unlike films that turn her into a murderess *(Criss Cross, Dead Reckoning, Out of the Past)*, and attempt (unsuccessfully, in my experience) to cover up social malaise with a patina of gynephobia, *Gilda* cannot (or does not want to) wholly suppress her. Viewers who know of Hayworth's long and unsuccessful struggle against her victimization by Hollywood (and men in general), will conclude that anyhow, despite the false ending, there was no way out for her, or Gilda.[11] But since they will reach this conclusion sadly, the movie, as ambiguous movies will do, thereby can turn the viewer against what seems at first to be an obvious message.

In contrast, no one will think about *Tootsie* or *Mrs. Doubtfire* for five minutes, because despite their apparently overt appeal to sexual uncertainty, the tension that ought to result is very quickly dissipated and made into a source of pure entertainment as well as ultimately clear-cut ideological satisfaction: men to the rescue! Good men, men who are just like women— only men! At the moment in *Mrs. Doubtfire* when we see Robin Williams's hairy legs peeping out from under his dress, we know that everything is still for the best in this best of all possible worlds: the world in which men, now happily humanized, can safely be allowed to go on ruling. Once a movie has promiscuously offered itself up to our enjoyment in this way, without making any real demands on us, there is nothing to think about. Feeling no unease or existential nausea, we know that we have been in the presence only of evasion or escape.[12]

Ambiguity, however, even unintentional ambiguity, is inherently risky. In the contemporary period, mainstream films, with their bloated budgets, opportunities for colossal profit or loss, and condition of being hostage to the makers of respectable opinion, leave their makers with little room for intellectual maneuver. Ordinarily the most they can achieve is disavowal without recuperation. That is, a film itself, as the product of the divided consciousness of its various creators, may give us reason to believe that the state of harmony with which it concludes is spurious; and so it falls short of its recuperative intentions. In *Philadelphia* Tom Hanks wins justice against the firm that fired him for having AIDS, and his death and funeral service bring about a kind of family reconciliation. But anyone who's been watching will have every reason to doubt the honesty of these quite arbitrary outcomes: especially in that the unparalleled feeling of heartbreak conveyed by Maria Callas's rendition of "La Mamma Morte" trumps the film's relatively feeble attempts at a "happy ending." Anyone who can listen to Callas and not recognize the reality of existential despair must truly be unable to "suck the marrow out of life."

One variety, however, of a more genuine textual ambivalence, and potential ambiguity of interpretation, is or was virtually inevitable in the conjunction of the commercial film form and American culture. We should not forget that the protagonist of our most enduring novel of young manhood, *Huckleberry Finn*, lights out for the territories precisely in order to escape from the demands of family, community, and even nation. Many of the writers and directors of classical Hollywood cinema were themselves deeply involved in that fundamental tension in a new context, as New Dealish or popular front leftism gave way to cold war liberalism. In *Viva Zapata!* and *On the Waterfront,* for example, director Elia Kazan and scriptwriters John Steinbeck and Budd Schulberg revealed their deep ambivalence about their own political beliefs, as they negotiated their passage from popular front leftism to cold war liberalism. The kind of filmmaking that resulted from their ambivalence cannot be simply willed.

The conclusion of Spike Lee's *Do the Right Thing,* by way of contrast, invokes the antithetical voices of Martin Luther King Jr. and Malcolm X, but nothing in the narrative itself has prepared us for either of them; their deeply theoretical visions of politics do not inhere in its essentially comedic premises. Hanging the picture of a black man on the wall of a white-owned pizza parlor in a black neighborhood may be a plausible metaphor for the visions of social justice they articulated, but it remains only a metaphor. When Lee throws a radio through Danny Aiello's plate-glass window, he may think he's fighting "the power," but that kind of cultural politics is hardly what King *or* Malcolm had in mind. Lee's ambivalence is undoubtedly felt deeply enough, but it does not seem to be especially felt within this particular filmic context. The conflicting liberal individualism, Marxism, and romantic anarchism that animated the making of *Zapata!* or the class consciousness and reconciled Americanism that are at war in *Waterfront,* are visible in every frame of those films.

Many socially critical mainstream films of that earlier period, though never breaking free of their dependence on the commercial structures of patriarchal capitalism, were visibly (or audibly) at war with themselves. Usually this did not reach the depth of Kazan's unresolved political trajectory, but was animated by a less interesting, simpler intellectual confusion that is still much more provocative than the cynical manipulativeness of contemporary artistic promiscuity. Especially among Westerns, for example, the conventional heroic and masculinist individualism of the genre were often conjoined uneasily with other values: with the rejection of all established and respectable institutions *(The Wild Bunch);* with a trite but powerful Freudian critique of patriarchy (*The Naked Spur, Man of the West,* and the other Westerns of Anthony Mann); with racial integrationism and even an implicit attack on myths of private property *(Bad Day at Black Rock);* and with both an affirmation of the family *and* a critique of conformity and myths of community *(High Noon).*

High Noon is an especially interesting example of how political confusion can leave the way open to viewer interpretation. In this respect, criticisms of that film as an example of cold war liberalism, or Howard Hawks's "pro-community" revision of it in *Rio Bravo,* are too simple.[13] That Marshal Will Kane's Quaker pacifist wife shoots an outlaw in the back to save her husband is not merely an oblique endorsement of the use of violence. It is also a clear statement that what stands above abstract moral principles and even the law, is not just the individual conscience but *the family.* This kind of personal loyalty has always been potentially at war with the state, even the cold war American state.

From a more comprehensive standpoint, the film would seem to offer a one-sided version of loyalty: Gary Cooper is loyal to his principles, Grace Kelly to Gary Cooper. But to stop there would be to substitute the literary criticism of a written text for the cinematic criticism of a visual one. *High Noon* is not an essay on loyalty, but a visual spectacle. What we see is crucial. At the film's climactic moment, what we do see is Will Kane trapped between the last two outlaws; when Ben Miller has finished reloading his gun, there is nowhere for Kane to go. All our visceral intuitions suggest that Will Kane is about to die. And in a sense, by the code of the West (that is, of Hollywood Westerns) he *deserves* to die: he's blundered and lost. When the fatal shot comes, and to our shock the gunman pitches forward to the ground, we haven't simply read an essay on the futility of nonviolence, or the duties of a loving helpmeet. We have also seen a vivid demonstration that the masculine individualism that, until now, we thought was being apotheosized by this movie, is not in the end enough.[14] Here "family" functions very clearly as a surrogate and (emotionally) utopian replacement for the "community," whose authorized leaders (businessmen, ministers, lawmen) have all deserted the hero. From the standpoint of the viewing community, most of whose members are neither feminists nor revolutionaries, not every endorsement of "the family" necessarily functions in the same way. Even today *High Noon* reminds us of this.

In this respect we can also learn something by comparing the end of *High Noon* with the end of the apparently right-wing "law and order" movie, *Dirty Harry,* in which (twenty years later) Clint Eastwood quotes Gary Cooper by throwing his badge into the river, out of disgust with "soft" judges and politicians who hamstring the cops (Cooper throws his badge in the dust). In both cases "law and order" is silently vindicated; the hero who has acted outside the law must give up his right to embody the law.[15] But Dirty Harry walks away alone; Will Kane rides away with his wife. *Dirty Harry* is nihilistic; the end of *High Noon* suggests a utopian longing that can't be realized in conventional, mainstream society. Though the film mounts a fierce attack on mass conformity, its equally unmistakable scorn for the town's businessmen (never criticized in *Dirty Harry*) and political leaders implicitly suggests a preference for a political countercommunity, though perhaps not one that Howard Hawks would have been comfortable with. *High Noon* is *not* just one ideological statement, nor does it offer indiscriminate stances for differently positioned members of the audience to adopt. Its implictly left-wing politics and liberal individualism are truly at war with each other, and this leaves it open to conflicting emotional responses and interpretations.

This kind of cinematic ambivalence or ideological confusion is possible because an individualistic and egalitarian libertarianism has always been at war in the American psyche with a repressive, puritanical authoritarianism: an authoritarianism that derives its strength precisely from the equal strength of the dark forces it confronts. The interplay of this source of moral tension with the formal structure of cinema is visible in James Stewart's tortured countenance in Mann's Westerns; in most of the films of, say, Humphrey Bogart or John Garfield; and more recently in some of the films of Al Pacino, Robert De Niro, and Mickey Rourke. These actors' defeated hero/victims embody an unconstrained individuality that is more vivid, more historically compelling, than the carefully contrived endorsement of "law and order" contained in the ostensible narratives of most of their films. (The ideological salience of this kind of ambivalence is hardly uniform; in *Patton*, e.g., George C. Scott's vivid portrayal of the authoritarian militarist as hero completely overwhelms whatever liberal intentions are visible in the screenplay.)

Is there, however, really the same kind of contradiction in our fundamental cultural values about gender and sexuality as appears in our feelings about the individual's relationship to the community? The effect of seamlessness, the absence of a visible author, and the very womblike nature of film projection, make of film a cultural form that strikes at and activates our deepest fantasies. And this form would appear to be the core source of whatever ideological messages we ultimately derive from cinema as an institution. The repression of homoerotic messages in classical cinema would seem to suggest that this kind of conflict is near the surface, but it is still mostly a conflict for and among men.[16] As to the intersection of sexuality with gender differentiation, in Mulvey's formulation cinematic ambiguity necessarily disappears precisely at this, the most crucial juncture of film and audience. The gaze that is activated by classical cinema is unequivocally male.

Making a visual spectacle of women highlights (fetishizes) their apparent castration, producing *in men* an anxiety that must thereafter be either avowed or disavowed. Avowal occurs as a controlling and ultimately sadistic voyeurism; disavowal as what Mulvey calls "scopophilic fetishism," or fixing on something about the woman's image to assuage the fear of difference. In either case, the "we" of my earlier formulation about the structure of cinematic narratives is a very peculiar and limited "we"; the gaze of the camera and thus of the spectator is always either voyeuristic or fetishistic. In a phallocentric civilization in which *women* are always the passive objects of the active male gaze and of male desire, the spectator is necessarily interpellated as a man, or men; the structure of a culture in which men look and women are looked at is reified and preserved by cinematic structure. The inhabitant of the mystified world need not be other than visually "active" if he is a male, since as a male he is apparently in control of the very apparatus of cultural production. And she cannot be other than passive if she is a woman, since she is indelibly on the wrong side of the camera. The male receives the illusion of being a controlling actor while remaining a consumer, and the woman receives the knowledge that she can only be an object of male consumption.

Central to Mulvey's thesis is that not just *any* woman but any woman appearing as visual *spectacle* (however that may be culturally defined) is the object of the male gaze. In this analysis, no visual cultural commodity of any kind can break out of the (patriarchal) subject/object dyad as long as the female subject is potentially desirable to men. Movies starring Divine may disturb that dyad, but not movies starring Rita Hayworth. The "resistance through charisma" of the great female stars of the "classical" period—Hayworth, Joan Crawford, Bette Davis, Marlene Dietrich, Katharine Hepburn—is evanescent; really no resistance at all. In the contemporary period seemingly socially critical television series with beautiful stars, such as *Cagney and Lacey* (Sharon Gless) or *Northern Exposure* (Janine Turner), can only repeat the essential relationship of cultural patriarchy while seeming superficially to question it. Contemporary patriarchalism is a loose rather than rigid social system. It is a system of informal cultural, social, and economic relationships rather than formal legal rules. "Token" women of any kind do not disturb the overall outlines of this system but rather confirm them, and desirable token women all the more so.

Even as a generality about classical Hollywood cinema, which was the subject of Mulvey's essay, her argument was overstated in its apparent universality. Some well-known instances of classical cinema are evidently elegies for the loss or even the hopelessness of manhood that do not need to be (and cannot be) explained by castration anxiety.[17] They do not erase women in the manner I discussed in Chapter 2, but rather present a tragedy of socially constructed male societies. If the viewer of these films is interpellated as a man, it is hardly as the kind of man he desires to be. Overstated as it was, however, Mulvey's thesis certainly captured the core of most dominant cinema: that all textual ambivalences aside, it is inscribed with the ideology not merely of a complacent humanism, but of male domination as well. Can it be possible to pass beyond this limit in a visual culture so totally dominated by men?

8 What the Male Gaze Sees: "Women You Don't Mess With"

Though ambiguity is inescapable, Hollywood strives desperately to escape it; the received wisdom about the mass audience is that for it anything is better than uncertainty. The kind of textual ambivalence, and consequent viewer ambiguity I've described in the previous chapter, is strikingly rare today, as the stakes of production have risen higher and higher. The feminist turn in American history most frequently is recognized or even tentatively endorsed and then, by the methods I've described, finally and clearly disavowed.[1] Sometimes, though, disavowal fails (as in the examples given in Chapter 4); the status quo ante is not, or is only barely, recuperated; and the cultural and institutional changes that have been pressing on American society are momentarily recognized as too strong to be easily repudiated. How this recognition manifests itself varies greatly from television to cinema, and from genre to genre. Looking more carefully even at the examples of tokenism I've given, there is something going on that invocations of "the male gaze" cannot fully account for. Our gaze has become a source of ambiguity: we are seeing what Laura Mulvey said we must see, but two decades after her initial intervention we are also on many occasions, if only subliminally or fleetingly, seeing something else.

One possibility for mainstream cinema is simply to appeal to a new audience; to invert the shot/reverse shot structure of classical cinema so that the active cinematic gaze becomes that of a woman rather than a man.[2] This is to go a step beyond the "women's movies" of classic Hollywood in which women were appealed to by the prospect of watching their own suffering. Despite *Desert Hearts*'s voyeuristic appeal to men, for example, we cannot look at it and not see the camera's and the spectator's gaze as the gazes of a woman; and there is no reason to believe that it privileges male over female voyeurism. Nor do I mean to suggest here that women, as argued by some post-Mulvey cultural critics, can take understandable pleasure in their own objectification. That implies objectification by a *man,* which is precisely what is absent in *Desert Hearts;* of the three facets of the male gaze (of the man behind the camera, of the male onscreen protagonist, and of an imagined male audience) at least two have been cut off.

Alternatively, it can be claimed that even when films seem to change the frame of men gazing at women, they still preserve the basic social order of dominance-submission, with the gender positions now reversed but nothing socially significant really happening. E. Ann Kaplan gives the example of films such as *Saturday Night Fever, Urban Cowboy,* and *The Electric Horseman,* in which John Travolta and Robert Redford are made into objects of a female gaze, as examples of this tendency. More recently, the tight-bunned fetishized male has become a regular part of the visual landscape, as in *Top Gun, Young Guns, Young Guns II,* and *Interview with a Vampire;* and male heartthrobs such as Tom Cruise, Christian Slater, Brad Pitt, Keanu Reeves, and Ethan Hawke can build a career on being marketed as an object to be looked at by females.[3] Even this amendment, though, does not account for films such as *Mortal Thoughts, Extremities, The Burning Bed, The Accused,* and *Thelma and Louise,* in which the shot/reverse shot methodology interpellates us into the persona not of a female gazing at a desirable male, but of a woman enraged by unforgivable male abusiveness.

In their tentative way, these movies attempt to appeal not to a new audience of women, but rather to an audience of "new women," alerted by feminism to new possibilities of spectatorship. The influence of this new genre has been so profound that by now members of an audience are likely to get impatient when they encounter a traditional female protagonist who is passive or hysterical in the face of attack, or who embraces her victimization rather than striking back against it. In a minor contemporary horror movie (the title of which I have unfortunately forgotten), the male lead and his female partner/sidekick drive up to an old house within which the usual unnameable horrors may be occurring. As in all such movies of the 1940s and 1950s he says to her nobly, "You wait here, while I check out the house." But this is 1993. "You've *got* to be kidding," she replies: explicitly rejecting the dominance-submission paradigm.

Television, of course, is full of such new women, in the home, the precinct house, the hospital, and outer space; Christine Lahti as the chief of surgery in *Chicago Hope* and Kate Mulgrew as the commander of Voyager in *Deep Space Nine* are emblematic. However, although television lives by making shows that appeal to a woman's standpoint, it cannot offer any *series* that would permanently place her in the role of angry social reformer, dissident, or revolutionary; that is not a state of mind in which to find the kind of distraction that advertisers want us to find. Movies, with their deeper claim on our attention, can go further; and have been doing so. As it turns out, though, the place to look for the winds of change is not, on the whole, in the fragments of visual culture that deliberately address women (e.g., *Boys on the Side, How To Make an American Quilt, Steel Magnolias*). In addition to once again providing suffering women for female audiences to gaze at, these appeal to a consciously "liberal" male gaze willing to swap some of its voyeuristic enjoyment for a brief rush of feel-good egalitarianism. This is an *ideological* pleasure not contemplated by the psychoanalytic perspective of most cultural criticism; and it recuperates the social order by relieving the male viewer of the obligation to do anything other than watch and enjoy.

For my purposes here, it is more important to address what is happening *ideologically,* at the cultural core that has always been addressed primarily to men. Earlier I've remarked that the majority of movies are daydreams of accomplishment and heroism; they belong to the various "masculine" genres of action, adventure, and violence. The dominant Hollywood assumption has always been that violent action is the most genuinely cinematic of all visual phenomena. Moreover, it does not really matter if Hollywood is wrong, for its position in the production and distribution of visual commodities has ensured that, the world over, audiences from many diverse national cultures have come to expect and anticipate violent action when they go to see a movie.

We should therefore look to changes in this arena to discover what visual culture in its present state can make of women who, whatever else they are, are not what they used to be. What is most important about the various action/adventure genres is that they privilege physical strength, combativeness, and skill—and therefore maleness. Women exist to be threatened or victimized and then rescued, or to be the hero's reward for his accomplishments. Even legitimate authority in the action genres is not only male but masculine; to be less than resolutely male in any way signifies a failure to deserve authority. What Griselda Pollock says of the female nude in painting is true also of the female protagonist in action cinema (as in most of the traditional cinematic genres, including even or especially "women's films"): "to look at and enjoy the sites of patriarchal culture we women must become nominal transvestites. We must assume a masculine position or masochistically enjoy the sight of woman's humiliation."[4] Looked at from the "masculine position" the action/adventure genres correspond to what George Mosse denotes as the "ideals of manliness" that are central to the reification we call the modern nation-state; and that sharply discriminate between "insiders who have accepted the norms" and "outsiders, those considered abnormal or diseased."[5] In the action/adventure genre, encompassing the two major subgenres of authorized male violence, the war movie and the police story, intrusive women have typically been treated as either one or the other.

Historically these genres thus constitute not merely an aesthetic category but also an ideology. They represent visual culture's most decisive erasure of women from public space. So powerful is their position in the metatext that even television's lugubriously liberal movies-of-the-week about women being mistreated by men or male-dominated institutions, do not basically challenge the moral hierarchy established by them. The demand that women be treated fairly, or equally, by calling on men to change *their own* behavior, reiterates the linkage of men to doing and women to being done.

One of the most interesting phenomena of contemporary visual culture, therefore, is the development within this most masculine of all preserves of a new genre (or subgenre) of films that, although in most cases clearly maintaining the fetishistic priorities of visual pleasure, seem to challenge or at any rate ignore the traditional allocation of privilege that accompanies it. Unlike *Dead Poets Society* or *Gilda* these movies are not diegetically at war with themselves; unlike *The River Wild* they do not inscribe a feminist statement only to erase it. As for the women in these films, unlike the tough-minded, independent women of the past (Crawford, Stanwyck, Hepburn), or the lawyers and businesswomen of today, they are not emblems of liberal tokenism (today, "power feminism"), and they are not put on the screen to appeal primarily to women. These films, rather, organize traditionally masculine narratives in a new way, without anyone noticing out loud that this is what they are doing. What happens, then, when *women* are put at the thematic *and visual* center of narratives of heroic action? When their erasure from public space is itself (momentarily) erased?[6]

At the least, some previous assumptions become suspect. Even the mythic quest, quintessentially male in the analysis of Teresa de Lauretis, can be narrated as though it is female.[7] Despite the efforts to recuperate their heroines for womanhood, this is obviously so for the *Alien* trilogy and for television's *Xena: Warrior Princess* (an exception to my previous generalization about television, in that the mythic cast of its narratives puts it firmly in the cinematic mold of storytelling). When in one episode of *Xena* a seer intones, "You must be the one: a woman with a dark past, strong and brave," we are without any doubt in the familiar (if unintentionally hilarious) realm of the epic quest. And after all, whatever the dubious appeal of *Huckleberry Finn* to modern young people, the most enduring epic quest in American popular culture is the heroic odyssey of a twelve-year-old *girl*, leading the men she has rescued in an attempt to return from Oz to her home in Kansas. More recently, in the persons of Jane Fonda *(The China Syndrome, Rollover)*, Meryl Streep *(Silkwood)*, Sigourney Weaver *(Gorillas in the Mist)*, Sally Field *(Not without My Daughter)*, Jessica Lange *(The Music Box)*, Carol Burnett *(Friendly Fire)*, Laura Dern *(Afterburn)*, Alfre Woodward *(The Agent Orange Story)*, Daphne Zuniga *(Pandora's Clock)*, or even "Wonder Woman" Lynda Carter *(The Last Song)*, what is otherwise recognizable as the heroic search is carried out by a woman; just as Rosanna Arquette's search for authenticity in Susan Seidelman's *Desperately Seeking Susan* is finally validated by another woman, the unmistakably countercultural Madonna.[8]

Of course MGMs decision to flatten Judy Garland's buxom teenage figure in a body corset symbolized the limit to Dorothy's, or any woman's, representation of the quest: just as the presentation of the woman as voice of reason—*Alien*, television's *X-Files*—serves to desexualize the female, and thus in a sense make it possible for her to be a hero despite (not because of) her gender. In the mainstream, the female hero must be sexless, or else she might express a predatory sexuality that is allowed only to the male; that much castration anxiety is too much.[9] In an image from *Aliens* that sums up this limit, a blush suffuses Ripley's face as her one male comrade, trying on his protective mode, affectionately shows her . . . his rifle, and lays it tenderly in her arms. It remains hers for the rest of the movie, while he becomes hopelessly crippled *and* disarmed (except for a comparatively tiny sidearm), quite as though the phallus itself has been overtly passed on by a director who's plagiarized from a previously undiscovered manuscript of Freud's.

This is not the kind of dominance-submission reversal Ann Kaplan has in mind when writing about *Urban Cowboy!*[10] Even the dominating Xena (played by Lucy Lawless, an actress six feet tall and heroically built, and wearing the standard revealing garb of women in ancient epics) usually manages to avoid any hint of assertive sexuality. In one episode she meets an old flame, who still has not entirely repudiated their once mutually wicked ways, and we know instantly that his death warrant has been signed (when Xena does briefly propose an alliance of equals it is with—who else?—Hercules). If the heroine did have a male sexual partner, what could be his role? Sidekick?

So the mythic heroine is usually a lone wolf (though Xena has a female sidekick). But then so has been the mythic hero; sex gets in his way too. Given that limitation, there has been tremendous change in popular culture. The perceived conflict between individual and society now extends to women; now a woman can be portrayed, even if only until her eventual recuperation (e.g., *The River Wild*), as the unreconcilable self that the dominant ideology never manages finally to disavow. The culture is not what it has been. Marx's image of revolution and disarray becomes yet more prescient, as we approach the moment when "*man* is at last compelled to face with sober senses, his real conditions of life, and his relations with his kind."[11] Voyeurism or fetishism still may undergird the framework of visual pleasure in these movies, though much less overtly so in some *(Rollover, The Music Box)* than in others *(Aliens, The River Wild, Xena)*. But the saliency of the fetishistic appeal has become indeterminate.

For example, Gina Rourke has remarked to me that what she liked most about "Xena" was that Lucy Lawless played her without overt appeals to fetishism. This was news to me, but as it turned out she was comparing Lawless to Sharon Stone and Linda Fiorentino, who shriek "dominatrix" to anyone in their range. Lawless is more like Deborah-Lee Furness in *Shame:* the most attention-getting aspect of her is her heroic character. If a man (inevitably) mingles fetishism with his appreciation of her heroics, that is still very different from the intermingling of fetishism and gynephobia (which itself may have an equivocal political resonance, as I argue below). In either event, scopophilic fetishism is now in competition with some other demand on male (let alone female) attention.[12]

How extensive is this change? Describing her efforts of three decades ago, the feminist science-fiction writer Joanna Russ says: "I had turned from writing love stories about women in which women were losers, and adventure stories about men in which the men were winners, to writing adventure stories about a woman in which the woman won. It was one of the hardest things I ever did in my life."[13] Now female adventurers are commonplace, not just in her own literary genre but also in cinema, if one knows where to look for them.

In *Airport 1975*, Karen Black steps out of the cockpit of the plane she has kept in the air until a pilot, Charlton Heston, could be lowered into it to land it and save the day; she receives a spontaneous round of applause from the surviving passengers. The applause is for having done a woman's job—stewardess—above and beyond the call of her duty. In the post-apocalyptic *The Blood of Heroes*, fifteen years later, Joan Chen plays the role of the underdog adventurer, up from the dusty roads of nowhere to join a team of losers who make their doomed "living" engaging in bloody gladiatorial combat. With everything at stake for herself and her teammates, she wins the decisive *mano-a-mano* with a male opponent from a far superior team, and is embraced by the cheers of the crowd in the big-city arena, without the slightest suggestion during the course of the narrative that her being a woman has made a difference.[14] In Maggie Greenwald's *The Ballad of Little Jo*, an independently produced Western, the most masculine genre of all has been given a female protagonist who masquerades as a man throughout the movie, without either betraying her femaleness or recuperating maleness in the manner of *Tootsie* and *Mrs. Doubtfire*.[15] The step from the earlier movie to the later ones may seem a logical progression, but it is an immense step nonetheless.

Some of these women, as in all classical quests, are losers; but some are also "winners." Some of them (Lynda Carter as a widow, Sally Field as a vengeful mother, Sigourney Weaver as a nurturer of gorillas) are ultimately motivated by conventional "female" role-playing. But in few of these films is the female body intentionally mystified or objectified; and in none of them (except *The Blood of Heroes*) is the female hero's quest validated or affirmed by a male authority figure.[16] In most of them, moreover, it would be meaningless to say that the camera's gaze or the audience's gaze is "male," unless we write women out of culture altogether. It would be an evasion of the obvious to deny de Lauretis's assertion that Western mythology is fundamentally phallocentric, or Mulvey's that visual culture is fundamentally voyeuristic. But there's no reason to believe that this phallocentrism is a *structural* necessity of the mythology of the hero, or *male* voyeurism a structural necessity of narrative cinema. If dominant narrative cinema is fundamentally phallocentric and voyeuristic, that is not because it is cinema, but because as dominant cinema it is part of the structure of dominance. Within that structure, though, obvious variations are without significance *only* if, again, one assumes that only total revolution is significant.

Another approach well short of revolution, yet still separated from simple immersion in the dominant ideology and its male gaze, is the choice of stylistic abstraction rather than Hollywoodian naturalism as a mode of narrative discourse. This is the approach taken, for instance, by the short-lived but highly original Lifetime Channel series, *Veronica Clare*, a program about a female private detective (though it was never clear if that was actually what she was, since she also seemed unaccountably to be the owner of a nightclub).[17] This television series did not present fractured or multiple viewpoints: "Veronica's" viewpoint was central throughout. However, being without any redeeming social message, and also being totally stylized and hermetic in its decor and mise-en-scène, *Veronica Clare* operated by distancing us from her world instead of drawing us into it. Hollywood social realism brings stereotypes to life even when ostensibly avoiding or overturning them; the Hollywood style insistently reminds us of conventional "reality." The refusal of "realism" is a strength rather than a weakness for those who would challenge convention.

"Veronica" (as everyone calls her) is not the Phallic Woman from Hell, who will blow you away as soon as look at you, or another comic-strip version of Wonder Woman (like Kathleen Turner in the *V. I. Warshawski* travesty of Sara Paretzky's tough-woman detective stories). Again, iconography is crucial. In *Cagney and Lacey*, as I've noted, Sharon Gless's beauty serves the ideological purpose of reconciling opposites, the "feminine" and the "masculine." Here, actress Laura Robinson's beauty, like the Art Deco, non-naturalistic mise-en-scène that surrounds it, is ironic. It does not soften the hard edges of her masculine toughness, since unlike Gless she has none to begin with, but rather shows up the banality of the conventional opposition.[18] And although the scripts are written by a man, Veronica is their narrator and so never the object of the camera's voyeurism. She seems always to be in charge of its gaze; even close-ups of her are used primarily to reflect her implicit commentary on the fears and follies of others (often, men). The male lead in the series is her partner in the puzzling nightclub; he is neither her lover (an absent person of no specific gender to whom she tells the stories in the form of letters), nor a source of wisdom or authorization for her. She never uses a gun except in desperate self-defense, and she's as vulnerable as any other ordinary woman in hand-to-hand combat with a reasonably fit man. Asked what her "weapons" are in one episode, she replies "my skill as a private investigator." In short, her portrayal tells us that there are ways of being attractive not reducible to pure feminized sexuality; and ways of being strong that aren't comprehended by hypermasculine aggression.

In an exemplary scene from the first episode of the series, which is a reworking of *The Merchant of Venice*, Veronica/Portia confronts an Italian gangster version of Shylock who has demanded his pound of flesh from her widowed aunt. The aunt's late husband had stolen (and gambled away) a million dollars from the mob; Shylock is under orders to retrieve it. Beginning as a tough guy speaking condescendingly to the little woman, he soon loses his air of superiority, and her gender quickly becomes irrelevant. So, too, does his: "I *like* confidence in a woman," he says early on in a parody of Sidney Greenstreet. "*I* like candor in a man" is her riposte, as though to say what will become evident, that his muscles and his weapons and his money are of no moment. Before long he has forgotten that she is a she. Gradually, even as he falls half in love with her, he becomes more afraid of an unarmed woman than he is of his employers: not because she is terrifying, but because what he wants above all is a soft life, and she will not let him have it.

Told by a policeman friend that she can't protect her aunt within the rules of the game, she replies that she'll "ignore the rules of the game and just cheat." She then proceeds to pay "Shylock" a derisory sum, steals it back from him with the connivance of friends, and blackmails him with the threat to tell "the Syndicate" what has happened. Making it clear to him that to recover his money he will have to kill her, and that this will not be easy, she forces him to look at himself. *He* has to decide whether the money is worth a duel to the death, for he can see that *she* has already decided her aunt's honor is. He gives in because her will is stronger. You can always get money somehow, but implacability is a lot harder to come by. He lacks it; she has it. Like "character" generally, that is not either a "masculine" or "feminine" trait (or white or black or middle-class or working-class); anyone with the requisite will can possess it, and anyone can exhibit it. Illustrating this simple truth, *Veronica Clare* dissolves conventional notions of sexual hierarchy, even while having nothing specific to say about them.

Sondra Locke's movie *Impulse* achieves a somewhat similar effect in a different genre. Like *Shame*, it was treated by (male) reviewers as just another police/action film, and crocodile tears were shed over the inability of a woman director (especially one known as Clint Eastwood's former companion) to make a "different" film.[19] But like *Shame*, *Impulse* is profoundly different from other films of its genre, in that its hero and the active agent of all its events is a woman. This is not a distinction without a difference. As the female protagonists of *A Question of Silence* know, this difference makes all the difference.

Played by Theresa Russell, she is a cop who first kills a holdup man, then allows a criminal to befriend her, steals a million dollars as an illicit witness to his murder, and becomes both hunter and hunted. This is a standard genre plot (cf. *The Big Clock* and its remake, *No Way Out*), but now turned on its head. Once again, moreover, the film's basic choice—how shall the female be presented?—is decisive. Russell has an unconventional body shape and inexpungable air of go-to-hell toughness that have always prevented her from ever playing a typical romantic lead in Hollywood.[20] Even the attempt to give her a romantic co-star, presumably in order to soften the movie's femaleness, falls flat on its face. The very secondary male lead (like the female lead of *My Darling Clementine*, instantly forgettable) seems woefully inappropriate to his assigned task. Partly this is because he is inadequate compared to Russell; but partly also, we come to realize (and is this not perhaps the same point?) because he is actually playing the standard *female* role of restraining the recklessness and immorality of an adventurous (male) lead.

The movie, however, is not about dominance-submission in another guise, but is about the woman as outlaw hero. Unlike Ripley in *Aliens* or Linda Hamilton in *Terminator 2*, this woman is never recuperated for the family or the community (or even the Law, which she has consistently broken). This inversion of previous genre codes highlights and, in a small way, subverts the fundamentally male construal of American individualism. When Shane rides off into the mountains, he takes with him the lost masculine utopia in which individual heroism and social stability are reconciled, and leaves behind him a reintegrated community that will become the United States. Because culture has never been able for long to conceal from view the masculine paradox, the dominant ideology rests unequivocally on a foundation of unambiguous womanhood. If Theresa Russell's departure from the community carried with it the same mythical resonance—as of course it cannot—the resulting cultural shock would be off the Richter Scale.

Typically, at the time of its release *Impulse* was inextricably linked by reviewers with another female cop film directed by a woman, Kathy Bigelow's *Blue Steel*. Less thematically coherent, the latter movie ultimately reveals itself as an updated slasher movie, starring the all-time "final girl," Jamie Lee Curtis, confronting once again the monster who has returned from *Halloween* and *Halloween II*. The final girl, as Carol Clover argues, is a hero for men and women both, and throughout *Blue Steel* Curtis takes evident pleasure in behavior coded as "male," and finally in blowing away the monster.[21] Her character certainly disavows the initial presentation of woman as perpetual victim, but (this being a horror movie) also recuperates it, and thus challenges

Hollywood's sexual stereotypes much less than *Impulse* does. Her role is less that of the woman as active agent in an activity typically reserved for men: he who makes things happen.

Here, *Impulse*'s truest counterpart is the excellent police thriller *Arizona Heat*, which, not surprisingly, was not even reviewed at all. This movie stars Denise Crosby as a lesbian policewoman who, without ever compromising her own stiff-necked counterideology or her own sense of herself (without, that is, becoming a humanized do-gooder), teaches her bitterly misogynistic and homophobic partner what good police work is really about; and finally saves his life. Like its heroine, the film goes so far off the ideological rails that it sank without a trace. The 1996 edition of *Video Movie Guide* describes *Arizona Heat* as a "run of the mill cop story about a tough but good policeman ... inheriting a female partner ... and tracking down a crazed cop killer."[22] What's fascinating is not that virtually every word in this capsule description is wrong, or that a minor parlor game is suggested by it (*"Philadelphia:* courtroom drama in which a lawyer sues his firm for firing him"), but that the reviewer of this movie has been unwilling to identify its protagonist.

With regard to all such cinematic examples one might ask, "So what?" Filling an out-of-the-way niche in the Hollywood metatext labelled "difference," they probably make no significant impact at all. Why should they? We should not expect culture to overturn itself: for that, "the arm of criticism must be replaced by the criticism of arms."[23] However, such cultural events do reveal something going on at the core of the dominant ideology; something dramatized by the bizarre treatment of *Arizona Heat.* Suppose we try to imagine a Hollywood in which these women were the rule and Clint Eastwood the exception. We cannot; these deviations are possible only because they're deviations, and are understood as such. (The same is true of Denzel Washington). Even in an age when women move into the professions in unprecedented numbers, take them too seriously and they will be called "unrealistic" portraryals, as they are. Ideology tells half-truths, but it rarely lies. For them to become the standard, as opposed to being at the margins, there would have to be a completed revolution, a world turned upside down. Who will play the role of victim, let alone helpmeet to a male hero, if women (or black persons) won't? However, that such movies are being made at all tells us that a major cultural struggle is taking place.

To be sure, the women in these films, and in the "quest" films mentioned above, have little in common with what is in fact the most common male portraiture of "strong women" in visual culture: the fetishized, phallic woman, who fights and kills just like a man; and the Medusa, *la femme castatrice,* who kills men just because she is a woman.[24] The phallic woman, who appears mainly in so-called exploitation films, made on the margins of Hollywood (and often far from it geographically), seems at first glance to be more directly apposite to Mulvey's thesis about voyeurism.[25] Yet there is much more to be said about even her onscreen apotheosis. One has to pay close attention to the subterranean spaces of visual culture to discover just how riotously these films have proliferated. The female heroes from the mainstream I have already referred to—Linda Fiorentino in *The Desperate Trail,* Sigourney Weaver and Jenette Goldstein (Vasquez) in *Aliens,* the bulked-up Meryl Streep in *The River Wild,* not to mention the even more formidable Linda Hamilton in *Terminator II,* and Angela Bassett in Kathy Bigelow's *Strange Days*—are merely the outriders of a "monstrous regiment": not of Knox's female monarchs or Hawthorne's "damned scribblers," but of female adventurers in roles (both heroic and villainous) previously reserved exclusively for males.[26]

The efflorescence of movies based on the exploits of women of violence is extraordinary.[27] Although I have said earlier that women can never pass the implicit test of physical equality, these are movies in which women do exactly that. How are we to understand them? We should begin by observing that there is one similar phenomenon in American cultural history: the body of serial films, made mostly in the period between 1910 and 1920, that Ben Singer calls "the serial-queen melodrama."[28] These serials also featured women of action and derring-do, but there were significant differences between them and the contemporary version; differences that highlight the originality of the latter. Most important, as we discover from Singer, these movies were not only almost explicitly about the "New Woman" of the period, but they were deliberately (if not exclusively) addressed to a female audience; both by what they contained (e.g., careful attention to "fashion") and what they omitted (the kind of fetishistic appeal designed for men's eyes and psyches).[29] The contemporary genre, in contrast, is clearly addressed to men (though as I note below its potential appeal might be more widespread than that). These are therefore not fantasies of representation for women, but fantasies of recognition, or misrecognition, for men. What is it about "new women" in the postliberation era that men (the creators of most of these films) imagine themselves (their audiences) to be imagining?

As a genre, new women's proximate source in visual culture (the serial-queen melodrama having long since disappeared from view) is probably the British TV series, *The Avengers,* which first reached the United States in the mid-1960s.[30] Even though its earliest episodes were not seen in the United

States until years later, it was especially Honor Blackman's role as "Cathy Gale" that came to define an entire movement in visual culture (though she and all her successors—Diana Rigg, Linda Thorson, and Joanna Lumley— were never quite equal in billing with Patrick McNee as "Steed"). Blackman's contract, somewhat similar to that of Gary Cooper's in the 1950s, called for her to put on her black leather outfit and beat up a man at least once in each episode. It led to her role as "Pussy Galore" in *Goldfinger* (and, this being mainstream cinema, to her losing a pitched battle with Sean Connery's James Bond); brought her endless fan mail and proposals of marriage from all over the United Kingdom; and together with Joseph Losey's film *Modesty Blaise,* prompted a young Anthony Lewis, then the *New York Times* correspondent in London, to deliver himself of one of the earliest recorded laments about the decline of Western (or at least British) civilization. Middlebrow opinion is almost never wrong about perceived threats to its hegemony; so we ought to take seriously the path that this cultural innovation was to follow.[31]

However, it is 1971, the year of release of *Ginger* with Cherie Caffaro, and *The Big Doll House* with Pam Grier, that probably deserves a special niche in cultural history. Indeed, the movies of Caffaro *(The Abductors, Girls Are for Loving, Too Hot to Handle)* and Grier *(The Big Bird Cage, Coffy, Foxy Brown, Friday Foster, Naked Warriors)* became so popular with the onset of the VCR explosion, that video mail-order outlets now sell them in boxed sets. They were shortly joined by the equally popular films of Tamara Dobson, *Cleopatra Jones* and *Cleopatra Jones and the Casino of Gold.*[32] Very few male actors, and hardly any other females, can make that claim.

At the time most observers would have attributed the popularity of Grier and Dobson to the contemporaneous surge of "blaxploitation" films, most of them starring male ex-athletes such as Fred "The Hammer" Williamson or Billy Dee Williams. Just as movies such as *In the Heat of the Night* and *Guess Who's Coming to Dinner?* were a direct liberal white response to a civil rights movement that constituted the "acceptable" face of racial protest, so "blax-ploitation" films were an evasive response by black filmmakers, to an "unac-ceptable" black power movement that could not be confronted openly (except to be denounced), by anyone who wanted to procure serious financing.[33] In this light, all those films represented a typical deployment of images of black "primitivism," at a critical cultural moment where the conjunction of race and sexuality, so frightening to whites, could once again be used to deflect substantive social criticism. However, that explanation does not satisfactorily account for Caffaro's equal success, nor for the fact that Grier's movies (and perhaps Dobson's) have outlasted those of their male counterparts, nor for the fact that in any event something else of profound significance was going on in the world of visual culture at the same time.

As to the last point, the white-oriented films that followed hard on their heels are by now numbered in the hundreds. Overall, they can be divided into two categories: conventional films of violence in which the male leads are displaced; or pure martial arts films in the style of Bruce Lee (Li) and later Chuck Norris et al.[34] The female martial arts field, especially, seems inexhaustible. The movies of Cynthia Rothrock—"Chuck Norris's pupil" and the genre's leading exponent—can hardly even be counted, in that by the time one has finished listing them another is on the video store shelves or the pay cable channels (*China O'Brien* and *China O'Brien II* are probably the most well known). But there are other karate-chopping, high-kicking stars such as body-builder and stuntwoman Kathy Long *(The Stranger, Knights);* plus, in addition to Dobson and Bell, a number of martial artists, stuntwomen, gymnasts, wrestlers, or body-builders, who've achieved minor stardom in this genre (among others Rachel McLish, Karen Shepard, Graciela Cassillas, Karen Chase, Kristie Phillips, Melissa Moore, Cat Sassoon, Sue Price, and Mimi Lesseos).[35]

The less purist but clearly related cinema of female violence (still often martial arts-saturated) has also made video and cable (if not box-office) successes out of Kathleen Kinmont *(Phoenix the Warrior, Roller Blade Warriors, C.I.A. Code Name: Alexa, C.I.A. Target: Alexa, Sweet Justice);* Shannon Tweed *(No Contest, Lethal Woman, Last Call, The Firing Line, Hard Vice);* Laurene Landon (first coming to attention in *All the Marbles,* a mainstream film about female wrestlers, but a cult star because of films such as *Hundra* and *Yellowhair and the City of Gold);* Joan Severance, a comic-strip heroine in *Black Scorpion* and *Black Scorpion II;* ex-hard-core star Traci Lords *(Not of This Earth, A Time to Die, Ice);* and cult figure Sybil Danning *(Malibu Express, Battle Beyond the Stars, Seven Magnificent Gladiators, L.A. Bounty, Panther Squad).*[36]

Brief reference to two of these movies may be useful in showing ways in which this genre overturns traditional expectations. *C.I.A. Target: Alexa* is hardly at the level of *Gilda,* but it is a minor masterpiece of the unreliable narrator fiction in its own right. We see the first part of the movie from the perspective of Lorenzo Lamas, Kathleen Kinmont's diegetic lover (and real-life husband), who suspects her throughout of being, as she has been in the past, a double agent—which means that so do we. The revelation that all along she has been playing a lone hand to save her daughter, but has been playing it faithfully, leaves both him and us out on a limb of male sexual mistrust, and firmly positions her as the misunderstood hero. In a more minor vein, when we learn in *Last Call* that Shannon Tweed was once a knife-thrower in a carnival, we know instantly that she will save the life of the hero by throwing a knife into the villain at the appropriate moment: a type of narrative prophecy and thus moral linkage once reserved exclusively for men.

There are also countless such movies adapted from the standard male versions of the action genres: the police story *(Hard Vice, L.A. Crackdown, Policewoman, Backstreet Justice)*; the undercover cop *(Catch the Heat, Angel Fist)*; the bodyguard *(Lady Eliminator, Guardian Angel)*; the reformed hero fleeing from the mob *(Breakaway)*; the teenager who stands up to the town bully *(Fire in the Night)*; the treasure hunt *(Enemy Gold)*; the international spy thriller (all the movies of Andy Sidaris, such as *Fit to Kill, Savage Beach, Guns, Hard Ticket to Hawaii*); vigilante narratives of the ambiguously heroic hitman *(The Silencer, Quick)*, or the rogue avatar of justice *(Lady Avenger, The Eliminator)*; the pseudoclassic swordplay epic set in ancient Rome or in some pre-or postcivilized time and place *(Barbarian Queen, Warrior Queen, Naked Warriors, Seven Magnificent Gladiators, Xena, Hundra)*; biker movies (*Chopper Chicks in Zombie Town*, not to mention *Shame* itself); versions of Richard Connell's story "The Most Dangerous Game" and its many screen incarnations, with the hunted man now recast as a woman and every bit as dangerous *(Warcat, Opposing Force, Nowhere to Hide, Blood Games)*; the "Dirty Dozen" rescue mission mounted against an impregnable fortress *(Commando Squad, Doll Squad, Seven From Heaven, Jungle Warriors, Hired to Kill, Nightforce, Under Lock and Key)*; time travel stories in the mode of the *Terminator* series *(Nemesis 2: Nebula)*; and postnuclear or post-apocalyptic films (such as *The Blood of Heroes* and *Knights*), which like the prehistoric films often foreground not just a female hero but a countercommunity of women (*Phoenix the Warrior* and its sequel, *She* with Sandahl Bergman, *Barbarian Queen, The Sisterhood, Hundra*).[37] Here too deviations from the mainstream are revealing. Consider, for example, the thriller *Blood Games*, a female version of *Deliverance* or *Southern Comfort* in which a traveling women's baseball team is besieged by a cliché of rednecks they've just defeated on the playing field. One of the women, just as in *Survive the Night* (see Chapter 3 above) insists on setting an ambush for their pursuers rather than continuing to run. Having been pushed around by men all her life, she declares, she's had enough; she's going to kill them before they kill her. In any mainstream film she'd be dead, especially after she strangles to death the one pursuer who's relatively innocent of malevolence. But she survives to kill again, and to walk away arm in arm with her sisters. The code is overthrown.[38] In *Blood Games*, as in many of these films, what Kirsten Marthe Lentz calls the thrill of "payback time" is now available to women—both in the narrative and, presumably, in the audience as well.

In many of these movies also, not only *Blood Games,* even if the female lead is not one of a community of women, her sidekick or backup is also a woman (or women). Women who win, and men who lose, as Joanna Russ put it: they are almost a drug on this particular market. It turns out that my count of titles and stars in the public library was misleading: not because it misrepresented the mainstream that libraries perforce replicate, but because it underrepresented the margins. There is a kind of reinhabitation of public space going on, though we must be very careful in characterizing it.

What distinguishes these films is not only that the heroine fights with and defeats men, who are often cast as sexual oppressors as well as criminals (only infrequently are other women the main villains). She is (or they are) usually also without her (or their) own domestic attachments (husbands or fiancés tend to get killed early on and become merely a motive for vengeance). Only rarely are women seen recuperating family structures or ideology, even when coming to the aid of other women or children. The fetishistic visual coding of these movies may ultimately disavow her threat to masculinity, but not her independence. When at the end of *The Stranger* Kathy Long rides out of the lonely town she has just cleaned up (on a motorcycle, not a horse), she leaves behind a reconstituted semifamily (the sheriff and the younger sister of his murdered fiancée) that we know she, like Shane, could never be a part of. As in *Impulse,* the myth of the quintessentially male hero who can't be fully socialized is stood on its head.

The problem with this figure from a feminist perspective is that *of course* she can't be recuperated for the family: female violence as a normalized role, unlike that of male violence, is and remains unacceptable. But the problem with her figure from the standpoint of the dominant ideology is equally as great: if female violence can be imagined as normalized, the essentialist understandings of patriarchalism are seriously undermined.[39] One can compare these movies with, say, a typical Lifetime movie-of-the-week such as *With Hostile Intent,* in which two policewomen battle sexual harassment in a "docudrama." Their accomplishment consists in fighting back against their victimization through the law; but for much of the audience they remain basically victims, symbols of recognition for angry masochists. The women in the female action movies are heroes outside the law, not victims.

Since the audience for these low-budget movies is specialized and apparently faithful, their producers can take risks that dominant cinema, always a hostage to "respectable" opinion, must avoid. All the same, something similar is happening in mainstream cinema itself. Though the dedication of James Cameron and his ex-wife Kathy Bigelow to presenting muscular women is exceptional, so is the extent to which the male character actors who played second banana to the heroes of action movies (Harry Morgan, of *The Ox-Bow Incident*, *My Darling Clementine*, and *Dragnet*, is the most familiar) have been replaced by women (occasionally even black or Latina women) who now fill the dual role of armed and dangerous backup, and partner in the exchange of witticisms.[40] Brigitte Nielsen as Arnold Schwarzenegger's fighting companion in *Red Sonja* was probably the first one of these in an important role, though Rene Russo of *Lethal Weapon 3*, *In the Line of Fire*, and *Outbreak*, is now the prototype; but the role, from Farrah Fawcett-Majors in *Sunburn*, to Kate Vernon in the made-for-cable *Probable Cause*, is becoming commonplace.[41] In *Lethal Weapon 3* Russo is actually backup to two men, Mel Gibson and Danny Glover—who himself, however, as a black man, is really also a sidekick for Gibson. Jennifer Lopez plays the same role in the more recent *The Money Train*, backing up Wesley Snipes and Woody Harrelson—and, as a carefully balanced Latina neither too dark nor too light—winding up in bed with Snipes.[42] It is only a matter of time before we will have white female leads with nonwhite female backups (*Aliens* having almost reached this state already).[43]

In mainstream Hollywood, however, leading women in an action role are still often treated as a joke.[44] This is the fate of, say, Turner in *V.I. Warshawski* and *Undercover Blues* (not to mention *The War of the Roses*); Whoopi Goldberg in *Fatal Beauty*; Geena Davis in *Cutthroat Island*, or Michelle Pfeiffer in the campy *Batman*.[45] Turner's treatment is the best example of the mainstream's unease with unconventional (i.e., not slender) women. To be sure, Kirsten Marthe Lentz sees *V.I. Warshawski* differently, as the first example of "payback time" for women: "The absolute lack of fear in the character, combined with her snide remarks [as she is being beaten up by gangsters], establishes a new subject position for women in film, one which ironically foregrounds her *agency* through the obviousness of her status as a *temporary victim*."[46] All of this is true (though not the claim of originality, unless perhaps if one's canvas is limited to Hollywood), but what it leaves out explains why some women have found *V.I. Warshawski* more unpleasant than charming. Turner/Warshawski is a major victim of the double standard discussed earlier. When we first meet her, she fulfills all the stereotypes of a sex-starved woman. A leading man can want sex, in which case he's an ordinary guy; or not want it, in which case he's too busy or a stoic. A woman who too openly wants sex is a joke; not to want it at all casts her as a dyke. The line, as I've noted, is difficult to draw for a woman and Turner, with her breathy, throaty voice and general ditzy-blonde affect, a wardrobe that emphasizes the fullness of her body, and wearing ludicrously high heels during many of her action sequences, crosses it all the time.

The directors of the "serious" nonmainstream films in this genre (not those that are really erotic comedies) handle this problem by depicting their heterosexual heroines with complete straightforwardness. Setting out to entertain men, they do not exhibit the uneasy consciousness of Hollywood's men, who want to suggest feminism but don't dare embrace it: to have it both ways. Cynthia Rothrock and Kathy Long are shown as obviously heterosexual women, but precisely because of their unalloyed fetishization, the single-minded text of their films, they are never subjected to sexual stereotyping by dialogue or camera.

During the early post-1960s period only Raquel Welch, in *Fathom, Hannie Caulder,* and *Kansas City Bomber,* managed to retain her dignity in mainstream action films starring a woman. Even Doris Day was made a mockery in the 1967 movie, *Caprice,* as have been aging (in the Hollywood sense) actresses such as Julie Newmar, Shelley Winters, and Angie Dickinson (*Big Bad Mama* and its sequel). Even today Hollywood, with its penchant for maintaining the status of women as victims, is more likely to make "tough" women villains or criminals: Lori Singer in *The Last Ride,* or Irene Cara and Tatum O'Neal in *Certain Fury.*

Of course actresses may love playing these roles, as backup or as villain, for the freedom they give from compulsory femininity.[47] They are, however, more imbued with compulsory ideology than those that uninhibitedly present the phallic woman as hero. The "postfeminist" approach of allowing actresses to revel in "tough guy" roles has nothing to do with any genuine physical toughness. James Cameron and Kathy Bigelow aside, mainstream Hollywood still will not allow a real jock or "mannish-looking" (i.e., muscular or just genuinely imposing) woman to get near a starring role, thus straining the bounds of credibility even more than would otherwise be the case.[48] As the noncareer of Patrice Donnelly, the attractive, athletic, and diegetically gay co-star of *Personal Best* testifies, it can be fatal to allow oneself to appear in such a guise.[49]

Still, it is suggestive that someone felt the need to add the character of Nancy Travis, tough waitress *extraordinaire,* to the American version of *The Vanishing;* or to remake *La Femme Nikita* almost frame-for-frame as *Point of No Return;* or to make an unlikely action star out of an aging Debbie Reynolds in the 1982 television movie *Detective Sadie and Son.*[50] Throwing punches at men's jaws has become virtually a contractual requirement for the female lead in any action movie (recall supermodel Cindy Crawford throwing them at the *male* lead in 1995's *Fair Game*, not to mention Elizabeth Berkeley turning into a black belt for the last two minutes of *Showgirls*). The transformation of Geena Davis from the cartoon figure of *Cutthroat Island* to the prototypical action heroine of 1996's *The Long Kiss Goodnight* (the failure and the success both directed by her husband) is emblematic. Screaming "suck my dick" as she drives a gigantic truck toward a rendezvous with enough high explosives to blow up Niagara Falls, Davis gives new content to the fetishistic male gaze and literal meaning to the term "phallic woman." Moreover, this revised gaze and meaning, both appealing now to gay as well as straight men, are emphasized even more by giving her a *black male* backup.

In addition to all this, women are more and more taking the lead in films that basically belong to the action genre even though they require less physicality from the actors. In many of these the female lead ultimately has to be rescued from her own intrepidity (*The Client* and *Coma*), or is demeaned beyond retrieval (Holly Hunter in *Copy Cat*). In some, however, the role reversal, however mechanical, is not disavowed. Recent examples of this tendency include Sandra Bullock (most famously) in *The Net;* Kim Basinger as a safecracker in *The Real McCoy;* Amy Madigan as an Air Force pilot and survival expert, framed along with her murdered husband for espionage, and on the run from an entire Air Command in *Nowhere to Hide;* Goldie Hawn as the coach of a men's football team in *Wildcats;* Pamela Anderson Lee of *Baywatch* fame as *Barb Wire*, reprising Bogart's reluctant hero Rick Blaine in a post-apocalyptic remake of *Casablanca* (and throwing a punch at the male version of Bergman); Joan Severance as a cop in *Criminal Passion;* Shannon Whirry in *Private Obsession;* Darlanne Fluegel as a nurse tracking down a "Freeway Killer" in *Freeway;* Linda Fiorentino and Kim Cattral as spies in (respectively) *Gotcha!* and the comic *Honeymoon Academy;* Kristi Swanson in the wonderful parody of teen films *Buffy the Vampire Slayer,* or Hilary Swank as the eponymous *Next Karate Kid;* and of course Sharon Stone in the Western *The Quick and the Dead*.[51] So too, in a different way, is the resurrection and celebration of female baseball players in *A League of Their Own*. The thoroughly egalitarian partnership between Alexandra Paul (of *Baywatch* fame) and Pierce Brosnan in two "Alistair Maclean" movies shown on the USA channel in 1995 is also indicative of this trend.[52]

Hollywood in the 1990s, in other words, is trying to create "women's movies" that men will also watch. What the public meaning of womanhood is to be in such movies, though, remains the source of deep confusion. As the political fate of Hilary Rodham Clinton testifies, the double standard has been replaced (or deepened) by the double role, which then becomes a source of resentment on the part of more traditional men and women. So the code is stretched but not repudiated and, as we shall shortly see, the phallic woman easily becomes the death-dealing Medusa.

Network television is somewhat different. Because of its crucial female audience it is much more open to "liberal feminist" themes of the movie-of-the-week kind, and during the 1970s even pioneered the presentation of women as authority figures: Suzanne Pleshette as a police inspector in *Alone in the Neon Jungle;* Theresa Graves in a similar role in *Get Christy Love.* At the same time television is usually much more cautious and conventional in its conception of its masculine audience. Thus two very good (by network TV standards) television action series pilots of the 1980s, *Lady Blue* with Jamie Rose as "Dirty Harriet," and *Foxfire* with Joanna Cassidy as a counterspy, never got past the pilot stage, though the first at least piled up huge ratings.[53] On the other hand, just as in the cinema we are beginning to see remakes of male-genre TV movies with female leads.

The misfit team or the apparently hopelessly ambitious athlete may now be women or a woman: *Oklahoma Dolls* or *Annie O.* (whose big game is in this genre always against men). Again, *Molly and Gina* (following the earlier series *Legwork*), is a typical version of the private eye *malgré lui;* except that the accidental detective here is the secretary of her murdered boss, who sets out to track down his killer with the help of another woman who is the only witness. A genial, unexciting movie, what is most extraordinary about it is its central "chase" scene. As long as the similar scene in *Jade,* but taking place entirely on foot at a walking pace ("the slowest chase in history," lead actress Frances Fisher affectionately called it), it makes gentle but unmistakable mockery of the entire smash-'em-up tradition of car chases that has become the staple of male action films with nothing to say.

More directly, *Sex, Love, and Cold Hard Cash* (see Chapter 3) has been remade as *Where's the Money, Noreen?* with Juliane Phillips as a woman who is released from jail after serving time for her part in a multimillion-dollar robbery. The changes to character are even more interesting than the mere fact of the remake. Phillips is not "really" guilty, as she was dragged into crime trying to protect her older brother. On the other hand, she really *does* know where the money is hidden, though we don't realize that until the very end: she walks away from the cop with whom she's made love, in order "to get away from her past," and she *also* walks away with the original swag, after carefully depositing large amounts of it with the church in which it was hidden, and with a homeless family who helped her. All of these changes from the original position her as essentially "innocent" and "good" in a manner that would not be necessary in a story about a man; or in a movie such as *The Desperate Trail,* which is forced into pushing at the boundaries of what is normally coded as "female" by the identity of its star.

However, our expectations of a traditional "damsel in distress" story are also shattered along the way. Although she is not presented as being especially tough, Phillips inter alia traps and faces down one of her trackers with a water pistol; knocks another to his death off a rooftop; and chases the original villain into an empty warehouse in a footrace which she wins, without bothering to call for any help. The few times she seemed frightened about being tracked, it turns out, she was playacting; most of the time she is just angrily determined —while deceiving everyone in sight, including the audience. What movies such as these demonstrate above all is that, as I've remarked earlier, most plots would indeed make as much sense (or nonsense) if the gender of the protagonists were reversed. We have only to break loose from the pseudorealism of male-dominated public space, in which fairy tales are set down in the midst of what looks like "the real world," to see other possibilities for storytelling.

Gender reversal thus teaches an important lesson. Still, like affirmative action generally, it is so far a means of recuperating hierarchy in the large, while making inroads in the small. The films in which women stand on the moral high ground, or uncover social corruption (e.g., *Country, Silkwood, Rollover, Stop at Nothing, Gorillas in the Mist*) are not incompatible with the Victorian (or Rousseauian) patriarchal code of the pedestal; their indictments of public power suggest that women can only be useful if they remain outsiders. As for the action films, the explicit apotheosis of female hero as imitation of her male counterpart, especially for those male viewers who watch both versions, is automatically a form of marginalization (another word for "tokenism"). It is also a means of repeating yet again, that the only legitimate source of moral authority is a willingness and capability to resort to physical violence.[54]

There is one problematic aspect, moreover, to all the films and television programs that invert genre stereotypes to give us tough or destructive female heroes, even those that are not especially voyeuristic. Their initial gender inversion aside, hardly any of these films deviate from the conventional visual, moral, and sexual (including racial) codes of dominant culture; the hulking, mannish, Latina, lesbian biker remains in someone else's dream.[55] Above all, Mulvey is certainly correct that, given the extent to which a particular relationship among gender, power, and the male gaze is inscribed in contemporary culture, any visual presentation of women (or girls) as spectacle, especially in the context of violent action and its directly visceral appeal, is almost certain to emphasize the fetishistic structure of our (male) viewing. In Russ's "Picnic on Paradise," one of the great adventure stories in the English language, the reader neither knows nor cares exactly what Alyx, its hero(ine), looks like; any more than we can visualize the hero's looks in, say, Geoffrey Household's classic *Rogue Male*.[56] She is tough, skilled, courageous, determined, and seems to have the whole galaxy after her as she shepherds a band of misfit tourists across the impossible landscape of "Paradise"; and that is all that we, female or male readers, need to know to feel the familiar thrill of underdog heroism. Put her on screen, though, and she must be played by someone, and as soon as she becomes not Alyx of the printed page but the very visible and overwhelmingly "there" Sigourney Weaver or Linda Hamilton or Kathy Long, her fetishistic appeal (to men at least) becomes inescapable.

Thus for most of the movies in the female action/adventure genre, the camera's gaze remains male. Glamour still rules; mise-en-scène invariably highlights the same striptease clubs and other excuses for showing scantily clad women that we encounter in traditional R-rated movies. Action remains the prerogative of men *or* of women who are "like men": fetishized women who carry weapons and throw punches with equal ease, and who at first glance do not redraw any lines between the sexes that are not centered on violence.[57] All of these movies privilege force (though this privilege is continually questioned in television's more politically self-conscious *Xena*).[58] Furthermore, even if they are not conventionally good-looking most of these new, if ghettoized, movie stars (e.g., Cynthia Rothrock, Kathy Long, Kathleen Kinmont) seem to have been chosen not just because they can imitate masculine heroics so well, but because they are also more than ordinarily attractive; thus confirming their essentially sexual appeal. In an odd twist, this is even more true of the movies that make the most of their ostensible "feminism": the post-apocalyptic or prehistoric films about Amazon women who inhabit a world in which all the men are predatory animals (except, usually, for one man who seems to be an anachronistic holdover from late twentieth-century sensitivity-training sessions). After all, what better way to show large expanses of female flesh than to make a movie about an entire *tribe* of good-looking women, especially when the sloppily bearded louts or mutants they encounter offer no competition to the fantasies of the male viewer? To be fair, the spy spoofs of Andy Sidaris aside, in most of these movies there is little or none of the T and A jiggling that made *Charlie's Angels* a bad joke; but the sexual text is eminently readable.

Such movies, then, even those from the cinematic mainstream, tend to turn the historical recognition of feminism into entertainment for men. The male viewer (such as myself) can enjoy their voyeuristic fetishism while disavowing, at the level of consciousness, the implicit hierarchalization of gender that usually accompanies male voyeurism. Moreover, since these films usually do not foreground a male character whose suffering might directly implicate the male viewer in his own masochistic tendencies, his enjoyment can go forward unaccompanied by the vertiginous gynephobia that is the implicit or explicit text of other film genres featuring violent women.[59] Any possible suggestions of thinking about role reversal in less fetishistic forms, or extending it into more socially meaningful arenas, are carefully contained. In the seriously macho version the women are mostly heroes from a male fantasy: "women you don't mess with," in the words of a Turner Network Television come-on for a nightlong festival of B-movie female action.[60] These films, that is, offer the pleasures of violence without guilt: a sort of passive version of carnival, a momentary *frisson* followed by relaxation into scopophilia. And as many of the martial arts films in particular are narratives of female revenge against men, these additionally (like the rape-revenge movies discussed in Chapter 9) enable the male viewer to have it both ways, by disavowing male violence against women while being relieved of the necessity to do anything about it.[61]

Still, disavowal and recuperation in these films is not nearly so diegetically straightforward as in more mainstream cinema and television, or as in those science-fiction television episodes about Amazon planets, or those panic-stricken episodes described earlier, in which the male leads are physically outclassed by their female partners. Moreover, what I have said here is not equally true of all entries in this ambiguous new metatext. For example, in the comic thriller *Sawbones* an unprepossessing young woman determinedly tracks down a serial killer while a male cop, the authorized investigator, in fact functions as her reluctant, disbelieving, and slightly buffoonish sidekick, always a beat behind the action. However, the expected rescue scene is followed by a totally unexpected dénouement in which she resists his attempts to make amends and have them become lovers. Ideologically, this moment is more shocking than any number of castratory climaxes: this is a Hollywood movie, starring a Baldwin brother, and yet she's actually just saying no![62]

More seriously, in *The Stranger* Kathy Long quite persuasively reprises Clint Eastwood's role in *High Plains Drifter*, in a pastiche that even features a Morricone-like score. One scene from the original, though, is signally absent:

the scene in which Eastwood makes Verna Bloom's day by raping her. Seeing the two films together is a revelation. Eastwood's film is not "better" (though it obviously deserves credit for originality), and for reasons to be discussed shortly I enjoyed *The Stranger* considerably more; except in the single sense that his depiction of the Western town as a fiery Hell, all in blazing red out of Antonioni's *Red Desert,* creates a kind of visual beauty that the inexpensive remake cannot equal. But the omission of the complacent rape scene, which originally told us that all this chronically fatigued woman needed was a good lay, makes us realize how inappropriate and finally ugly that "beauty" really was when torn from its original, critical, context.[63]

On second glance, therefore, these movies, if for the most part hardly oppositional, and despite their general conformity to the stereotypical racism with which all American movie and television production searches out its villains, are often different from Hollywood's run of the mill. In the action/adventure genre (as opposed to the rape-revenge or horror genres), visual pleasure is less frequently taken in the suffering of women, even when that is necessary to advance the narrative. Of course, the extent and significance of this difference have limits given less by the filmic texts than by the patriarchalist social setting within which they are received. There is no escaping the fact that some, and perhaps very many, men will take pleasure in *any* visual presentation of male dominance or sadism, no matter how overtly the text works to position it as a moral negation. So those among these movies which are built around an assault or assaults on a woman (or women) by men, have at best an ambiguous visual text—unlike, say, *A Question of Silence,* in which the only physical violence visualized is the killing of the store clerk by the women. Still, in many of the movies in this genre (e.g., *China O'Brien, Guardian Angel, The Stranger, Quick, Code Name: Alexa*), the issue hardly arises, or does not arise at all.

More significant, attractive or not, most of the actresses mentioned here (that is, those who unlike Weaver and Hamilton are restricted to the action genre) are also far from the usual mold of femaleness that dominant cinema has made familiar. They certainly couldn't be strippers in R-rated movies, but they couldn't play Cagney or Lacey either. Few of these women would have such success as most of them have had, were it not for the creation of this new genre and the discovery of this different way of being "female." They are not mainstream stars enjoying a one-time flirtation with toughness, à la Weaver or Streep or Hamilton or Michelle Pfeiffer in *Batman*. Rather like John Wayne or Clint Eastwood, they are icons of physical strength; they incur no death warrants by being physically aggressive or resistant to male domination.[64]

There is therefore an uncertainty, an *ambivalence,* in the appeal that they make to the audience. The lead actress—and she is absolutely the lead—though determinedly heterosexual is very definitely not there to be the beautiful but passive woman who'd "be so nice to come home to."

Iconography remains decisive; no man can look at Lucy Lawless or Sigourney Weaver or Cynthia Rothrock and think that she is there merely to confirm his own fantasized heroism by becoming his property. There are no helpmeets here, and no exchange of women (except, as noted above, in those few films from the mainstream that make the heroine the token of racial relationships). Without providing us with anything genuinely new to put in its place, these women represent the passing of that icon. This phallic woman, this fetish, is ambiguously both a re-presentation (in her fetishization) *and* a disavowal (in her non-normative iconography and behavior) of her forebears.

Moreover, the outright fetishism of the genre is itself ideologically ambiguous: however the texts may be read by male viewers whose relationship to women in any representation is always sadomasochistic. As we've seen, for example, the films of director James Cameron revel in appeals to fetishism. By way of contrast, in the original *Alien,* directed by Ridley Scott (also the director of *Thelma and Louise*), Sigourney Weaver seems to represent nothing so much as the embodiment of pure reason until the voyeuristic final scene.[65] Even in dominant cinema, apparently, it makes a difference who makes a film. But on the other hand, if Cameron were to call himself a sexual egalitarian (as he almost certainly would), it would be hard to deny him without a lot of complicated (and perhaps counterproductive) explanation.

How are we being interpellated, after all? As I've noted earlier, we have the same response to Ripley's transformation as we have felt at the birth of the male hero from cinema's inception—and perhaps more than that, insofar as the original viewers of *Aliens,* at least, were conscious of witnessing the birth of a new kind of hero.[66] Even the evident familialism of *Terminator II* and *Aliens* is equivocal, for the families they invoke are hardly sites of male domination, the man being absent from one and clearly subordinate in the other. In these and many similar contemporary films female morality, of the kind that the enthusiasts of separate spheres put on a pedestal, has been separated from gender hierarchy even when it is recuperated and preserved. What remains from the traditional ideological code is fetishistic voyeurism (which in Cameron's movies now seems to be directed at women as much as at men), and the distinction between doomed sexual women (Goldstein) and surviving chaste women (Hamilton, Weaver). Even this coding disappears in his *The Abyss* (supposedly made as a sort of apology for *Aliens*), in which bickering equality characterizes an equivocal heterosexual dyad, and the woman (Mary Elizabeth Mastrantonio) is the one chosen to engage in the final quest.

No other film in the female action/adventure genre is so large in its visual impact, or as fortunate in its casting, as *Aliens*. Still, it is evident that a great many women (even those who detest watching horror films) enjoy or even love watching not only Sigourney Weaver and Jenette Goldstein, but also Deborra-Lee Furness and Linda Hamilton and Lucy Lawless (the latter two both treated virtually as poster queens by, for example, *Ms.*).[67]

Why might this be so? A comparison may help to clarify the issue. At first glance it could be thought that *Wonder Woman* was television's predecessor to these stories, especially to *Xena*. However, seeing that good-humored comic-strip side by side with *Xena*, any viewer must be struck by the fact that both diegetically and iconographically Lynda Carter lacked (or was not encouraged to exhibit) the physically intimidating presence of Lucy Lawless as Xena. When Lawless/Xena (on more than one occasion) says warningly to a man who is about to attack her, "You don't want to do this!" there is a suggestion of fundamental role reversal (not to mention an unmitigated appeal to male masochism) that was never developed in *Wonder Woman*. That is, women watching these movies are most certainly not, as Pollock puts it (see above), required to either "assume a masculine position" or "masochistically enjoy the sight of woman's humiliation." The gaze of the camera and the gaze of the intended audience may remain male, but the diegetic gaze that confirms the meaning of the visual text is a *female* gaze. It goes without saying, furthermore, that *men* who look at visual culture for experiences that enable them to sadistically "enjoy the sight of woman's humiliation," will not find it here; the power of the male audience's gaze has been to that extent curtailed.

Second, precisely because the heroes of these movies are *women*, most of these films are automatically about that central figure of the American individualist tradition, the underdog—blood brother to the misunderstood hero represented in another genre by Rita Hayworth's Gilda. When we watch Hollywood's male martial arts films, for example, we are often witnesses to something repellent and ugly—and no less so because, say, Chuck Norris (or in the gun-toting version, Eastwood or Charles Bronson) is righting some alleged wrong. Because they are beating up and killing other men *whom they can beat up and kill,* their behavior is in the end merely sadistic.[68]

Thus Chuck Norris's *The Octagon* and Cynthia Rothrock's *China O'Brien* could both be described, by a moviegoing computer (the author perhaps of the entry on *Arizona Heat* quoted above) as being, ideologically, about vigilante action in the pursuit of justice. But *The Octagon* as it presents itself to us has nothing to do with justice or with the courage of the noncomformist individual. It is about vigilantism as sadism, and its "individualism" is that of the cut-rate Nietszche Howard Roark in Ayn Rand's *The Fountainhead*. *China O'Brien*, conversely, features a heroine who is heroic because she can do what no one has any expectation of her being able to do; and does it on behalf of a much more egalitarian vision of the "community." Whereas the overwhelming odds that confront Norris, (the early) Eastwood, and Bronson always feel obviously trumped up once the fists and bullets start flying, the odds against Rothrock really *are* overwhelming, and she is heroic rather than vicious.[69] Her quest thus does have something to do with justice and nonconforming—that is, liberal—individualism.

Of course the overall outlines of the dominant ideology—American individualism—are recuperated. But the standard (male) version recuperates it as the strong protecting the weak against the ignoble forces of due process: as incipient fascism. The female version emphasizes the genuine conflict in the dominant ideology, the tension between community and individuality, without allowing them to be welded together in the patriarchal form of authoritarian populism: the woman as hero cannot do that even if she wanted to. That form of linkage being denied, an ideological fault line is highlighted rather than papered over. In a historical moment when the cult of "musculinity" in general provides reassurance in the face of (what many men perceive as) threats to national and personal identity, the female version functions differently than the male, even though both appeal primarily to men.

To return to an earlier comparison, *High Plains Drifter* valorizes rape and vigilante vengeance together. *The Stranger* associates vengeance with the punishment of rape (or attempted rape) and thereby (as does *Shame*, to which it is generically related) splits vigilantism from its association with sadistic male violence. *High Plains Drifter* never gets beyond a simple delight in that sadistic violence. *The Stranger* preserves the delight in violence, presumably with the added attraction of sexual fetishism; in focusing our attention, however, on the righting of wrongs—specifically wrongs against women—by a woman, it puts us on the side of something more than brute force. *The Stranger* is a fantasy: there's no way that Kathy Long could clean up a town all by herself (though one doesn't doubt it watching her). But neither could Clint Eastwood; on any credibility scale, both these films are at the zero point. In both films, for example, the hero has apparently occult powers, such as resistance to bullets, but this similarity too marks a significant change.

Traditionally in culture it is the *male* body that is strong and invulnerable; the female body fragile and needing the male's protection. The martial artist who takes ten or twelve killing blows to the head and then gets up to dish them out in his turn, or the hero who is shot in the side or leg, bandaged by his faithful female companion, and then immediately resumes action with a slight limp, is a visual metaphor engendering this traditional mythos (often as unintentional comedy). Eastwood's imperviousness to harm merely carries this metaphor to new heights (and incidentally strengthens a viewer's suspicion that *High Plains Drifter* is really a ghost story). Attribution of the same powers to Kathy Long, who like him (and unlike "powerful" women in horror movies) remains free of any taint of monstrosity, begins to de-gender the myth of the hero.

Many viewers, perhaps especially female viewers, will take his role seriously but giggle scornfully at hers. But that is to give in to pseudorealistic preconceptions and expectations that have no place in the midst of what is in either case a moral fable *and* a general statement about sex and gender. Once we rid ourselves of those preconceptions the remake, though it can obviously make no claims to narrative originality, is in fact a more exciting, more interesting, and more pleasurable movie. Moreover, it can be all these things without giving into the conventional association of masculinity with force, and of femininity with passivity. It's worth adding also that, contrary to my earlier remarks about sex in R-rated movies, the one scene of graphic sex in this movie most definitely does not end in the missionary position, but rather with Long firmly—and not murderously—on top. Nor has she been either coyly reluctant or predatorily seductive; instead she exhibits the kind of ordinary sexual desire that Hollywood traditionally cannot allow women to express (as in *V.I. Warshawski*), since it repudiates the double standard at the heart of conventional civilization.[70]

All of this is dependent on context. For one thing, cultural commodities are not produced outside the international circuit of capital, but are obviously a part of that circuit. Because of their low-budget nonconformity, many of the female action/adventure films are filmed outside the United States, and perforce participate in a neocolonialist discourse.[71] Some of them are therefore racially coded or occasionally explicitly racist in the same way as are Hollywood's naturalistic explorations of the "urban jungle" (even when some of the ostensible good guys are black, as in *Strange Days*). The heroine is white, as is perhaps her chief sidekick or love interest (or her entire tribe in the prehistoric or post-apocalyptic genres); nonwhite women tend to be nightclub strippers or other versions of "exotica erotica." The villains, more likely to be drawn from the local population if they are not rogue CIA agents, may range from the merely swarthy to the threateningly oriental.[72]

It is also important just what social role the heroine occupies. For example, in *Lady Blue*, a remake of *Dirty Harry*, Jamie Rose does a Clint Eastwood imitation with such grinning, scenery-chewing gusto that she actually makes the part *more* sadistic, in comparison with the flat stoicism that he brings to it. But from its opening shot of a bathing beauty caught in the sights of a giant rifle barrel, *Dirty Harry* itself is a veritable stockpile of sadistic imagery; Sigourney Weaver at her most heroically maternal could not change that. Moreover, the violent woman as villain (Louise Lacavaliere in *Strange Days*, Jenette Goldstein in *Fair Game*, Famke Janssen in *Goldeneye*) can be as sadistic as her male counterparts, though she signs her own death warrant in accomplishing this transgression.[73] These movies don't abolish our obsession with violence; visual culture cannot do that in any way.

Still, there *is* a potential difference in just how the social role of violence is expressed (the racism is unrecuperable). We can see this by comparing, for example, *Cagney and Lacey*, with its liberal feminist pretensions, to the more ostensibly egalitarian (what is erroneously called "postfeminist") USA cable series *Silk Stalkings*, the longest-running cable network show of the 1990s and television's most visible entry (before *Xena*) in the female action genre. *Silk Stalkings*, set in Palm Beach, features two cops, originally played by Rob Estes and Mitzi Kapture, who solve crimes in the milieu of the rich and famous.[74] There is no feminist subtext of discrimination, or gender hierarchy; here are just two equals on the go. Each is susceptible to the other, and to outside sexual interests, on an equal basis; each comes to the other's rescue on occasion. (This ostensible equality, which might produce skepticism in the viewer, is given more credibility by the fact that Kapture has about 90 percent of the personality visible on the screen, and the hopelessly bland Estes about 10 percent).[75] The result, however, is that much more so than *Cagney and Lacey* this show stands for the democratization of uninterrogated violence, of "law and order" as an ideology. Locale and motif—two working stiffs stalking the extraordinarily criminogenic well-to-do—give extra weight to the "classless" component of this ideology.[76]

So too, again, does iconography. Kapture's televisual persona consists mostly of a permanently cynical grimace, and a scornful voice that always lets us know the wine was really vinegar, but all of this is aimed only at the wealthy citizenry, never at her own occupation and its social or political structuring. Whereas Kapture was the most refreshing new face on television for the first year or so of *Silk Stalkings*, by its fifth year she'd become an oppressive bore. This fate never befell Sharon Gless, whose character could not be pinned down to a single, repetitive ideological note. Always having it both ways,

Cagney and Lacey did succeed from time to time in manifesting a kind of textual ambiguity; *Silk Stalkings* manifests only conservative smugness. Give Kapture an Hispanic surname, make the partners' commander (now a Jewish male) a black woman with some Asian ancestry, and we could give up civil rights politics altogether: just settle back and watch the show. This is always the intention of visual culture in any event, as evidenced by its consistent intertextuality. A commodity like *Silk Stalkings,* not in spite of but because of its "egalitarianism," fits in perfectly with that intention. Rather than leading us to question the overall perspective of the male-oriented law and order series, it reinforces that perspective.

Thus we have to be very careful in assessing the female action genre; its various expressions are far from identical. As a whole, however, it does often present us with texts that are not what we are used to. Furthermore, and perhaps most crucial, female action/adventure movies are but one element in a much larger cultural tendency that cannot help influencing the way they appear to us. Even television advertising has begun to foreground athletic and adventurous women in commercials for beer, automobiles, and credit cards.[77] To take an example from another realm of popular culture, since Marcia Muller published her first Sharon McCone mystery in 1977, the mystery and detection field has become wide open to the introduction of female detectives and cops who are active agents of destiny, who are tough in their own ways rather than "like a man." The same is true of the science-fiction and fantasy field, so that a feminist bookstore may have shelves full of books in that genre, and not a single one by Joanna Russ. In both these genres, moreover, men have begun to try to create believable female protagonists, just as women (though in considerably greater numbers) are creating male protagonists who don't reason with their fists. Hardly any of this output depends on fetishization (which is in any event much harder to achieve on paper than visually). And of course, behind all this literary and visual work in culture, stands the flowering of interest in and attention to female athletes from Martina Navratilova to the UConn Huskies women's basketball team—and beyond that, the unremitting debate as to whether women should be serving in combat in the military forces.[78]

Unlike the movies and television programs discussed in Chapter 6, those I've been discussing here do not valorize difference; for the most part, rather, they attest to the inability of male-oriented visual culture to imagine it. They don't interrogate violence but democratize it, as when Ripley ends the debate about how to deal with the aliens by declaring, "I say we go into orbit and nuke the site." Moreover, their interpellative effect, if there is one, must be different. I've said, for example, that *The Stranger* and *High Plains Drifter* are both fantasies, and so they are. The most obvious fantasy can work the magic of interpellation, though, only if the phantasmic world it creates is in some recognizable way a correlative for the material world we inhabit, and within which we are prepared to be interpellated. If Clint Eastwood cannot clean up an actually existing small town, he can symbolically rule it—and the world, by extension of both it and the masculinity he stands for. For both women and men, conversely, interpellation by female action movies can only remain at the level of fantasy; it may hail us into a desired subject position (that of equal), but not a familiar one.

For all that, every time we see even the least of these movies—which, though they are mostly truly trashy, are no more so than their male equivalents[79]—we're reminded that even dedicated scopophiliacs can sometimes get it right. Though the movies in this new genre are not thematically at war with themselves in the manner of *Gilda* or *Dead Poets Society*, their texts are truly ambivalent, and cannot simply be explained as male fetishism doing its usual work in visual culture. "Fetishism" is a description, not an explanation. There is an infinity of possible representations of male fetishism; for an explanation we want to know, Why *these* commodities at *this* time in *this* place? And here we should think back to 1971, the year of the first Cheri Caffaro and Pam Grier movies.

By far the most visible, the overwhelmingly visible, gender news of that time in the United States was the news of "women's liberation." The female action genre, with all its potentialities for super-voyeurism, was an obvious avoidance response to the issues raised by the women's liberation movement.[80] But it was also not an implausible response. It made and still makes a certain kind of sense, or else the genre would not have proceeded to proliferate as it has. As Samuel Delaney said of Joanna Russ in 1968, "Alyx, whatever her suffering at the hands of male editors (or critics), is not a feminist figure—as some male readers have taken her for. She is rather a figure of proto-feminist consciousness."[81] Her protofeminism, though, was liberating in its time; three decades later a male protofeminism that long since ought to have been surpassed becomes mechanical. Still, the ideology of which more traditional forms of voyeurism are the behavioral token is crumbling. Not every appeal to male fetishism is the same appeal; and this one is so clearly a sublimated attempt to confront a changing reality in the sexual division of labor that it highlights the putative change every bit as much as the fetish.

We could say that the action/adventure films with female heroes directly address the impact of contemporary feminism. However, by confusing two kinds of "strength," the more simple-minded contributions to these genres (which is most of them) manage to avoid any kind of confrontation with the real issues feminism raises; and to deflect its counterideological implications. There's nothing unique about this; it's the general Hollywood standard, and films that celebrate the moral character or social embeddedness rather than the physical prowess of men are almost as rare. In that sense, the action/ adventure genre achieves a kind of subcultural equality that we only fail to notice because most of the time we don't take it as seriously as we would if it were about men. In movies such as these, if only in fantasy, women are now becoming imaginable as "the individual," the mythic bedrock of liberal capitalism. The bi-gendered hero, a doer of heroic deeds men can identify with even though (or, as Carol Clover argues, because) she inhabits the body of a woman, has a secure niche in visual culture.[82] The ideological implications of this regiment for that social order, realized in a material form rather than as a fantasy, are potentially as fateful as Mary Tudor's effect on the institution of hereditary monarchy.

9 What the Male Gaze Sees: The Wrath of the Medusa

The shakiness of male self-satisfaction is perceptible in those genres in which feminism is recognized more symptomatically, as a kind of contagious disease, a disease that can only be warded off by embracing it in the guise of horror rather than confronting it as political or social statement. These are films not about women as fighters but about women as *killers*. Here the female protagonist appears implicitly or explicitly as castrator, and thus these films also generate an ambiguous, double-edged appeal. But their edges are much sharper; glamour now kills. Their rampant gynephobia suggests again that the makers of visual culture detect a profound social upheaval on the horizon and, however much they might fear it, have a divided consciousness about its meaning.

Most apparently explicit here is the cycle of rape-revenge films (of which *Thelma and Louise* is an enfeebled mainstream imitation, and *Girls Town* a comic, bloodless variant), in which vengeful victim/heroines go unpunished (*Lipstick, I Spit on Your Grave, Violated, Sex Crimes, Sudden Death, Model by Day, Savage Instinct*); women join together for collective vengeance (*Ladies Club, Rape Squad*); and no one requires a male dispensation for her vengeance, as does Sandra Locke in Clint Eastwood's *Sudden Impact*. Unlike *Shame* or *The Stranger*, these are a version of the classic horror film in which the female, the "Final Girl," slays the male monster (compare *Texas Chainsaw Massacre II* and *Halloween*); but now the monster is at bay, and the roles are reversed. The film is about her pursuit of him rather than the other way around.[1]

This genre, however, is far from being either stylistically or ideologically monolithic, and to say that a movie "belongs" to it is not necessarily to describe that movie's psychopolitics. As a comparison of the two most notable "classics" of the genre demonstrates, in some (perhaps most) of these movies something more than gynephobia is at their ideological core.

Ms. 45 is probably the most famous of all rape-revenge movies. However, despite its reputation it is actually an allegory in the European art-film tradition, inspired directly by Polanski's *Repulsion* and Roger Corman's *Masque of the Red Death*, and saturated with imagery from Cocteau's *Orphée* and Bergman's *The Seventh Seal*. As the literally named "Thana," double-rape victim Zoe Tamerlis is initially mousy and unprepossessing. Upon managing to kill her second attacker, though, she is transformed. Now, cloaked and hooded from head to toe, and made up in flaming red lipstick, she stalks the streets of New York as the seductive Angel of Death (the film's more revealing alternate title), killing every man she meets. Finally, at a Halloween Masque, dressed in leather boots, black stockings and garters and a black minidress, all surmounted by a nun's habit, she undertakes a final massacre. Just in case we should miss the point, she stares long and hard at a reveller who is quite convincingly cross-dressed as a virginal bride before shooting him; she deliberately holds her fire, however, on a woman who has just stabbed her in the back.

Ms. 45 is a stylistically delirious movie aiming at (though not reaching) the status of poetry. The rape scenes in it are brief, ugly, and invite no eroticization of the female body, or of the act. More than any other movie in American cinema, its subject matter is the erotics of death, and nothing else. There is therefore no way any man, except one who fancies himself in the role of the Grim Reaper, can be interpellated as the Death Angel; she is most definitely not, as in slasher films, a female avenger with whom males can vicariously identify.[2] Interpellating the male viewer, rather, as the enthralled subject/

victim, the film belongs squarely in the romantic masochist tradition of Keats's "La Belle Dame Sans Merci" or "Lamia." The elements of misogyny this tradition notoriously contains are a far cry from the pleasure in the brutal exercise of power that the voyeur of, say, *High Plains Drifter* may feel. This movie, then, indeed merits the appellation "gynephobic" to describe a consciousness divided between fear and desire.[3]

The almost equally famous "classic," *I Spit on Your Grave*, though often linked with *Ms. 45*, could not be more different; it is also more representative of the genre. Stylistically, it represents the acme of grim, brutal naturalism. During the unbearably lengthy rape scene that takes up most of the first half of the movie, the naked victim is covered in mud and blood, her attackers are made to seem like maddened animals, and among these northern rednecks the only man capable of securing sympathetic male identification is a retarded boy who is coerced into participating by the others. In actuality the viewer, male or female, is interpellated as a sophisticated middle-class urbanite caught, like the protagonist, in a horror-movie version of the American small town. Unlike *Ms. 45*, which always positions the viewer to be staring into the face of Death, *Spit* visually unites us with Jenny Hills as she strangles, castrates, axes, and dismembers her victims during the entire last half-hour of the movie. Moreover, they are the guilty ones, whereas most of Thana's victims are "innocent" (in the same sense in which the victim in *A Question of Silence* is innocent).

In this version of the genre, therefore, the male consciousness is not so much divided as reintegrated. This vengeful woman is a universal hero, and this movie is not about the masochistic erotics of death. It is instead (or at least also) about the sadistic erotics of violence. We are interpellated as her/him the virtuous killer; Camille Keaton ("Jenny Hills") as Charles Bronson. (As though to emphasize this reading, one of the most recent additions to the genre, *Dirty Weekend*, was directed by Michael Winner, director of all of Bronson's *Death Wish* films.) This judgment, to be sure, offers another example of the inescapable effects of gender on viewing. Barbara Creed writes that *"I Spit on Your Grave* is still misogynistic in its representation of women. It is important to note that the scenes in which Jennifer carries out her revenge are deliberately eroticized. Woman is monstrous because she castrates, or kills, the male during coition." Since misogyny is a male condition, however, this is true only if Jenny Hills seems "monstrous" to male viewers. My own response was that she was rightfully taking enjoyable vengeance on a bunch of evil creeps, and to cheer her on. Since I've never felt this way in a Charles Bronson movie, and indeed find them unwatchable, this is undoubtedly a sexualized response—how could it be otherwise? But it does not fit Creed's description of "misogynist," any more than—perhaps more questionably—the rape scene in the same movie fits any possible definition of "erotic."[4]

From the perspective of this comparision, it's clear that films in this genre may be, but are not necessarily, resistant in some degree to the dominant ideological readings of sex and gender. There are all sorts of different paths that they may follow, and it is crucial which are chosen. For example, they may, like *Dirty Harry* and the *Death Wish* cycle, adopt the reactionary position of making due process of law the enemy, as does the 1996 mainstream derivative *Eye for an Eye*. Some, such as *Ms. 45*, may go out of their way to avoid treating rape as a sexual, and therefore erotic act. *Shame* is noteworthy, in that the only rape has already taken place off-camera when the movie begins. Moreover, at one point in the Australian original the young pack of would-be rapists attacks an elderly grandmother, making it crystal clear that rage, not lust, is their trigger. But only a few movies in the genre escape the coding of voyeuristic eroticization as the corollary of the act of rape (which is anyway difficult to escape insofar as many men will be able to find the erotics of sadistic power in the act, no matter how it is treated visually).

In any event, their oppositional positioning of the camera's gaze aside, most rape-revenge movies are assimilable as simple inversions of the *Death Wish* saga; especially as their heroines are almost always "innocent victims" and their rapists obviously coded as deviant or socially marginal.[5] Straightforward representations of our historical predilection for vigilante violence in the name of justice, they call to mind nothing so much as those frequent, contemporary images of white women practicing with their handguns on the target range, getting ready to defend suburbia against the inner-city hordes spilling out of their barrios.[6]

Nor is this a casual analogy. To my knowledge, there has never been a rape-revenge film in which the victim was black and the rapist(s) white. Even cult superstar Pam Grier was never allowed to carry out this particular fantasy, for its implications are too upsetting. Moreover, that the female victims in these movies are always reasonably attractive enables us to understand rape as a purely *sexual* phenomenon, and holds at arm's length the more unsettling notion that rape is about the assertion of male sexuality and power rather than the alleged inability of some men to control their understandable lust.[7] By and large, that is, any potential spillover effects of the genre are safely contained (or at least, can be contained). In this regard it's instructive, I think, that whereas *Adam's Rib* and *Cagney and Lacey* are the creations of women in part or in whole, the rape-revenge cycle is almost entirely the handiwork of men.

Ideologically, we can see the genre not only as an invocation of sadistic violence, but also as a logical outcome of the masculine psychodynamic described in Chapter 5. Like the law-and-order film of which it forms a subgenre, it enables viewers—here specifically male viewers—to denounce as deviant a social behavior engaged in by people just like ourselves. This move interpellates us as members of a virtuous community within which we are exempted from the implied indictment. It is like dividing the sides for a pickup basketball game into "shirts" and "skins," but with more complexity. In this game all New Age sensitive males (a category that in Hollywood comprehends just about everyone but Bruce Willis and Sylvester Stallone) wear shirts around women and children (see *Kindergarten Cop*); but in those action genres where the serious business of beating up other men goes on, real men are all reduced to skins.

The rape-revenge cycle at first separates, so to speak, the men from the men, but finally speaks to all of us. Those scenes, so lovingly depicted in all of these movies, in which the vengeful rape victim blows away, castrates, or otherwise destroys her tormentors, serve several purposes for the shirt-wearing masculine audience. They fetishize the woman, enable male viewers to identify "innocently" with the commission of sadistic violence *by a woman,* and relieve men of a traditional responsibility for being women's protectors. This loss of an ideal vocation perfectly mirrors the loss of a real vocation away from the silver screen. "You make your own living, and I don't have to hold the door open for you." It is a considerable improvement on our earlier treatment of rape in visual culture, but it has its own historical determinants. If women are less frequently conceived of as the site of a male contest over property, this may be part of the general tendency described by Barbara Ehrenreich as a male "flight from commitment."[8] So men sympathetic to but threatened by the feminist project can feel themselves to be "taken off the hook." Women can take care of themselves if they'll just learn karate and get a gun; it's not men's problem.

Nonetheless, there will often be at least some ambiguity, if only in a limited sense, inscribed in our reception of these texts. To some extent this new attitude is significantly different, and potentially *politically* different, from the male-centered, voyeuristic attitude toward rape (epitomized in *High Plains Drifter* and Samuel Peckinpah's *Straw Dogs*) that Molly Haskell describes in her discussion of earlier films about that subject, *From Reverence to Rape.*[9] There was no textual ambiguity in those films, but rather only an occasional emotionless invocation of "the law" set against the clear visual enjoyment of the act. Now the act has a price, and that price is embedded in the traditionally *male* symbolization of vengeful heroism.

Here again dominant culture, as always during periods of transition, is working against itself. Catharine MacKinnon has argued that "rape, as legally defined, appears more a crime against female monogamy (exclusive access by one man) than against women's sexual dignity or ultimate integrity," and this has undoubtedly been the norm (though reformers, some of them influenced by MacKinnon's work, have begun to make incremental changes in the law of rape).[10] But for a long time it has not been the norm in rape-revenge movies, in a majority of which (*Thelma and Louise* most famously) the victims are not attached to any man at all.[11] However else the male spectator is positioned psychodynamically, as a would-be hero of his own life he is positioned ineluctably as the *female* avenger; and this, as Carol Clover argues, is novel.[12]

On the whole, then, the genre's invocation of the phallic woman in the guise of killer seems to suggest not so much a different, frightening way of being a woman, as a different, more universalized way of being a man. Moreover, its overt appeal to fetishism, as that of female warrior films, is too disreputable, James Cameron and Kathy Bigelow aside, for mainstream Hollywood—for, one might say, the Hollywood that is actually located in geographical California. As we have seen, the female action hero appears there partly as travesty, mostly as sidekick, and only occasionally in a less drastic version as the protagonist. As for mainstream rape-revenge films, *Lipstick* is primarily a woman-in-peril narrative (as opposed to the man-in-peril thematic of the genre); *Sudden Impact* has a male protagonist; *Thelma and Louise* is really a female buddy film; and *Eye for an Eye* shows that mainstream Hollywood (no one more so than star Sally Field) is still only comfortable with straightforwardly sadistic action.

It is thus *Ms. 45* rather than *I Spit on Your Grave* that prefigures the development in Hollywood of a mainstream genre that looks at the new woman as woman: only to turn back in fear from what it sees.[13] This is the genre of the new *noir* cinema, in which "woman" is confronted not as the phallic warrior or killer, but as the Medusa, whose wrath is uncontrollable: the Sharon who turns a man to stone. Now the object of "the triple male gaze" stares back at the voyeur—and her gaze is death. To see the genuinely divided consciousness of contemporary gynephobia, this is the genre we have to look at. It includes movies like *Body Heat* or *Blood Simple* or *Basic Instinct* or *Fatal Attraction* or *The Hand That Rocks the Cradle* or *Final Analysis* or *Malice* or *Romeo Is Bleeding* or *Kill Me Again* or *Dead On* or *Eve of Destruction* or *The Last Seduction*; or the veritable flood of their straight-to-video / cable clones, such as *Obsessive Love, The Temp, Body Chemistry, Traces of Red, Those Bedroom Eyes, Lethal White Female, Sins of the Night, Night Angel, The Perfect*

Bride, Prey of the Chameleon, Snapdragon, Scorned, The Substitute; or the nicely titled *Basic Obsession, Naked Obsession,* and *Animal Instincts;* or even made-for-TV movies, such as *Dying to Love You.*[14]

This list too could go on forever, and be perhaps even longer than a list of female action movies. In an obvious sense, moreover, these films are quite different from the action genre in that they represent male Hollywood hunkered down in its foxholes. In an era when straightforward contempt for women is hard to justify, obsessive gynephobia is an obvious stand-in.[15] But again something else is happening in them as well: an ambiguity that is probably more structural than intentional. Women you love to be terrified by, the protagonists of these films might be called, but the gynephobic terror is also a form of recognition: "Something is happening and you don't know what it is, do you, Mister Jones?" In this contemporary version of traditional film noir (actually closer in theme and tone to the horror movie), the rage of actresses such as Crawford and Stanwyck has escalated to total warfare. In some of these films, even, the Medusa is finally triumphant in her war against men, like the monster who will return for one or more sequels, so that our sense of moral closure is hopelessly confused; recuperation fails. *Basic Instinct* and *The Last Seduction* are the most prominent of these, but there are many more. By comparison, even television's most "shrewish" women, with their continual verbal putdowns of every man in sight, are merely cultural snobs, wanting their men to pay attention to them instead of guzzling beer or watching football. Cinema's women are killers.[16]

Michael Douglas did not invent the character we meet in *Basic Instinct* and *Fatal Attraction* (and later also in *Falling Down* and *Disclosure*) out of thin air; he clearly tapped into the Zeitgeist, or part of the Zeitgeist, as well. This bizarre self-pity of the powerful confronted by the relatively powerless (how many actresses in Hollywood can procure major film financing as easily as Michael Douglas can?) begs for a larger explanation. Obsessive fear is inescapable testimony that there is something to be afraid of. In male-dominated cinema that "something" can apparently not be externalized beyond fascination with an imaginary female toughness, or hysterical fantasies about female vengeance: vengeance that is activated as uncontrollable lust, but otherwise seems completely unmotivated. Even though they too are only symbolic testimony to change rather than a rational exposition of it, these films cannot be confined to the simplicities of their genre limitations or their overt sex appeal.

And sometimes they are more. To take the most notorious cases, even *Fatal Attraction*, the film that more than any other unleashed the genre of what has been called "backlash" cinema, is considerably more ambiguous; like *Gilda*, it has two texts. On the one hand, the film recuperates Reagan-era misogyny without too much difficulty, splitting femaleness into a duality that carries out the program of moral linkage to perfection. One side of this duality, the independent career woman Glenn Close, is coded as sexually active, predatory, destructive, and finally psychotic; her desperate desire to have a child only underlines the instability of her social role. The other side, Anne Archer as the good wife, is coded as sexually passive to the point of being symbolically chaste, accepting sexual activity but never initiating it (like Kim Cattrall in *Breaking Point,* no one ever accused *her* of giving them the best night of sex they ever had). She has no apparent life outside her home and family; much of the time when we see her she is putting on makeup and getting dressed. Moreover, the film's iconography (so richly contrived that it would take an entire essay to explore it), emphasizes this duality at every turn; as in the contrast between Close's witchlike and almost repellent appearance as the film progresses, and Archer's eroticized chasteness: a contrast that retrieves female passivity from its potential critique by Close's character.[17]

This recuperation of misogyny, however, is not paralleled by any comparably obvious recuperation of the ideology of the family. Here the text's ambivalence creates a void that the male viewer must fill from his own psyche. In neither of this film's two versions is the impotent male protagonist left with a type of masculinity that most men would publicly wish to emulate.[18] In the original ending, his haplessness is confirmed as he is framed by his suicidal, vengeful mistress for her own "murder"; in the revised ending, intended to be more acceptable to all viewers, but presumably especially to men, only his wife can slay the Medusan monster he is unable to defeat in single combat. Imagine a Western in which two strong women fight a climactic gun duel for a hapless man, and we can see how thoroughly this film has departed from the traditional code of masculinity.[19] Though she publicly embraces him afterward, ostensibly recuperating his patriarchal role, his bathetic weakness still leaves the male viewer unable to find a sympthathetic identification, except as masochistic male victim without any redeeming sexual liaison, or as partner in a monogamous heterosexuality that is absolutely closed off from the freedom of public life. We can be voyeuristically attracted to Close, whose availability symbolizes that freedom for men, but again we must pay the price.[20]

Whatever the ultimate female-to-female combat of *Fatal Attraction,* like that of *Aliens,* is about—and heterosexual monogamy would seem to be the most likely candidate—it is not about the preservation of patriarchy as a system of unqualified male domination. The clear narrative intention of *Fatal Attraction* is to throw men back into the nuclear family, but that has never been what modern patriarchy is about. Modern sexual hierarchy is based on the double standard—precisely what this movie repudiates, in that its message is to foreclose sexual adventurism as an option not only for women but also for men. In thinking about the ideology of the nuclear family, we have to remember that being "head" of it is much, much less than what many men want or expect out of liberal individualism. The text that confers that role on Douglas is there to be read, but it carries with it narrative baggage that cries out for more recuperation than the film can securely provide.

Basic Instinct and *The Last Seduction* are different from this and from most of their clones. In each of them the female lead's contempt for men spills over the boundaries of the "normal" and the "natural," and becomes something other than merely entertaining or system-confirming. *Basic Instinct* is perhaps still the most disturbing, because the most unmanageable, exemplification of the genre. Michael Douglas, in his repeat portrayal of male self-pity, can find no help anywhere when confronted with Sharon Stone (nor can any other man in sight). As a woman who is always on top both sexually and intellectually, and who advertises her pleasure in making us think she's lying even (or especially) when she claims to be telling the truth, she incarnates femaleness as the unknowable masquerade it is in a gynephobe's nightmare.[21]

Basic Instinct has been described by some feminist viewers as the most appalling possible document of misogyny, homophobia, and antifeminist backlash. It has been seen by others as a celebration of women's liberated, self-determining sexuality (by, for example, two reviewers in *Ms.*), or as an invocation of the fetishist male's terror of gender distinction and, correlatively, a monument to his masochism.[22] It has also been seen as a right-wing populist version of class conflict, and (like *Ms. 45*) as an expression of the American puritanism that links sex inextricably with death. None of these characterizations is "wrong"; all of these elements are there. Still, there is another text that is equally "there," and that at a key moment speaks for itself. This moment, which defines everyone's character thereafter, occurs during the interrogation of Stone, when she starts to light a cigarette and the chief detective tells her that "this is a no-smoking building." "What are you going to do, charge me with smoking?" she responds contemptuously, and promptly goes on lighting up. At this moment Catherine Trammell is placed firmly in the long line of American wiseguy heroes that includes Philip Marlowe, Sam Spade, Rick Blaine, and even Dirty Harry Callahan. Later on, when Douglas, now under interrogation himself, repeats her line, the movie's reconstruction of gender roles is confirmed: *she* is the All-American tough guy, he's the loser. This reconstruction is beyond gynephobia; it gives us a subtext that's not about murder and sexuality but grace under pressure. Who will read this subtext remains open, but again it is there to be read.

This suggestion of a text beyond gynephobia is even more applicable to *The Last Seduction,* which unlike its predecessors does not trade in castrative imagery. Of the two male leads (really, supporting actors), one is a would-be rapist and the other a wife-beater.[23] Given this background, Linda Fiorentino's manipulative and murderous contempt for all men, and the overt role reversal between her and weak male lead Peter Berg, seem to many female viewers to be a breath of fresh air. In a sense, this film's complete amoralism is the most radical statement Hollywood is capable of making. Morality in dominant culture is primarily sexual morality, and sexual morality is primarily about female subordination. It could be said that *The Last Seduction* is *A Question of Silence* without female solidarity—again the real absence from all these films. (See, in contrast, my earlier discussion of *Shame* and of *Stop at Nothing.*) In the absence of an ethic of solidarity linking individual behavior to a counterideology, to collective opposition, the Medusa remains only an attractive monster.

But she is a monster of ambiguous significance. To be sure, these are far from being the same film. Like *Silence of the Lambs, Basic Instinct* trades in a putatively "feminist" subtext for sheer homophobia. And with self-pitying Mike Douglas at its visual center, it never gets beyond its gynephobic—and homophobic—fascination with the Other. *The Last Seduction,* contrarily, is narrated entirely from the point of view of Fiorentino. If male viewers want to position themselves as white male victims in the Douglas mold, they will have to do it on their own; in this film there is definitely a text beyond gynephobia. Still, the films have a good deal in common. Their invocation of cultural disarray is unmistakable, and it takes them well beyond the alleged transgressions of soap opera. Dystopian rather than utopian, anti-fairy tales in which a fang-toothed Red Riding Hood lies in wait to devour both wicked wolf and innocent woodchopper (who are really one and the same), they suggest the existence of a *dis*order too profound to be recuperated or assimilated; they are therefore potentially subversive of established culture.

This is not to say that such films don't interpellate men in a masochistic position that is ultimately pleasurable; pleasurable is what masochism is intended to be.[24] To be devoured by Fiorentino or Stone, even while possessing them, might be a price many men would be willing to pay. The point, however, is that this transaction is subversive; it points, as Freud might have said, to the "discontents" rather than the joys, of civilization. It is thus not surprising that, despite the unmistakable and acute gynephobia manifest in these images of *la femme castatrice,* many women (including the star of *Fatal Attraction,* Glenn Close) have seen a powerful statement in them, loosely characterized as "women determining their own sexuality"—though Close could only have come to that conclusion by ignoring the presentation of her alter ego, Archer. Stone and Fiorentino (both of whom have publicly enjoyed their filmic personas) would be on firmer ground.[25]

How these movies might credibly be interpeted in this way can be seen more clearly by comparing them with *Falling Down,* the film that Mike Douglas made subsequent to *Fatal Attraction* and *Basic Instinct. Falling Down* is pornographic in the self-indulgence of its own violence. Yet even it carefully elides the implicit racism that its most enthusiastic viewers would surely want it to proclaim. As the terminally redundant Tom Wilson / Douglas descends through the Third World inferno that Los Angeles (and by extension the United States) has become, the movie repudiates racism, anti-Semitism, and even homophobia. "What kind of vigilante *are* you?" the neo-Nazi weapons collector who incarnates all those bigotries asks him. A good question: in fact his only ethnic or racial enemies are people who don't speak English as well as native-born Americans do. Aligning itself with the English-firstness of such luminaries as Jacques Barzun, Saul Bellow, and Arnold Schwarzenegger, *Falling Down* seems to be about nothing so much as the Third Worldization of America. But in fact that is not its final story. The horror that awaits our "hero" in the Eighth Circle of Hell is not Dante's "pimps, panders, and flatterers," but an ex-wife with a restraining order.

Though the white man is the victim in *Falling Down's* view of the world, the ultimate definition of Tom Wilson's victimhood is not deracination but emasculation. More than racism, it is misogyny that fuels the narrative and drives it to its conclusion. And what makes this misogyny "work," so to speak, is that we are not given a genuine female protagonist opposite Douglas. Fleeting glimpses of Barbara Hershey (has a great actress ever been so underworked in any movie?) do not provide either male or female viewers with an alternative source of interpellation. Only Robert Duvall's "good cop" does that, but for the most part his role is designed to help us thrill to the chase, and to create suspense as to whether Wilson will reach his final destination. *Fatal Attraction,* in contrast, gives Close equal weight with Douglas, until the narrative arbitrarily turns her into a psychopath and the film begins *its* descent into sheer misogyny. *Basic Instinct,* as I've argued, positions Stone as an alternate version of the American tough guy hero; and *The Last Seduction* gives us only the consciousness of Fiorentino to take seriously. In other words, looking at *Falling Down's* misogyny, we can see more clearly the way in which the gynephobia of these films is qualified (though less so in *Fatal Attraction*) by a potentially interpellative text for women, and an ambiguously patriarchalist text for men.

In sum, even the most gynephobic among the films in this genre manifest a textual ambiguity beyond that of the earlier films noirs on which they are loosely modeled. In those movies the directors and writers, unable to make direct political comments, substituted an atmosphere of social paranoia that depended on misogyny for its visual concretization. In the contemporary version, nothing is standing in for anything else; the political and social paranoia it suggests is about gender and sexuality *tout court*. It is the independent power of their gynephobic fetishism—male masochism—that gives the films their particular, and vertiginous, ambiguity. Traditional misogyny, whatever its psychoanalytic roots, was based on men's contempt for women as social beings. Now that contempt is stood on its head, and appears—since these are men putting their thoughts into the minds of women—as a kind of self-contempt.

As Carol Clover points out, there is little independent attention paid to fetishism, especially masochistic fetishism, in Mulvey's original discussion of visual pleasure. Calling it "fetishistic scopophilia," she assimilated it to voyeurism: perhaps because as of that point in time dominant cinema had hardly manifested the more overt, specialized kind of fetishism that is now, as I've remarked, one of its regular if still only secondary features.[26] The differences, however, are crucial.[27] Voyeurism as a mode of sexuality has a profound phantasmic component, but its salience is primarily ideological. Its public message is of men controlling, or desiring to control, the bodies of women.[28] No act of male voyeurism, whatever a particular man's psychic economy may be, can be innocent of this ideological positioning.

There are varieties of fetishism that are quite different. If the fetishistic male is interpellated by the fetish, it is not into a conventional, let alone a dominant, social role, but into a variable and unpredictable drama that takes place only in his imagination. Though fetishism in visual culture is at the same time obviously voyeuristic, it is voyeuristic in a manner somewhat unlike that described by Mulvey, for whom the essence of voyeurism is that the male viewer vicariously controls the object of his gaze. On the contrary, the fetishistic voyeur may be enthralled by the fetish (recall *Basic Instinct*); he may be not the bearer of a domineering visual obsession, but the (momentarily) powerless victim of a sexual obsession. That is, fetishism may be sadistic and controlling, but may also be, in the fetishist's fantasy world, sadomasochistic and ambiguous, or simply masochistic. In Barbara Creed's words, "Mulvey's theory of the sadistic male gaze, which seems to describe so well the structure of spectatorial relations in other genres, does not explain the very different structure of looks that is constructed in the horror film." [29]

Unfortunately, until recently it was impossible to find a concrete discussion of male sexual fantasy at this level in film studies, as opposed to Freudian or Lacanian theorization at a very general level. For feminist cultural critics, a discussion of male sexuality as variable rather than monolithic could be seen as calling into question straightforward and thus politically satisfying notions of masculinity or male power.[30] Moreover, for obvious reasons women do not especially want to look at visual cultural commodities that are so clearly designed for the consumption of men. Most feminist cultural critics have seen every Hitchcock movie available, but are much less likely to be familiar with the marginal titles described here and in Chapter 8. On the other hand, men do not discuss their own sexual fantasies in public; to do so is literally to expose themselves. Only women, it would seem, can do that for them (as in the pop psychology studies of Nancy Friday, or the more recent work of Shere Hite). Thus only with the publication of Linda Williams's pioneering study of cinematic pornography *Hard Core*, has it been possible for the average non-viewer of that genre to discover just how ambivalent (and just how unlike the assumptions about it that go into the pseudoscience of "pornography" studies) is its portrayal of male sexual desire. Similarly, only with the publication of Carol Clover's equally detailed study of the horror film, and then Barbara Creed's analysis of cinematic castration anxiety, has male masochism in concrete cultural manifestations received its first public discussion.[31]

Unlike voyeurism, male masochism has no essential, monolithic, ideological saliency: its politics are indeterminate. Perhaps it is a convoluted path to the reaffirmation of male dominance, as is, for example, often said of the British upper-class (male) predilection for undergoing scenes of bondage and humiliation, but it is certainly not the most direct path.[32] In fact, to get a clearer view of Hollywood's gender-bending obsession, we should look not at these ambiguous cultural commodities but at the real thing in misogyny. Probably the best place to see that in operation is not in movies or network television but on television's music video channels: MTV and VH-1. The songs and especially video representations that we see on these channels, over and over again feature women who are portrayed as nymphomaniacs and masochists, who want nothing more than to be the receptacles of men's insatiable lusts, no matter how violently and demeaningly the latter are portrayed.[33] In cinema proper, what is most striking is the outburst of movies, referred to in Chapter 3 above, about serial killers who get their kicks (and apparently ours) by strangling or mutilating one woman after another.[34] The apotheosis of this genre in the 1990s must be seen as a direct answer to Glenn Close (*Fatal Attraction* appeared in 1987) and later Sharon Stone: getting them back under control. But so too is such an apparently "innocent" film as Woody Allen's *Crimes and Misdemeanors,* in which we get straightforward misogyny and the normalization of sexual hierarchy. It's too bad that Angelica Huston had to be eliminated, but Martin Landau has to do what a man's gotta do—and gets away with it to general diegetic satisfaction (a conclusion repeated by Chazz Palminteri's cheerful murder of Jennifer Tilly in *Bullets over Broadway*).

The vengeful woman movies could not be more different. As Clover points out, in "slasher" movies and rape-revenge movies, both of which do typically feature graphic violence against women, young men (overwhelmingly the audience for these movies in theaters and in video rentals) are ultimately interpellated as victimized *women* who fight back against and finally destroy the (male) monster who has victimized them (often plural monsters in the rape-revenge film). To the question, How is this possible? Clover offers several answers, not all of them consistent with each other. For example, the "Final Girl" in slasher movies is invariably boyish and sexually chaste: Jamie Lee Curtis in *Halloween* and *Halloween II* being the prototype for these roles. In a chapter entitled "Her Body, Himself," Clover speculates that the violent Oedipal drama these films are encoding would be too threatening to young men if the slayer of the monster (read: father) were outrightly like themselves.

At the same time, she notes, such movies do not disturb the traditional ideological coding of "loose" versus "chaste" women (the former almost always dying in slasher movies), even while they are creating a "universal hero"; in contrast, the aggressively sexual women of the woman-as-monster movies are murderous by virtue of their not being chaste. But though these movies in either case thus seem superficially to repeat the conventional ideological codes of moral linkage, their texts are more complicated; their psychosexuality much more ambiguous. Sundered from its association with powerful, active men, and powerless, passive women, the code loses the core of its ideological meaning. Whatever we are to think about the murderousness of the protagonists in these genres (especially the rape-revenge and the female killer films), the last thing these women are is the passive recipient of men's sexual or social domination. Just as women may be better off in the worlds of action, science fiction, and other marginal genres, where the fascination with their fantasized strength paves the way for ambiguity in its presentation and in the interpretation of its social meaning, so they may be better off amid the ambiguities of a cinema that is enthralled by rather than dismissive or contemptuous of them. Again, what is essentially a dynamic of conflict is being played out in public, rather than being hopefully waved away.

It is striking how much a part of visual culture's explanatory framework feminism has become, even while its radical implications are frantically disavowed and the traditional order recuperated. Thus, as Elizabeth Young points out, misogyny and homophobia clearly determine the narrative of *Silence of the Lambs* (men of uncertain masculinity kill women because women are sexually threatening to them), but who is being interpellated in what social role is more ambiguous than that. Jodie Foster / Clarice Starling is posed as the object of Anthony Hopkins / Hannibal Lecter's domineering gaze, but never as the typical female victim; instead she is always resistant and at last the triumphant Final Girl of slasher movies. Like that figure, she is chaste; as are those other icons of female rationality, Ripley in *Alien* and *Aliens;* and Scully in the 1990s television series *X-Files.* Though a completely realized female figure still eludes dominant visual culture, here a feminist perspective seems to have become, comparatively speaking, part of that culture.[35] In sum, although feminism is seized on and then denatured by Hollywood for the usual purposes of pleasure and profit, it is not so easily domesticated. It is reduced in such a way as to be capable of encompassing many conflicting viewpoints; still, in many respects that is an advance over being able to encompass none at all.

Thus ideological theories of "backlash," or psychoanalytic theories of castration anxiety, are unsatisfactory as explanations of this new turn in cinema. The appeal of a certain type of actress in the role of destroyer has always "rested on masculinity's desire for and dread of an active and powerful female sexuality." It was Theda Bara, not Sharon Stone or Glenn Close, who declared that "the Vampire that I play is the vengeance of my sex upon its exploiters."[36] Similarly, the question, "Is it not really remarkable (we ask ourselves in amazement), when one considers the overwhelming mass of this transparent material, that so little recognition and attention are paid to the fact of men's secret dread of women?" was asked not by a contemporary commentator on cinematic gynephobia, but in 1932 by the psychoanalyst Karen Horney.[37]

All the same, today's gynephobic movies *are,* as I've noted, strikingly different from the 1940s films noirs they sometimes seem to imitate; and their female protagonists especially are a far cry from the femmes fatales who made film noir what it was (or English romantic poetry what it was). The 1940s women, even at their most murderous, were ordinary women (except for their beauty), turned outcast because there was no other way for an independent woman to be conceptualized in the Hollywood imagination of that era. To-day's murderous women are not ordinary. In the first place they do what men do, occupationally. Before we meet Fiorentino as a thief and murderer, we meet her as a hard-nosed boss of men. Stone's omnicompetence frightens every man she meets; and the real problem of Close is that, unlike Archer, she is in professional competition with Douglas. In the second place, these women are extraordinary in their single-minded (and misanthropic) ruthlessness, and in their proficiency at fighting and killing. Overall, therefore, the fear they inspire is not the 1940s fear of an independent woman, but the much greater fear of a woman who is independent *just like a man*.[38] Moreover, it is not simply fear induced by hatred and resentment, but also fear associated with obsession—and if we are to believe the repeated evidence of the camera, enthrallment.

Forties films noirs were usually movies about strong men brought to their knees by a malignant fate, most often coded as "woman." Burt Lancaster, Humphrey Bogart, John Garfield, were the stars and the real protagonists of any movie they appeared in, even on their deathbeds. But the male leads of the contemporary genre identified here, even though they technically are the "leads," are most often weaklings who seem to exist only to be seduced and murdered, unless rescued by another woman; it is the women who dominate the films, thematically and iconographically. Whether she wins or loses, the terrifying brilliance of the plot with which she has ensnared her victim is what the films are about. The sense that marked the earlier films noirs, of a "masculinity" worthy of respect even in defeat, has now virtually disappeared. Because it has not been replaced by a positive appreciation of possible new roles for men and women, these films are "noir," but they recuperate nothing that upholders of the dominant ideology should really find worth recuperating.

What is the unnameable fear that these movies express? What is the motiva-tion that cannot be named? When men create women who see them as the enemy, what exactly is it they think they are the enemy of? The men who run Hollywood undoubtedly have their own reasons, from alimony payments to concerns about their institutional power, for their love-hate affair with man-killing women who seem to be an unstoppable force of nature (unless stopped by another woman). But the movies wouldn't be made and made again unless someone else wanted to watch them, and unless they made some kind of sense to both a male audience (they are voyeuristic and fetishistic) *and* to a female audience (many of them lack the more strictly masculine appeal of the action genre). And they do make sense, beyond their parading of good-looking women's bodies, and beyond the longing of female viewers for portraits of strong women to take to their hearts.

Here we can only be speculative, but the crisis of sexual relations they hint at ("explore" would be too charitable a word) is not simply ideological. Nor is it simply a response to the feminist revolution, for its main tendencies were diagnosed more than three decades ago by Betty Friedan and Paul Goodman: the obsolescence of traditional sex roles in late industrial society.[39] The crisis of ideology and sexuality is a *material* crisis. The contemporary action hero and the superwoman/superbitch are a response, *by men,* to the apparent absence of satisfactory vocation for men and women, respectively. Because there is no comparably rich body of visual culture created by women, we cannot really compare what men are seeing to some concrete alternative; thus interpretative description must be considerably more interpretation than description.[40] Still, there are clues, both within and without the metatext itself.

To men the contemporary crisis appears as a lack of opportunities to be a man, and a dearth of women who will accept a man who is less than that. To women it appears as a lack of nonoppressive ways to be a woman, and a dearth of useful men. In either case the new genre's appeal has deep roots in the social structure.[41] "Backlash" is then not so much a response to the feminist revolution as it is a signal of, or an accompaniment to, that revolution's incompletion; of our inability, for understandable political and historical reasons, to develop new institutions and structures that can provide more than the occasional rectification of individual injustices.

Thus the cinematic dominatrix, far from being simply the outgrowth of a resurgent misogyny, is integral to a more general cultural efflorescence that also includes both male and female "musculinity" (to borrow Yvonne Tasker's wonderfully evocative neologism); and so links the Medusa back to the phallic woman.[42] In short, the dominatrix and the woman warrior both are a *result* of feminism and a *cause* of gynephobia or misogyny. As women get tough, the men must get even tougher: "The stronger women get, the more men love football." Or, more generally, "a gleeful use of cunning and high spirits against brute force, a reliance on subterfuge have almost faded from heroic myth today. In the prevailing popular concept of masculinity . . . the little man, the riddler or trickster, has yielded before the type of warrior hero, the paradigm of the fittest survivor."[43] But we don't have to look as far as Charlie Chaplin for a countermodel.

When Clark Gable took off his undershirt in *It Happened One Night,* women swooned over a rather ordinary body; his appeal lay not in his physique but rather in a ringing statement of sexual availability that was blazoned by the contrast between this quite trivial instance of noncomformity and what was still a publicly puritanical culture. On *Baywatch* today he wouldn't even be noticed. When Arnold Schwarzenegger or Sylvester Stallone and their many imitators strip down to a buff of unbelievably well developed and well oiled muscles, their appeal lies not so much in a revealed sexuality (of which Schwarzenegger and Stallone both have very little), as in their caricature of ordinary masculinity. Any ordinary man could identify both with Gable's sexuality and with his actual body (if not his extraordinary good looks). No one can identify with Schwarzenegger's body. His bodily violence, like Stallone's, or Jean Claude Van Damme's, or Steven Seagal's, points to the impossibility that adult masculinity has become, rather than to any possibility of attaining it. Moreover, any male could hope to be what Gable was in that movie: a journalist. But the new masculinists don't do anything that has social meaning at all, except when they imitate policemen or some other purveyor of authorized violence; they have no other vocation. (In Schwarzenegger's best roles he's a robot from the future.) The only manhood, then, that can be clearly distinguished from womanhood is manifestly absurd; the teenage male fantasy that its avatars appeal to is not sexual wistfulness but bewilderment and, underneath, rage (most visible as such, perhaps, in the new generation of superviolent video games that boys can play at home or in malls).

The figure of the superbitch or Medusa in her many incarnations—malevolent killer, ball-busting lawyer, take-no-prisoners businesswoman—thus speaks directly to the unease with which society confronts the woman who pursues "masculine" success: she is taking away all that remains. Most critics have not noticed that the aspect of Catherine Trammel's persona inspiring the most awe in *Basic Instinct* is that *she has a B.A. in psychology from Berkeley!* And she's a *writer!* The tone in which these aspects of her persona are recognized is extraordinary. Schwarzenegger (along with Clint Eastwood that most self-conscious of masculinists) knew what he was doing when he recommended Sharon Stone for the role, on the basis of her having done her own martial arts stunts with him in *Total Recall.* The phallic woman is tough, the Medusa is smart: and they are the same person, linked together by the fact that each of them is doing what only men are supposed to be able to do.

The female action movies do not raise these issues so starkly; in most of them sex is downplayed and thus sex and violence are not so intimately linked.[44] Their ambivalence is about the public role of women, not the meaning of their sexuality. Ambivalence about female sexuality, on the other hand, entails gynephobia, even if, as in *Basic Instinct,* there are other texts there to be read by women or men. The ideological significance of gynephobia in this context is that there is no male equivalent of the superbitch, no fear inspired by the figure of the well-oiled male killing machine: a man who behaves like that is not threatening and may even be considered admirable; the latent male rage to which he appeals is *on his side*. What is a man to do when there's no such thing as a man any more? The Medusa thus has a social meaning wholly aside from the uneasy mix of male masochism and longings for vengeance against feminism that fuel such fantasies, and also aside from the understandable tendency of many women to identify with *any* image of female strength, however male-determined. Her appearance, together with that of the fetishized phallic woman, returns us to the fact that three decades after the birth of the new feminism, there still aren't enough ways in which women can plausibly be depicted as both forceful individuals *and* women, within the confines of an ideology that, for reasons already discussed, understands individuality only as violent *action*.

There has certainly been change, because society has changed. The femmes fatales of 1940s film noir had to die: what else was there for them to do as independent women? How would they even make a living? The ending of *Gilda* is risible because we know that Gilda would never settle for being Glenn Ford's hausfrau (though Hayworth would happily have done so). She certainly could not have become a lawyer or a businesswoman, as Jane Fonda or Sigourney Weaver might. In context, even the fact that today's female stars are much better educated than their predecessors has great significance (aside from Katharine Hepburn, who among the latter had been to college, much less graduate school?).

The gender difference remains determinative, though. It is why today's movies are double-edged, whereas the earlier ones were not. When Humphrey Bogart and James Cagney played misunderstood or even mad-dog killers from the lower depths, they could milk their roles for audience sympathy without compromising their masculinity or losing their aura of essential decency. Everyone watching them understood the message that it's tough to be a man in a pitiless world, but much better to be a bad man than no man at all. No one in the audience thought that their movies must have been made by misanthropes, or were intended to appeal to misanthropy. Rampant masculinity was implicitly criticized in some of these movies from Hollywood's classical period (especially those of Anthony Mann and Douglas Sirk in the 1950s), but only as a deformation of what remains the normative standard. No one watching Bogart as a mad-dog killer in *High Sierra*, or Cagney in *White Heat*, would have thought, "How frightening men can be when they're out of control!" (If anything, some of those movies, *White Heat* being the most notorious example, blamed women—the smothering mother out of parlor Freudianism—for the fate of the men.)

The masculine sense of a wholly independent self still sets the normative standard for right action in our civilization (or the American version of it). As long as that is the case a male protagonist (Stallone, say) can engage in what we would otherwise consider totally ruthless action and fascinate us with his determination, rather than being perceived (except by those of us who are squeamish) as perverse. He may even, like Bogart and Cagney—or John Garfield, James Stewart in Anthony Mann's Westerns, Robert Stack in Douglas Sirk's *Written on the Wind,* or Robert De Niro and Mickey Rourke today— seem a tragic figure.[45]

Conversely, in mainstream Hollywood the option of leaving her femininity behind to be an individualistic social actor is still rarely available to a woman, unless a subtext implicating her in violence and perversity is appended to it. Even the more sympathetic apotheosis of Woman as Hero for a mainstream audience will still encounter obstacles to its expression. The chief of these is not so much her fetishization for the males in that audience, which is highly expectable though not inevitable, but the unlikelihood that a male-dominated industry can finally take the revolutionary social implications of her figure seriously. Films about transgressive heroines made on the margins of cinema can be stylized for male fetishistic tastes, and otherwise be entirely straightforward, as they have no pretensions to social significance. Mainstream versions are more likely than not to be subverted: as by degrading Sara Paretzky's socially critical and feminist private eye, V. I. Warshawski, into a grotesque cartoon whose cinematic creators succeed only in mocking the female body; or by depicting supposedly independent female attorneys who are helplessly attracted to male serial killers and rapists (*Defenseless, Love Crimes, Jagged Edge,* and so forth); or, most of all, by turning the transgressor into the Medusa.[46] Ripley is a real female hero, but she's probably better off in outer space; that is why, finally, most of the transgressive female heroes we meet exist, like their male counterparts, only on film sets.

Several things become clear as we canvass the possibilities of explanation for this complex phenomenon. First of all, an immense amount of relatively painful disavowal is going on in contemporary visual culture, and it cannot help leaving a variety of ideological residues behind it. Therefore, any analysis that sees *only* phallocentrism, misogyny, tokenism, and recuperation in contemporary visual culture, is incomplete. What has happened, primarily, is that Hollywood (one should say here, male Hollywood, which is most of it) is at last unable to deal with the excess energy of "its" women. This energy, much like that of the screen goddesses of the classical period, cannot be totally contained by a cinema (or television) unable to think through new roles for women in an imaginative way, but doomed instead to present them only as either castrating horrors, or as imitators of male violence and toughness.[47]

At the same time, fantasy is the deepest level at which films capture our attention, and ideological interpellation in the context of that phantasmic overflow is considerably less than fully predictable. Who can say what happens when, if at all, fantasy is consciously or semiconsciously verbalized as ideology —especially as men's feelings about their own sexual experience are largely opaque to women (and even, publicly, to each other)? What we can say is that the possibilities are ambiguous.

To return to the example of *Gilda*, some critics have assumed that Rita Hayworth's humiliation at the hands of Glenn Ford activates or appeals to feelings of sexual sadism in male viewers. As Richard Dyer points out, however, and as I have argued in Chapter 7, it's quite possible that (some, many) male viewers identify not with Ford but with the more charismatic Hayworth, and share her feelings of anger and humiliation.[48] Gilda/Hayworth, though completely distinct from the kinds of active heroines (Final Girls) Carol Clover discusses in *Men, Women, and Chain Saws* (as well as from the casta-trices discussed here), is in a different way an exemplification of the possibility of recognizing the woman as "Her Body, Himself."[49] Since one of the ideologi-cal pleasures of male sexual identity (here I can only speak of men, for obvious reasons) is to identify with the underdog who is ultimately vindicated, and since most people are not triumphant about anything of great moment, the fantasy of vindication is a rewarding one. But what if the underdog is a woman? Nothing in psychoanalytic theory, not even Freud's theory of castra-tion anxiety, tells us what the male viewer's attitude toward her must be. Perhaps, as her fantasy lover, I have the uniquely male satisfaction of knowing I can possess her. So as a male viewer I can have it both ways, and in this I may seem privileged compared to a female viewer. On the other hand, the very condition of my identification with her in the first place was my recognition of Gilda as she who cannot be possessed.

As for the more contemporary female fantasy figures I have been discussing in these pages, viewers of these films must confront (as those of *Gilda* need not) the possibility that conventional social roles are neither natural nor fixed. Seen in this light, the "victim feminism" of a movie like Jane Campion's *The Piano* has much more to say about the possibilities of transforming gender roles in the late nineteenth century, but a lot less to say about those same possibilities in the twenty-first, than a movie like *Alien*, or *Arizona Heat*, or *Shame*, or a television series such as *Veronica Clare*.

The only thing we can say for certain is that the structural gendering of commercial cinema (and television), as described by Mulvey, is still its dominant tendency. But it is no more than that, because sex/gender structuration is itself only the dominant tendency of our culture, not the whole of it. Normative heterosexuality—familialism—can no longer be deployed with quite so much confidence as in the past to provide individual resolutions to social problems, because the heterosexual family is now visible *as* one of those problems. The possibility of cinematic (and to a lesser extent televisual) ambiguity, even on this fundamental point, remains as open for men and women in their viewing as it is in their other social activities: not very much more than a possibility, but also not much less. Spectatorship itself, in sum, is an ambivalent activity; but that is not the crucial point.

There *is* something to feel ambivalent about: the divided consciousness of a hegemonic ideological structure that is under severe attack, now manifested culturally as a developing new text—or, perhaps, several new subtexts. The (male) spectator of these texts may be a sexually sublimated voyeur, an ambivalent fetishist, or a single-minded hunter of friendly or hostile ideologies, a sexual egalitarian or a patriarchalist, or all of these at once. He may still be having it both ways, but one of them now is novel, is a different way. The female spectator may be a confirmed victim, a celebrator of the female body and female strength, an uneasy observer of her own divided consciousness, or an angry revolutionary, or all of these at once.[50] Wherever men or women stand, visual culture offers something for them to grasp at.

For the most part these cultural commodities are merely symptomatic and obliquely expressive rather than confrontational or truly subversive. "Paying attention to" a disturbing cultural event is a far cry from embodying it. Male-dominated visual culture, like American culture generally, is not genuinely pluralist, in the sense of valuing different subcultures with equal attention and respect. But again like the culture at large, it is at least notionally pluralist, and it has begun to be more than faintly plural.

Its limitations are still immense. Perhaps most indicative of them is that (*A League of Their Own* aside) the few movies about female athletes usually show the fantasy of their defeating men, rather than the reality of their defeating other women. Only men *really* count; what women do with other women is interesting only if it's about men. Moreover, men still have it both ways, enjoying our fetishism while playing with "difference." Furthermore, real or imaginary changes in gender relations by themselves do not begin to get at that core of American social organization and culture in which the construction of racial and sexual "Others" fuses national with personal identity. Thus in mainstream visual culture there are no female versions of Denzel Washington or Wesley Snipes, nor any gay or lesbian heroes (*Arizona Heat* and, more recently, *Bound,* aside). Today, that is, the black body can be eroticized, as it always has been, and yet also be heroic: as long as it is so safely "masculine" as to remain within the bounds of the imaginary "nation."

These absences and exclusions tell us clearly that cultural hierarchy still mirrors social hierarchy: attenuated but still powerful. The invisible here, is evidence of the visible elsewhere. As long as cultural production is monopolized, in the form of resurgent capitalism and of more troubled yet still powerful patriarchy and racism, change in the politics of representation has stringent built-in limits. But material reality, and the divided consciousness that reflects it, is becoming too fragmented to be sutured together merely by the operations of ideology. Despite all the complaints about its white, middle-class bias, contemporary feminism—and the egalitarian ideal it reflects—is in Marx's words a theory that "has seized the masses," and thus has become "a material force" in its own right, bringing to light fissures and ruptures that we have felt but in most cases have not yet consciously assessed.[51]

Women as unsocialized, outcast heroes; women in quest of dangerous secrets; women pursuing vengeance; women engaged in physical combat; women as killers—all are tokens of our fragmented reality. Hollywood is not only a report, nor only a continuing inquest on, that reality. Movies and television programs cannot by themselves change the class/sex/gender/race system, but in showing changes that are ineluctably occurring they become part of the process of change. Hollywood is also a major part of that material reality. And what Hollywood is daily showing us, and will undoubtedly have shown us even more strongly by the time these words reach print, is that there are cracks in the pedestal. The cracks are widening, and Hollywood, even as it engages in the rearguard actions I have described here, is helping to widen them.

NOTES

Introduction

1 By cultural commodities I mean those "works and practices of intellectual and especially artistic activity" that are created for profit, and sold to a mass public on an impersonal marketplace. See Raymond Williams, *Keywords: A Vocabulary of Culture and Society* (New York: Oxford University Press, 1976), 80. "Visual culture," as I use it here, refers only to fiction film and television; "nonfiction television"—documentaries, news, and the like— properly belongs under the rubric of "information culture," or propaganda: on which see Elayne Rapping, *The Looking-Glass World of Non-Fiction TV* (Boston: South End, 1987); Edward S. Herman and Noam Chomsky, *Manufacturing Consent: The Political Economy of the Mass Media* (New York: Pantheon Books, 1988); and Michael Parenti, *Inventing Reality: The Politics of the Mass Media* (New York: St. Martin's, 1986). A good but already dated discussion of recent Hollywood cinema, from a standpoint somewhat similar to mine but less oriented toward an appreciation of cinematic ambiguity, is Michael Ryan and Douglas Kellner's *Camera Politica: The Politics and Ideology of Contemporary Hollywood Film* (Bloomington: Indiana University Press, 1988). Michael Parenti's *Make-Believe Media: The*

Politics of Entertainment (New York: St. Martin's, 1992), is the best overall treatment of the general topic indicated by its subtitle; nonetheless, it is more a selective attack on the propaganda value of Hollywood commodities than a guide to the ways in which their more subtle ideological themes are propagated.

2   The necessity of viewing mass culture as two things at once, normally confirmatory but also potentially disruptive, is argued by Robert A. White in "Mass Communications and Culture: The Transition to a New Paradigm," *Journal of Communications* 33, no. 3 (Summer 1983): 2–30.

3   See, for example, Susan Jefford's dissection of 1980s masculinity in *Hard Bodies: Hollywood Masculinity in the Reagan Era* (New Brunswick: Rutgers University Press, 1994); Ryan and Kellner, *Camera Politica;* and Parenti, *Make-Believe Media*. See also Elayne Rapping, "The View from Hollywood: The American Family and the American Dream," *Socialist Review* 13, no. 1 (January-February 1983): 71–92, and her "Liberation in Chains," *Cineaste* 17, no. 1 (1989): 4–11.

4   This insuperable logistical problem aside, an equally insuperable problem for a statistical reckoning with Hollywood is that it's impossible to reduce movies to a quantifiable unit of analysis that can be faithful to the seamless quality of fantasmatic narrative. Conservative critiques of Hollywood especially are all either tendentiously anecdotal, as Michael Medved's *Hollywood vs. America: Popular Culture and the War on Traditional Values* (New York: HarperCollins, 1992), or deploy a naive and illusory "social science" to cover up what is actually pure propaganda, as in the work of Stanley Rothman. See, for example, Stephen Powers, David J. Rothman, and Stanley Rothman, *Hollywood's America: Social and Political Themes in Motion Pictures* (Boulder, Colo.: Westview Press, 1996), or S. Robert Lichter, Linda Richter, and Stanley Rothman, *Prime Time: How Television Portrays American Culture* (Washington, D.C.: Regnery, 1994).

5   Conservatives were making up a story about the "liberal" press corps, for example, just at the moment when its posture toward Ronald Reagan was visibly "on bended knee," and the whole terrain of political discussion on television and in newspapers had shifted drastically rightward. Compare S. Robert Lichter, Stanley Rothman, and Linda Lichter's *The Media Elite* (Bethesda, Md.: Adler and Adler, 1986), with Mark Herstgaard, *On Bended Knee: The Press and the Reagan Presidency* (New York: Pantheon Books, 1989).

6   There are, of course, other ways of reading visual (or any) texts than through an ideological lens. For a brief but tremendously helpful exposition of this point, see Annette Kuhn's introduction to the collection of essays *Alien Zone: Cultural Theory and Contemporary Science Fiction Cinema*, ed. Kuhn (London: Verso Books, 1990), 1–14.

7   Pam Cook, in *The Cinema Book* (New York: Pantheon Books, 1985), 245.

8   A brief exemplary account of epistemological realism in this particular context might be helpful. *Thelma and Louise,* for example, is a "buddy movie" about two women on the run from the law. A particular audience might view them as, "deep down," symbolically two cross-dressing men, say; and draw all sorts of original and interesting interpretative analyses from that viewing. But they remain women, and the notion of them as "really men" could only make sense precisely because we know they are really women.

9   In this respect Marxian ideological critique has a good deal in common with the technique of deconstruction, in that they both demand a "suspicious reading" of cultural texts. The deconstructionist critique of language, though, in some sense cuts much deeper than does the Marxian critique of social structures. As well, Marxians have traditionally been loath to

interrogate the premises of their own founding texts. On a rapprochement between the two, see Michael Ryan, *Marxism and Deconstruction: A Critical Articulation* (Baltimore: Johns Hopkins University Press, 1982).

10   But see, for example, Laura Mulvey's suggestive, analogical assimilation of Freud to Marx in her "Some Thoughts on Theories of Fetishism in the Context of Contemporary Culture," *October* 65 (Summer 1993): 3–24. The most crucial intervention in the long effort of critical theorists to reconcile Marx and Freud is still Herbert Marcuse's *Eros and Civilization* (Boston: Beacon, 1955).

11   For a fuller account of the limitations of psychoanalytic critique in the ideological field, see Virginia Wright Wexman, "The Critic as Consumer: Film Study in the University, *Vertigo*, and the Film Canon," *Film Quarterly* 39 (Spring 1986): 32–41.

12   None of whom is in any way responsible for the uses or misuses to which I put their work. In particular, Linda Williams's *Hard Core: Power, Pleasure, and the "Frenzy of the Visible"* (Berkeley and Los Angeles: University of California Press, 1989), and Carol Clover's *Men, Women, and Chain Saws* (Princeton: Princeton University Press, 1992) were the direct inspiration both for my decision to undertake this work, and for the form the work has taken on, but I doubt that they would approve of the latter.

13   For example, Mary Anne Doane, in *Femmes Fatales: Feminism, Film Theory, Psychoanalysis* (New York: Routledge, 1991), concludes that its "disruptiveness" of "the given sexual knowledge . . . can define, for feminist theory, the deadliness of the femme fatale" (14). This conclusion is similar to the one I reach about the femme fatale in Chapter 9, and the writings of Doane and others I refer to in that chapter have helped me reach it. But I do so without embracing the psychoanalytic paradigm that enables them to suggest that generalization, and in that sense my work is parasitic on theirs.

14   Given this approach, my analysis is based, and could only be based, on the personal viewing of thousands of American movies and commercial television programs—although, in not a few cases, on a detailed account of television programs by other persons. The justification for this distinction is that, once one knows what the main characters in a television series look like, there is almost nothing else to "see"; visual mise-en-scène is only there to highlight either wisecracks or morally earnest dialogue. The leftover effects, the excess we call "beauty," that make the best cinema what it is, so that we can never surely rely on a purely expository account of a movie to tell us what we really need to know about it, are entirely absent from (commercial American) television.

15   Mimi White, "Ideological Analysis and Television," in *Channels of Discourse, Reassembled: Television and Contemporary Criticism*, ed. Robert C. Allen, 2d ed. (Chapel Hill: University of North Carolina Press, 1992), 170. White, of course, does not mean to imply that visual culture is the only such system; nor do I.

16   A careful reader will note that my wording, which is typical for this kind of discourse, seems to imply that females have no race, black people have no gender, and lesbians have neither. The implication, more or less forced on me by a structural, and overdetermined, defect in our common language, is unintended. On this point, see Elizabeth V. Spelman, *Inessential Woman: Problems of Exclusion in Feminist Thought* (Boston: Beacon, 1988).

17   See, for example, Deidre Pribhan, ed., *Female Spectators Looking at Film and Television* (New York: Verso, 1988).

18   Consider, for example, the erasures of African Americans and women described in Chapters 1 and 2 below.

19 In any event, even the most persuasive postmodernists are unable to carry out their own program to the bitter end, and invariably retreat to an endorsement of political ideals that can only be justified, or even referenced, from a realist standpoint. Compare, for example, Judith Butler's invocation of "the radical democratic impetus of feminist politics" with her later announcement that "my question is not whether certain kinds of significations are good or bad," in *Feminist Contentions: A Philosophical Exchange,* by Seyla Benhabib, Judith Butler, Drucilla Cornell, and Nancy Fraser (New York: Routledge, 1995), 51 and 138. No matter how hard we try, we cannot recognize democracy as a "signification" without already knowing what it signifies. And how can we avoid misrecognizing it—as in, say, the grassroots solidarity of American women who in defiance of the (male) authorities genitally mutilate their own daughters? In my view, the most useful efforts to navigate the epistemological morass are Stuart Hall's "The Problem of Ideology—Marxism without Guarantees," in *Marx 100 Years On,* ed. Betty Matthews (London: Lawrence and Wishart, 1983), 57–86; and Kate Soper, "Postmodernism, Subjectivity, Value," *New Left Review,* no. 186 (March-April 1991): 120–28.

20 For a more extended presentation of this argument, see my *Retrieving Democracy: In Search of Civic Equality* (Totowa, N.J.: Rowman and Allenheld, 1985), 219–24.

21 Michael Taussig, *The Nervous System* (New York: Routledge, 1992), 10.

22 In this I again depart from the methodology of contemporary cultural studies, which tends to require belief in the trustworthiness of the author as a theorist.

23 Robert Warshow, *The Immediate Experience: Movies, Comics, Theatre and Other Aspects of Popular Culture* (New York: Doubleday, 1962), 27. This is a posthumous collection of essays; the quotation is from a review of popular culture in *Commentary,* in 1954.

24 The self-description contained in the textual sentence is of course purely ideological. It implies the existence of a community (men? white men? white American male academics?) that in no way really exists as such: an abstraction brought into being only to negate other possible descriptions of self. "Heterosexual" is even more suspect, for that is not even a verifiable sociological category at all, and as a so-called identification may cover up more than it "reveals." Chapters 8 and 9 of this book, especially, are about male fetishism, which, in Freud's explanation of it, serves various functions, among them suppressing one's knowledge of one's latent bisexuality. In reading those chapters, therefore, the reader must be aware that my viewing of visual culture is likely also the viewing of the kind of Jewish male who, as Paul Breines puts it, does "not want to appear to be [a woman]." Paul Breines, *Tough Jews: Political Fantasies and the Moral Dilemma of American Jewry* (New York: Basic Books, 1990), 36.

25 Thus, for example, bell hooks argues (in her *Black Looks: Race and Represenation* [Boston: South End, 1992]) that "mainstream feminist film criticism in no way acknowledges black female spectatorship," and especially the "possibility that women can construct an oppositional gaze via an understanding and awareness of the politics of race and racism," (123); see also her *Yearning: Race, Gender, and Cultural Politics* (Boston: South End, 1990). For thinking about the racial culture of television from an African American perspective, Herman Gray's *Watching Race: Television and the Struggle for "Blackness"* (Minneapolis: University of Minnesota Press, 1995) is essential; as are, more generally, Jannette Dates and Williams Barlow, eds., *Split Image: African Americans in the Mass Media* (Washington, D.C.: Howard University Press, 1990); Colin MacCabe and Cornell West, eds., *White Screens, Black Images: Hollywood from the Dark Side* (New York: Routledge, 1994); and especially Marlon Riggs's documentary film histories of black stereotypes, *Color Adjustment* and *Ethnic Notions.*

26 To take just one example, though I am aware of my own whiteness, I cannot possibly see it in cultural commodities in the same way as does a nonwhite critic such as bell hooks. See her "Representations of Whiteness" in *Black Looks*, 165–78.

27 Thus creating an endless regress of self-reflexivity from which no escape is possible.

28 See Laura Mulvey, "Visual Pleasure and Narrative Cinema," *Screen* 16, no. 3 (1975): 6–18. This essay has been reprinted in many collections both of film theory and of feminist cultural studies. As Deborah Linderman summarizes it (in "The Mise-en-Abîme in Hitchcock's *Vertigo*," *Cinema Journal* 30, no. 4 [Summer 1991]): "spectatorial fantasies of transcendence through intratextual scenarios of voyeurism and fetishism [are] enacted by male characters" (61).

29 The most viciously inquisitorial of these is Michael Medved's *Hollywood vs. America*; on this point, see especially his chaps. 2 and 6–12. The family resemblance of his title to postwar assaults on "unAmericanism" is intentional, not accidental.

30 These remarks about feminist film studies have the intrinsic shortcomings of any such generalization. They do not apply, for example, to the work of Linda Williams, who has made a notable effort to try to see what men are seeing when they view hardcore films; or to Carol Clover's work on the horror film. Still, even their considerations of the putative male viewer are for the most part psychoanalytically abstract, and any concretion that might be granted to them remains largely at the level of implication.

31 For example, Susan Jeffords's *Hard Bodies* is a detailed account of one kind of male-oriented genre that I discuss in Chapter 5. However, it is essentially a woman's account of what men might see when looking at a certain presentation of the male body; for obvious reasons, she cannot provide a man's account of that. Nor does she note, given this focus, how problematic it may be to determine what men see when they gaze at the "hard bodies" of *women*.

1 Ideology, Gender, and Visual Culture

1 The secondary and textual literature on ideology would fill a five-foot bookshelf. An analytic and historical development of the subject that is closest in spirit to my brief remarks here is Mike [Michael J.] Cormack, *Ideology*, Batsford Cultural Studies (London: Batsford, 1992). For a lengthier discussion of some subsidiary but crucial themes treated cursorily in the following pages, see Philip Green, " 'I Have A Philosophy, You Have an Ideology': Is Social Criticism Possible?" *Massachusetts Review* 32, no. 2 (Summer 1991): 199–217.

2 Louis Althusser, *Lenin and Philosophy, and Other Essays*, trans. Ben Brewster (New York: Monthly Review Press, 1971), 162. I should say here that it is possible to adapt aspects of Althusser's critical conception of ideology for use, as I do throughout this chapter, without thereby committing oneself to his complete philosophical system, in which "Marxist science" is opposed to ideology, and the subjection of persons to ideological discourse is held to be a functionally necessary requirement of social order. The purely negative critique of ideological mythmaking has its own problems, to which I shall refer; but they are not nearly so serious as they become when that critique is combined, as by Althusser, with a positive (scientific and functionalist) deployment of the concept. See note 7.

3 This approach to "ideology" gives no warrant for the notion that only persons belonging to the class of "intellectuals" are capable of either self-understanding, or the understanding of society and its cultural expressions. The fictitiousness of the (partially) fictitious community is not an artifact of some arcane system of knowledge. It is visible to any persons capable of

perceiving an evident discrepancy between how they are said to live and how they see themselves actually living, even though they may not be able to produce a complicated theoretical explanation of the discrepancy. Indeed, Marx thought that precisely because of the depth of its exclusion from the (fictitious) bourgeois Republic of equals, the formally uneducated proletariat was the class *most* capable of distinguishing myth from reality: "Law, morality, religion, are to [the proletarian] so many bourgeois prejudices, behind which lurk in ambush just as many bourgeois interests." In a different way, this is what Antonio Gramsci meant when he said that everyone is an intellectual, even though only a few people have the social function of intellectuals. See "The Manifesto of the Communist Party," in *The Marx-Engels Reader*, 2d ed. (New York: Norton, 1978; originally published 1972), 482; and Gramsci's *Selections from the Prison Notebooks of Antonio Gramsci*, ed. and trans. Quintin Hoare and Geoffrey Nowell Smith (New York: International Publishers, 1971), 9.

4   Jacqueline Rose, "Feminism and Its Discontents," in *Sexuality in the Field of Vision* (London: Verso, 1986), 90.

5   In Herbert Marcuse, *Eros and Civilization: A Philosophical Inquiry into Freud* (Boston: Beacon, 1966).

6   Herman Melville's Bartleby in "Bartleby the Scrivener," who repeatedly refuses to act because "I would prefer not to," and Christopher Tietjens, the tragic hero of Ford Madox Ford's trilogy *Parade's End,* who decides that there is no reason ever to get out of his bed again, are perhaps the most unnerving confrontations with the possibility of meaninglessness in the history of fiction. "Bartleby" was shown as a short play on the Public Broadcasting System; we can be fairly certain it will never be made as a mainstream movie.

7   Althusser, *Lenin and Philosophy*, esp. 174 and 182. As many commentators and critics have noted, there is sometimes an apparent paradox inherent in his deployment of the concept "interpellation," especially in the suggestion that the quintessential act of interpellation is our subjection to the Law's recognition. If our consciousnesses are fully constituted by interpellation, are we less than fully human in its absence? Aside from the elitism inherent in this stance (either Althusser was somehow interpellated as a Communist philosopher in a bourgeois social order, or else he arrived at his knowledge in an independent manner he denies to everyone else), it also renders the possibility of human emancipation unimaginable. Alternatively, if there is a pre-ideological self, if we are all potentially self-reflective in the absence of ideological interpellation, then its effects are arbitrary and contingent, and as a concept interpellation can bear little explanatory weight. The escape from this paradox lies in rejecting sociological functionalism and historical determinism. Yes, ideology is necessary for social stability; but social stability itself is not guaranteed by the operations of either society or history. Thus human emancipation remains conceivable, even if not immediately practicable.

8   The best extended discussion of how visual culture came to be conceived of as both an apparatus for the transmission of hegemonic discourses *and* a site of ideological struggle, is Stuart Hall, "The Rediscovery of 'Ideology': Return of the Repressed in Media Studies," in *Culture, Society and the Media,* ed. Michael Gurevitch et al. (New York: Methuen, 1982), 56–91. As to the former, "what [is] at issue [is] no longer specific injunctions, by A to B, to do this or that, but a shaping of the whole ideological environment: a way of representing the order of things which [endows] its limiting perspectives with that natural or divine inevitability which makes them appear universal, natural and coterminous with 'reality' itself. This movement . . . is indeed the characteristic and defining mechanism of 'the ideological' " (65).

9   The tradition of slapstick comedy, of which Lucille Ball and Sid Caesar were the last great American exponents, is the most noteworthy exception to this generalization; its hints of subversive anarchy stem from its rejection of naturalism. The disappearance of slapstick from American television (traces of it, and of non-naturalistic farce, can still be found in cinema) is probably evidence of a kind of triumph of the accommodation to hegemonic ideology described by Herbert Marcuse in *One-Dimensional Man: Studies in the Ideology of Advanced Industrial Society* (Boston: Beacon, 1964). It should be said that Marlon Brando, whose historical reputation is built around his supposedly having introduced "naturalistic" acting into visual culture, actually did something quite different. He is the one Hollywood actor who has consistently drawn attention to the fact that he is an actor; thus he occasionally conveys a kind of critical awareness of authorship that we usually associate with European cinema.

10 See Kuhn's *The Power of the Image: Essays on Representation and Sexuality* (London: Routledge and Kegan Paul, 1985): "A photograph stands as evidence that whatever is inside the frame of the image 'really' happened, was 'really' there" (26); "The visible is all" (32); "Pornographic images participate in photography's more general project of privileging the visible, of equating visibility with truth" (40); and "As spectacle, cinema [claims] a peculiar credibility on behalf of the visible" (65). The major work on classical Hollywood film style is David Bordwell, Janet Staiger, and Kristin Thompson's *Classical Hollywood Cinema: Film Style and Mode of Production to 1960* (New York: Columbia University Press, 1985). An excellent summary is "Classical Hollywood Cinema" by Mary Beth Haralovich in *The Women's Companion to International Film*, ed. Annette Kuhn with Susannah Radstone (Berkeley and Los Angeles: University of California Press, 1994; originally published, London: Virago, 1990).

11 Stanley Kubrick is the one "Hollywood" artist who has consistently rebelled against the Hollywood style, as opposed to those many writers and directors who have only pushed slightly at the ideological boundaries of American liberal orthodoxy. What I call "style" is much more pervasive than the mere denotation of a political position. *The Killing; Dr. Strangelove; or, How I Learned to Stop Worrying and Love the Bomb; A Clockwork Orange;* and *Full Metal Jacket* are especially interesting as stylistic deviations, and look almost "un-American" in their context.

12 An understanding of what is *absent* from dominant visual culture can be gained by reading, for example, the science fiction of women such as Ursula Le Guin, Marge Piercy, Anne McCaffrey, Joanna Russ, Marion Zimmer Bradley, Mercedes Lackey, C. T. Cherryh, or Elizabeth Moon. Even better, one can see the all-woman production of *Henry V* put on by The Company of Women, the theatrical group co-founded by Carol Gilligan and actress/director Kristin Linklater. It is fascinating, for example, how Henry's "wooing" of Catherine in the last act visibly becomes not a seduction but a rape, without a word of Shakespeare's original text being changed.

13 Hortense Powdermaker's classic *Hollywood, the Dream Factory: An Anthropologist Looks at the Movie-Makers* (Boston: Little, Brown, 1950), is still the best account of this process.

14 For the best discussion of genre or episodic television as a narrative style, see Sarah Kozloff, in "Narrative Theory and Television," in *Channels of Discourse, Reassembled: Television and Contemporary Criticism*, 2d ed., ed. Robert C. Allen (Chapel Hill: University of North Carolina Press, 1992), 67–100.

15 Now that auteur theory is common parlance, Hollywood movie directors often "sign" their films in one way or another; but this is the last one hears of their authorship.

16 On narrative television and its distinctiveness from cinema, see especially John Ellis, *Visible Fictions: Cinema, TV, Video* (New York: Routledge Books, 1982), esp. 111–71.

17 Nor did it prevent Mill from doing the same; see his *The Subjection of Women* (Arlington Heights, Ill.: Harlan Davidson, 1980; originally published 1869), 48 (the last paragraph of chap. 2).

18 For example, the world's foremost concert percussion soloist, Evelyn Glennie, even after becoming totally deaf at age thirteen, took up percussion with the full support of her family and her male mentor, himself a great percussionist.

19 See Susie Orbach, *Fat Is a Feminist Issue: The Anti-Diet Guide to Permanent Weight Loss* (New York: Paddington, 1978; reprint, New York: Berkeley Books, 1985).

20 On the new heroine, see Chapter 8.

21 Karl Marx, *Capital* (International Publishers: New York, 1977), vol. 1, part 1, chap. 1, sec. 4, "The Fetishism of Commodities and the Secret Thereof."

22 To repeat, these remarks about interpellation concern only the content and form of cinema and television, not any actual effects they might have on behavior.

23 The uninflected naturalism of Hollywood can only be understood in contrast with its opposite. For example, an American television watcher would have to see a product of British television such as *Pennies from Heaven* or *The Singing Detective*, even to begin to comprehend what non-naturalistic television might look like.

24 Though as Mark Crispin Miller points out, this becomes less and less true of movies designed as ads for the products of their multinational studios/sponsors. See his "Hollywood the Ad," *Atlantic Monthly* (April 1990): 41–68.

25 There are television programs (that is, news-format documentaries such as *Sixty Minutes* or *Frontline*) that occasionally encourage viewer activity to right some apparent wrong. These are exceptions to my generalization, but usually rather feeble exceptions. Picking up a phone or writing an angry letter is the most organized activity they encourage us to take part in.

26 I use the awkward term "patriarchalist capitalism" in preference to "capitalist patriarchy." I do not thereby mean to imply that political economy is more fundamental than the economy of gender. Rather, "patriarchy" is an inaccurate description of the contemporary sex/gender system, as would be instantly clear to anyone who had ever set foot in a real patriarchy. Unfortunately, there is no term for describing sex/gender economy as accurately as "capitalism" describes political economy.

27 Anyone who has ever seen Antonia Bird's British television film, *Safe* (about two homeless and desperate teenagers) or Ken Loach's film *Ladybird Ladybird* (about an Englishwoman deprived of her children one after another by so-called social services, material deprivation, and her own genuine inability to cope) will know what I mean. Charles Burnett's *Sidewalk Stories* is the only American film that comes close to this effect; it was not made in Hollywood.

28 Robert B. Ray's *A Certain Tendency of the Hollywood Cinema, 1930–1980* (Princeton: Princeton University Press, 1985) is the best discussion of the ubiquity of this theme in American cinema.

2 Erasures

1 See Benjamin Barber, *Jihad vs. McWorld* (New York: Times Books, 1995).

2 See the comments of Judith Williamson in *Deadline at Dawn: Film Criticism, 1980–1990* (London: Marion Boyars, 1993), 250–51. On the erasure of proletarian labor in a classic of the

feminist canon, see Laura Green, " 'The Successor of these Poor Girls': Class, Gender, and the Limits of Individualism in *Jane Eyre*," *Dickens World* 7 (Summer 1991): 17–30.

3 Marx, *Capital* (New York: International Publishers, 1967), 1:72.

4 The power of this ideological hierarchalization crosses race lines as well, as evidenced in such 1970s black-oriented shows such as *Good Times, Sanford and Son,* and *What's Happening!* in all of which wisdom was to be found among the unemployed or underemployed residents of the ghetto; see Herman Gray, *Watching Race: Television and the Struggle for Blackness* (Minneapolis: University of Minnesota Press, 1995), 77.

5 In visual culture, iconography almost always tells the story. The difference between Tom Hanks and Peter Sellers is precisely the difference between ideological sentimentality and satire.

6 See Stanley Aronowitz, "Working Class Culture in the Electronic Age," in *Cultural Politics in Contemporary America,* ed. Ian Angus and Sut Jhally (New York: Routledge, 1989), pp. 135–50.

7 Ibid., 149. In *Criminal Behavior,* as though illustrating Aronowitz's point, Farrah Fawcett chooses tough-looking, sexy cop A. Martinez over soft, epicene judge Cliff De Young.

8 The best full-length study of Hollywood's labor relations is a Ph.D. dissertation, "Motion Picture Craft Workers and Craft Unions in Hollywood: The Studio Era, 1912–1948," by Michael C. Nielsen (University of Illinois at Urbana-Champagne, 1985; available from University Microfilms International, Ann Arbor, Mich.). The most revealing brief account is Denise Hartsough, "Crime Pays: The Studios' Labor Deals in the 1930s," *Velvet Light Trap,* no. 23 (Spring 1989): 49–63. See among other (but not many other) accounts, Louis B. Perry and Richard S. Perry, *A History of the Los Angeles Labor Movement, 1911–1941* (Berkeley and Los Angeles: University of California Press, 1963); Murray Ross, *Stars and Strikes: Unionization of Hollywood* (New York: Columbia University Press, 1941); Larry Ceplair and Steven Englund, *The Inquisition in Hollywood: Politics in the Film Community, 1930–1960* (Garden City, N.Y.: Doubleday, 1980); and Dan Moldea, *Dark Victory: Ronald Reagan, MCA, and the Mob* (New York: Viking, 1986). It's typical of the success with which Hollywood has erased its own economic history that the authoritative *The American Film Industry,* rev. ed., ed. by Tino Balio (Madison: University of Wisconsin Press, 1985), has twenty-two essays, but only eight pages (271–79) of the editor's introduction to part 3 ("A Mature Oligopoly, 1930–1948") devoted to labor relations.

9 See Jane Feuer, *The Hollywood Musical* (Bloomington: Indiana University Press, 1982; 2d ed., Houndmills, Basingstoke, Hampshire: Macmillan, 1993), chap. 1. *Summer Stock* is the paradigm instance.

10 Laura Mulvey, "Some Thoughts on Theories of Fetishism in the Context of Contemporary Culture," *October* 65 (Summer 1993): 10.

11 See "Women in Hollywood," special issue of *Premiere* (1993): 35.

12 Interestingly, the strongest representation of women on television occurred during the 1980s in the new genre of black-oriented programs, though again mostly in writing and production rather than directorial roles.

13 Mulvey has modified her original formulation of the problem of "visual pleasure" somewhat, particularly to address the problem (elided by her in *Screen*) of female spectatorship; see Mulvey, "Afterthoughts on 'Visual Pleasure and Narrative Cinema' Inspired by 'Duel in the Sun,' " *Framework* 15–17 (Summer 1981): 12–15. On the meanings and uses of "glamour," see Kuhn, *The Power of the Image: Essays on Representation and Sexuality* (London: Routledge

222 Notes to Pages 39–42

and Kegan Paul), chap. 1 (written in collaboration with Frances Borzello, Jill Pack, and Cassandra Wedd).

14 Fittingly, the same issue of *Premiere* that highlights the statistics of women's exclusion from power in Hollywood, has interviews with Jodie Foster, Sally Field, and Demi Moore, in which they complain about their treatment—and are focused in the most glamorous possible, gauzy soft focus.

15 See her remarks in *Vanity Fair* for February 1994.

16 In the minor thriller *Liquid Dreams,* the protagonist is a woman who is virtually omnipresent, as though doing a one-woman stage show; yet the credits of the film read "Starring Richard Steinmetz." Has anyone ever heard of Richard Steinmetz?

17 Obviously, if this were literally true, this whole book would be otiose, because we would be living in a different civilization. Rather, by "story" I mean a bare-bones outline of the plot. For example, the 1996 film *Eraser* is about a man who helps people disappear completely. There is a *literary* character, "Jane Whitefield," who does exactly that in two exciting, well-reviewed books by Thomas Perry; the first, *Vanishing Act,* came out well before *Eraser.* Did the authors of *Eraser* read *Vanishing Act?* Do bears hibernate?

18 This is most visible of all in the video games that boys and young men play at shopping malls, in which male heroes battle male villains with the very occasional help of female sidekicks.

19 See *TV Guide* for New England, the week of 21–27 January 1995. I have counted episodes of *Cops,* even though these purport to be nonfictional. Anyone who accepts that pretense has probably not read this far.

20 That is also sometimes true of Angela Lansbury's *Murder, She Wrote,* depending on the protagonists of the mystery she solves.

21 As reported by Pat Aufderheid, in *In These Times,* 9–15 December 1987, p. 21.

22 To clarify a much-abused term: when I use the word "realistic" approvingly, I mean "enabling us to appreciate how some aspect of the social world actually does function." When I speak pejoratively of Hollywood's "realism" or "pseudorealism," I mean the multiplication of surfaces—New York's streets, California's freeways, white skins and dark skins, the overt signs of gender differentiation—that let us think we're looking at the actual world while concealing its nature from us.

23 Susan Brownmiller to the contrary, therefore, male voyeurs are not the advance guard of rapists. Rapists are not voyeurs who've slipped the leash; some men who commit rape may be unable to contain their secret sexual lust for women, but most are misogynists who can't contain their desire to dominate or hurt women. A male voyeur, except for those whose voyeurism has itself got out of control, is most likely a man who has thoroughly internalized the sexual prohibitions of conventional morality.

24 On this point see chapter 2 of Jane Tompkins's wonderful *West of Everything: The Inner Life of Westerns* (New York: Oxford University Press, 1992).

25 Peter Biskind and Barbara Ehrenreich, "Machismo and Hollywood's Working Class," in *American Media and Mass Culture: Left Perspectives,* ed. Donald Lazere (Berkeley and Los Angeles: University of California Press, 1987), 201.

26 Mulvey argues inferentially that it would have been less inflected with the dominant ideology, and that is certainly true: the dominant ideology is what attractive women sell. But Mulvey doesn't say that movies such as her own *Riddles of the Sphinx* would be more pleasurable than dominant cinema. Quite the contrary: her argument is, or was, that "visual pleasure" is what has to be abolished.

27 Perhaps "win" would be a more precisely correct word than "buy," as most Hollywood success stories are about luck rather than accomplishment; that is, they are about the conjunction of exceptional skill with a fortuitous opportunity for heroism.

28 *Criminal Behavior,* referred to above, is the perfect example. Classical cinema's elegies for lost manhood, in which women completely—or almost completely—disappear (e.g., *All Quiet on the Western Front, Angels with Dirty Faces, I Am a Fugitive from a Chain Gang, Brute Force*) clarify the meaning of this structure. Where there are no women to be won, there is nothing to be gained.

29 See *TV Guide* for 21–27 January 1995.

30 See Mulvey's "Afterthoughts," as cited in note 13.

31 To understand these films as a method, one would have to see their functional critique, John Cassavetes' *Gloria,* an uninhibited *hommage* to a self-defining woman (i.e., his wife Gena Rowlands).

32 If the cinematic spectacle were *sexually* spectacular, the male market for hard-core would be considerably diminished.

33 On the role of the female consumer in patriarchal capitalism, see Amy Bridges and Batya Weinbaum, "The Other Side of the Paycheck: Monopoly Capital and the Structure of Consumption," *Monthly Review* 28, no. 3 (1976): 88–103. On the development of the American advertising industry and "consumerism," see Stuart and Elizabeth Ewen, *Channels of Desire: Mass Images and the Shaping of the American Consciousness* (New York: McGraw-Hill, 1982); and for a theoretical overview, Sut Jhally, *The Codes of Advertising: Fetishism and the Political Economy of Meaning in the Consumer Society* (New York: Routledge Books, 1990).

34 See Ella Taylor, *Prime Time Families: Television Culture in Postwar America* (Berkeley and Los Angeles: University of California Press, 1989), chap. 5, for a documentation of this generalization, even though she values 1970s workplace comedy/dramas more highly than I do.

35 See Williamson, *Deadline at Dawn,* 65; and Joan Smith, *Misogynies: Reflections on Myths and Malice* (New York: Fawcett Columbine, 1989), 21–35.

36 That Melanie Griffith wins both the job and the man that Weaver loses is not a case of piling it on: it's the same result seen in two different ways. *Becoming* a family woman validates the career; never having been one vitiates it. On the subject of independent women in recent cinema, see Elizabeth Traube, *Dreaming Identities: Class, Gender, and Generation in 1980s Hollywood Film* (Boulder, Colo.: Westview, 1993).

37 See for example the 1994 episode of *Who's the Boss?* in which Samantha has to be cajoled into going to college, while her younger stepbrother is already preparing to become a famous doctor. One would never know from watching teen TV that a majority of medical school admissions are now women.

3 Ideological Destinies

1 On the transformation of domination into hegemony, see Howard Winant, *Racial Conditions: Politics, Theory, Comparisons* (Minneapolis: University of Minnesota Press, 1994), chap. 3.

2 *Psycho,* in 1960, was so terrifying precisely because, for the first time in audience memory, fate was completely severed from desert. The absence of that linkage is what makes a true horror movie.

3   Thus during the 1995 season of television's *Baywatch* there was a female character whose sole function was to give responsible advice to the main protagonists. She was much less bosomy than the other female regulars: a contrast which suggests that her iconographic role was to insulate certain kinds of moral positioning from the heroics and romance that are otherwise the show's staple narrative elements. It is the latter, then, that constitute the "real" morality of the series.

4   Thanks to Jennifer Accongio for this reference.

5   See Judith Williamson, *Deadline at Dawn: Film Criticism, 1980–1990* (London: Marion Boyars, 1993), 39.

6   See Chapter 9, note 30.

7   Joan Smith, in an essay entitled "There's Only One Yorkshire Ripper," in her *Misogynies* (New York: Fawcett Columbine, 1991), demonstrates that the Yorkshire police actually lost a chance to catch the Ripper early on in his career, because they assumed his victims had to be sexually "guilty" and so misclassified both victims and nonvictims.

8   Shannon Faulkner, the first woman to enroll at the Citadel, could tell us all about this.

9   See the article, "Good Girls, Bad Girls, And How TV Scrambles the Signals," by Betsey Sharkey, in the *New York Times* Arts and Leisure section, 17 September 1995, p. 1. Sharkey begins a general discussion of the fine line Hollywood must tread when treating women's sexuality with the following anecdote: "Not long ago, Brett Butler, star of the hit ABC Comedy 'Grace under Fire,' was stopped by a fan on the street. 'She told me she didn't think it was right when Grace slept with a man,' Ms. Butler recalls."

10 As one observer put it about an episode of *Home Improvement*, "the characters were basically divided into three types: male, female, and fat." And, "the one extremely overweight character on the show is the one who the males don't accept for their ritual fixing of the car" (Lisa Hix, in an unpublished paper).

11 For a taste of what such a movie might be like, one could do no better than see the amateurish but quite wonderful independent film, *Lesbionage*.

12 Weaver has remarked that as soon as she walks into a room she knows whether she'll be able to work with the men in it: if a man remains seated while shaking hands with her, his male chauvinism will be unappeasable. This kind of calculation is routine in Hollywood history: witness the pairing of Sophia Loren and Alan Ladd in *Boy on a Dolphin,* she being put in a ditch for all the scenes, including kissing scenes, that perforce had them side by side.

13 The immediate trigger of his final rage is her cutting remark that he can't even be sure the child would have been his.

14 Most, though not all, of the time, it does not even matter when the director is, as in this case, a woman.

15 *Jacob's Ladder* is a rare exception, and even it pulls its counterideological punch at the last minute.

16 See Chapter 9 for a further discussion of this genre. On the films of Gorris, see below.

17 *The Asphalt Jungle* is in large measure a critique of the law-and-order genre. I shall have more to say about this kind of hard-to-find cinematic ambiguity in Chapter 7. A professor of psychology once said to me, scathingly, that I only liked *The Asphalt Jungle* because I was really an anarchist at heart; that still seems to me the best compliment a Hollywood film can merit.

18 As in *Salt of the Earth.* See Martha Ackelsberg, *Free Women of Spain: Anarchism and the Struggle for the Emancipation of Women* (Bloomington: Indiana University Press, 1991).

19   Antonio Gramsci, *Selections from the Prison Notebooks of Antonio Gramsci*, ed. and trans. by Quintin Hoare and Geoffrey Nowell Smith (New York: International Publishers, 1971), 12.

20   Tony Garnett, the producer of British TV's *Between the Lines*, discussed in Chapter 6 below, remarks that although for public relations reasons the London Metropolitan Police were willing to give complete cooperation to the making of what was an unabashedly critical and presumably "realistic" series, he immediately discovered that he had to make one major compromise: the real language of London policemen simply could not be reproduced on television, for there was very little of it other than obscenity. Needless to say, this single omission completely falsifies the nature of policemen as social beings.

21   In the same way, in movies about political institutions the internal enemy who momentarily obstructs national unity may be a psychopathic officer (e.g., *Attack*, or *Seven Days in May*) or a corrupt politician (*Mr. Smith Goes to Washington, Born Yesterday*, the Rambo movies) or businessman *(Aliens)*, who must be removed from his position of authority for the moral universe to be righted; that is, returned to its normal and natural order.

22   When I first saw *Aliens* at the local mall, at the precise moment when Ripley strips down to her undershirt and picks up her weapon, a man in the audience leaped to his feet, thrust his clenched fist in the air, and shouted "Go!"

23   Apparently Gene Roddenberry, the original creator of *Star Trek*, had intended to make her a central, and explicitly lesbian, character in the new series. When he died just as it got under way, the new producers quickly scrapped her part.

24   In the British television series *Band of Gold*, a prostitute, who in the initial episode has seemed to be the character we are supposed to identify with sympathetically, is murdered, leaving behind two children and a babe in arms. Her friends keep asking, "What will become of her children?" and no reassuring answer is ever given. I cannot recall even once seeing such a dénouement from Hollywood, in fifty years of consuming its visual commodities.

25   Sometimes of course these ideological destinies are overdetermined. In *Aliens*, for instance, Weaver is both a nurturer *and* desexualized; Jenette Goldstein (Vasquez) is a tough cookie *and* a fetishist's dream: there is no way she can survive that combination.

26   As bell hooks points out in a commentary on Madonna's video "Like a Prayer" "the taboo expression" of white female sexual agency "is choosing to be sexual with black men. Unfortunately, this is a continuation of the notion that ending racist domination is really about issues of interracial sexual access"; see her *Yearning: Race, Gender, and Cultural Politics* (Boston: South End, 1990), 60–61. Access, that is, of men to women—though even this is carefully regulated, as the fate of Lawrence Fishburne in *Bad Company* testifies. The only such "romance" I can think of that concludes unproblematically is that between Raquel Welch and Jim Brown in *100 Rifles*: two sex objects meeting, or more to the point colliding, on equal terms. Black women partnering (or hoping to partner) white men, as during the 1993 season of the soap opera *All My Children*, are less frequent, since (1) black women are a relatively smaller segment of any potential viewing audience than are white women, and (2) to secure the attention of most white men the question would have to be posed the other way around.

27   Of course the image of black men that Washington et al. convey is still submerged in the much more frequent image of, as Ishmael Reed puts it, "black men . . . shown naked from the waist up, handcuffed, and leaning over a police car" (quoted by hooks in *Yearning*, 74).

28   The last two are designed for what bell hooks calls "selling hot pussy"; see hooks, *Black Looks: Race and Representation* (Boston: South End, 1992), chap. 4. As for Latina women, the

situation is changing, as they have come to hold an intermediate cultural (or rather sexual) position. Thus in the 1995–96 season, the soap opera *All My Children* featured a Latino family with three daughters, two of whom were sexually involved with white men, and one with a black man. In *Criminal Behavior,* discussed briefly earlier, Farrah Fawcett chooses a Hispanic cop over a white judge. And see my discussion of *The Money Train,* below.

29   See Chapter 8.

30   This point perhaps needs clarification. As compared with my imaginary scenario of the lesbian hero on the run, or with the actual movie *Lesbionage,* the gay women in these films are themselves malevolently violent.

31   This is by no means to say that women may not find great pleasure in watching her perform, or just in looking at her hard body. On the whole question of female spectatorship I can only report what women have told me, or have written publicly. See for example the discussion of *Terminator 2* by Kirsten Marthe Lentz, "The Popular Pleasures of Female Revenge (Or Rage Bursting in a Blaze of Gunfire)," *Cultural Studies* 7, no. 3 (October 1993): 374–403. The topic of female action/adventure heroes is taken up at length in Chapter 8.

32   See Carol Clover, *Men, Women, and Chain Saws* (Princeton: Princeton University Press, 1992), 33–36.

33   Kally Lloyd-Jones in *The Women's Companion to International Film,* ed. Annette Kuhn with Susannah Radstone (Berkeley and Los Angeles: University of California Press, 1994; originally published London: Virago, 1990), 109.

34   Joan Acocella remarks (in a private communication) that ballet more than any other art form is primarily about exploring the capacities of women; in this case, the use of the female body in ways that men cannot emulate (e.g., women's greater thigh rotation and more supple waists). Narratively and thus visually this exploration is for the use of men, as in the lifts that signal man's greater social as well as personal power. But that ideological signification diminishes and may even disappear under the greater symbolic weight of purely kinesthetic pleasure in the elaborations of female movement.

35   I have Lisa Hix to thank for this formulation.

36   Kate Ellis, "Gimme Shelter: Feminism, Fantasy, and Women's Popular Fiction, in *American Media and Mass Culture: Left Perspectives,* ed. Donald Lazere (Berkeley and Los Angeles: University of California Press, 1987), 223.

37   Gina Rourke notes of the episode of *Home Improvement* in which Jill decides to go back to school, that "she chastises her husband and sons for being louts, unsupportive, and unwilling to pick up the slack on the domestic front."

38   Typically, though she is a working woman we never see her working.

39   Actually not the latest. That honor belongs to Tony Danza on the 1995 series *Hudson Street* when, in reply to his son's counsel to "just be yourself, dad," he replies, "That's why your mother left me." Rueful or not, we can hear the unspoken epithet at the end of that sentence.

40   Anne Deutsch drew this to my attention.

41   Herman Gray, in *Watching Race: Television and the Struggle for "Blackness"* (Minneapolis: University of Minnesota Press, 1995), V. 82, points out that in the wake of *The Cosby Show,* most black-oriented sitcoms "provided familiar (and comfortable) renderings of black middle-class family life in the United States"—which, as he also notes (on p. 79) were not distinctively different from television's renderings of white middle-class family life.

42   See, most notably, Tania Modleski, *Loving With a Vengeance: Mass-Produced Fantasies for Women* (Hamden, Conn.: Archon Books, 1982); and Martha Nochimson, *No End to Her:*

Soap Opera and the Female Subject (Berkeley and Los Angeles: University of California Press, 1992).

43   "The soaps aren't a reflief from the domestic routine which oppresses their viewers but a confirmation of it: watching them becomes another unshirkable daily chore." Peter Conrad, *Television: The Medium and Its Manners* (London: Routledge and Kegan Paul, 1982), 71.

44   "Subversive" readings of vulgar texts run the constant danger of being foolish in their efforts to rescue vulgarity for a more productive "reading." In this regard the following comparison, from Nochimson, *No End to Her,* is surely the most fatuous attempt ever at recuperating popular culture aimed at women for feminism: "Beauty in conventional screen fiction also establishes an exclusive norm. Hollywood reduces beauty to mastery. . . . It is the erotic possession of the glamorous woman by the camera eye. . . . Beauty [however] in soap opera is the beauty of dialogue, mutuality, and connection. It is the aesthetics of intimacy in the family story" (194). This confusion of the gaze (women presumably don't want to possess other women) with what is being gazed at (sheer glamour reiterated over and over) makes all analysis unnecessary, since anything can be made into its opposite.

45   See Modleski's comments on the villainess in *Loving With a Vengeance,* 94–98.

46   In Great Britain, where censorship of film and television is official, the censor's attention to detail is greater and the public's knowledge of it more extensive. Thus it's a matter of common knowledge that *erect* penises are totally prohibited; to be shown, they have to be either soft or, in the words of one art critic, "leaning against something."

4   Recuperating the Sexual Order

1   Sacvan Bercovitch, *The Rites of Assent: Transformations in the Symbolic Construction of America* (New York: Routledge, 1993), 355.

2   Hartz, *The Liberal Tradition in America: An Interpretation of American Political Thought since the Revolution* (New York: Harcourt Brace, 1955).

3   Even though television's repetitive episodic nature militates against formulaic resolutions of any kind, whole series have been elaborations of this convention, such as *Moonlighting* or *Anything But Love.*

4   "[P]opular genres often function in a way similar to the way myth functions—to work through social contradictions in the form of narrative so that very real problems can be transposed to the realm of fantasy and apparently solved there." See Gina Marchetti, "Action Adventure as Ideology," in *Cultural Politics in Contemporary America,* ed. Ian Angus and Sut Jhally (New York: Routledge, 1989), 187.

5   Marchetti, in "Action Adventure," has an excellent brief discussion and summary of the necessary tension in mass popular culture between ideological conformity and uneasiness or apparent resistance.

6   See Stephanie Coontz, *The Way We Never Were: American Families and the Nostalgia Trap* (New York: Basic Books, 1992).

7   The term "postfeminist" is a cant phrase, used alternately to denigrate the accomplishments of feminism or to deny the necessity of continuing its historical project. "Postliberation" is accurate, in that the revolutionary program of the early women's liberation movement has indeed been swept aside by reform, reaction, and the awful inertia of the present.

8   Mary Ellen Brown, *Soap Opera and Women's Talk: The Pleasure of Resistance* (Thousand Oaks, Calif.: Sage, 1994), 112.

9   Oriana Noel Lewis pointed this out to me.

10 This theme, as noted earlier, is later repeated on a 1995 episode of the television series, *The Marshal*.

11 "The outlaw hero" is Robert Ray's useful phrase to describe one of Hollywood's most ubiquitous "thematic paradigms," the story of the unsocialized hero who must be reintegrated into society. See Robert B. Ray, *A Certain Tendency of the Hollywood Cinema, 1930–1980* (Princeton: Princeton University Press, 1985).

12 For an informative and detailed, but slightly overenthusiastic consideration, see Elayne Rapping, *The Movie of the Week: Private Stories, Public Events* (Minneapolis: University of Minnesota Press, 1992).

13 Judith Mayne calls this phenomenon, "the door that swings both ways." See Judith Mayne, "*L.A. Law* and Prime-Time Feminism," *Discourse* 10, no. 2 (1988): 30–47. The various creators of *L.A. Law* may indeed have been the best in the business at producing a sustained, rhythmic, oscillation between "conservative" and "liberal" approaches to the legal system. So perfectly were they attuned to viewer consciousnesses that I found myself, episode after episode, being on the verge of turning off the set only to be "rescued" (or were they being rescued?) by a sudden lurch to the Left. See below.

14 Megan Kennedy called this episode to my attention. On Debbie Allen's role in rescuing the Black sitcom *A Different World*, see Gray, *Watching Race: Television and the Struggle for "Blackness"* (Minneapolis: University of Minnesota Press, 1995), 96.

15 Compare the unrelenting nightmare of the British television drama *Safe*, which is not genteelly "about" homelessness but, like *Ladybird, Ladybird*, impales us on shrieks of pain.

16 If the general were an intellectual, we can speculate, the working-class guy would finally be positioned as morally superior to him. See Chapter 2.

17 Viewers who want to satisfy their urge to identify with a female victim will have little luck even if they manage to reject the ostensible narrative as ridiculous: how can we really empathize with *anyone* mindless enough to have wanted a sexual liaison with such a creep?

18 See Jeanine Basinger, *A Woman's View: How Hollywood Spoke to Women, 1930–1960* (New York: Knopf, 1993), for this argument.

19 Marina Warner, in *Managing Monsters: Six Myths of Our Time* (London: Vintage, 1994), 2–3.

20 On the painful record of Hollywood's homophobia, see Vito Russo's classic *The Celluloid Closet*, rev. ed. (New York: Harper and Row, 1987). This is an immensely knowledgeable portrayal of the dialectic between revelation and suppression of images and themes of homosexuality in Hollywood cinema. A 1995 documentary film version, produced by Robert Epstein and Jeff Friedman, and updated through the 1990s, was shown on the Public Broadcasting System. As the examples discussed below suggest, gayness is no longer primarily an absence, and it now appears when it does as the occasion less for outright homophobia than for nervously liberal unease.

21 This is spelled out in such bibles of conservative ideology as George Gilder's *Wealth and Poverty* (New York: Basic Books, 1981), and Charles Murray's *Losing Ground: American Social Policy, 1950–1980* (New York: Basic Books, 1984; 2d pbk. ed., 1994). None of this has anything to do with social reality, for the economic order would collapse without the extensive participation of married women. The best way to understand these assaults on female independence is even less as attempts to restore patriarchy than as attempts to restore the domestic service class.

22 "The times cried out for a hero," the voice-over continues, and this incantation is followed in short order by a close-up of actress Lucy Lawless's breasts. This kind of "having it both ways" is a more subtle version of the *TV Guide* ad for *Dateline NBC* (in the issue of 25 November-2 December) in which the headline "Strip Clubs Exposed" is juxtaposed with the very erotic picture of a stripper.

23 As Gina Rourke points out, this is the method of obviating the need for a feminist consciousness by letting us know that "men really *love* women."

24 This is in fact the normal way of arranging talk about race relations in the United States: any ordinarily capable black academic, for example, can become instantly famous by denouncing affirmative action, or trumpeting the cultural failure of African Americans in the inner city. On the Charlie Rose show after the Million Man March on Washington, the producers carefully arranged to have three *black* (male) critics, and no whites, criticizing the march.

25 Compare the 1994 episode of *Law and Order* in which the prosecuting attorney is a white woman and the judge is a Hispanic male: integrationist overkill with a vengeance.

26 It is certainly not coincidental that the director of this movie is an African American. Even so, he can't resist casting a white woman as the judge presiding (initially quite harshly) over the trial of an accused black man.

27 In just the same way the possibility of unbridgeable barriers is also elided in Hollywood, as in "civil rights" films such as *Mississippi Burning, The Long Walk Home, In the Heat of the Night, Guess Who's Coming to Dinner?, The Defiant Ones, Driving Miss Daisy,* and *The Autobiography of Miss Jane Pittman.* Hints of racism (hard to avoid given Hollywood's commitment to social realism) are usually nicely balanced—as when in *Dirty Harry,* having met a black bank robber we are promptly introduced to a black surgeon. See the extended comments of Benjamin A. DeMott in his *The Trouble with Friendship: Why Americans Can't Think Straight about Race* (New York: Atlantic Monthly, 1995).

28 Readers of Michael Parenti's *Make-Believe Media: The Politics of Entertainment* (New York: St. Martin's, 1992), or Michael Parenti himself, may notice a remarkable similarity between my description of this episode, and his own (pages 82–83 of his book). I can only say in apology to Michael that I in fact wrote this particular paragraph quite a few years ago, when this project was barely under way, and have made no attempt to rewrite because there's really no alternative description that would be as accurate. That we both saw this episode in virtually identical ways offers support, perhaps, to my methodological assumption that there is a *text* in there, beyond whatever the audience out here sees.

29 The political vacuum of *The Big Chill* is most apparent when seen in the context of the declarative politics in John Sayles's *The Return of the Secaucus Seven,* the non-Hollywood predecessor of which it is an obvious pastiche. The scene in the latter movie in which Jeff and Maura proudly recite their police records as antiwar activists to a disbelieving officer ("criminal trespass, criminal trespass, disorderly behavior, inciting to riot, criminal trespass," and so forth) has no counterpart in *The Big Chill.*

30 Judith Williamson, *Deadline at Dawn: Film Criticism, 1980–1990* (London: Marion Boyars, 1993), 56. Compare Herman Gray's comment, speaking of "the Black moment" on network television, that "it is possible . . . to recognize, indeed celebrate, the presence of African Americans, Latinos, Asians, Native Americans, and women and the particularly distinct tradition, experiences, and positions they represent without disrupting and challenging the dominant narratives about American society" (*Watching Race,* 87). Movies such as *Mississippi Burning, In the Heat of the Night, Hearts of Dixie, The Long Walk Home,* and *Driving*

Miss Daisy, as well as black-oriented television programs in the wake of *Roots,* with its outcome in "human triumph" (Watching Race, 78), exemplify the tendency described by Williamson.

5 Media Structures and Dominant Ideas

1 Chomsky and Hermann, Parenti, and also Herbert I. Schiller in such works as *Information and the Crisis Economy* (New York, Oxford University Press, 1986), and a few other media critics of their stature, have undertaken the task of description with both rigor and imagination. Anyone attempting to do theoretical work in this area is building on their work and owes them a considerable debt of gratitude.

2 From "The German Ideology," excerpted in *The Marx-Engels Reader,* 2d ed. (New York: Norton, 1978), 172–73.

3 Marx puts this point most clearly in a comment on Greek art, about which he says that it "presupposed Greek mythology, i.e., nature and the social forms already reworked in an unconsciously artistic way by the popular imagination. This is its material . . . is Achilles possible with powder and lead? Or the *Iliad* with the printing press, not to mention the printing machine? . . . The charm of [Greek] art for us is not in contradiction to the undeveloped stage of society on which it grew. It is its result, rather, and is inextricably bound up, rather, with the fact that the unripe social conditions under which it arose, *and could alone arise,* can never return." *Grundrisse* (London: Penguin Books, 1973), 110–11; my emphasis.

4 The real, and it may yet be fatal, problem of oligopoly in this cultural field is at the distribution end: the disappearance of independent bookstores in the wake of predatory competition from giants such as Barnes and Noble.

5 For example, Hollywood films are distributed at home and abroad in blocks, and any theater owner who wishes to show one of those films must buy the entire block; this leaves little opportunity for showing non-Hollywood films. Block booking, although it increases the number of cinemas, in the form of mall or downtown multiplexes, actually *decreases* the chances for the showing of independent films. In addition, to revert to the comparison with publishing, it only costs more to publish a blockbuster historical romance by James Michener than a minimalist "anti-novel" by Ronald Sukenick because Michener has to be paid more for his work; the technical costs of production are roughly similar. Aside from the cost of hiring stars, this is not at all true in cinema or television.

6 See Stanley Aronowitz's remarks, in "Working Class Culture in the Electronic Age," in *Cultural Politics in Contemporary America,* ed. Ian Angus and Sut Jhally (New York: Routledge, 1989), for an incisive description and analysis of the extent to which the cop has become *the* Hollywood version of a working-class hero.

7 Producers and audiences aren't stupid; both are aware that organized society is a good deal less than ideal. Thus the prevalence in American cinema (much less so on television) of that ambivalent figure the unofficial or outlaw hero, from the "left-wing" Rick Blaine to the "right-wing" Dirty Harry. See Chapter 4, note 11.

8 Consider, for instance, the moment when the uneducated, working-class protagonist of *Il Postino* is called forward to read his poetry at a gigantic Communist party rally; or the moment in *The Ox-Bow Incident* when William Eythe diffidently pushes his way through an angry mob to cast a lonely vote against a lynching led by his father.

9 Medved, *Hollywood vs. America* (New York: HarperCollins, 1992). As the demographic pro-file changes, so will Hollywood (and is probably doing so as I write these words).

10 Patricia Holland, "Thrill and Bills," *New Statesman and Society,* 22 April 1994, p. 36.

11 Wendy Brown, *States of Injury: Power and Freedom in Late Modernity* (Princeton: Princeton University Press, 1995), 189.

12 For a close discussion of this point, see Peter Biskind and Barbara Ehrenreich's "Machismo and Hollywood's Working Class," in *American Media and Mass Culture: Left Perspectives,* ed. Donald Lazere (Berkeley and Los Angeles: University of California Press, 1987), 201–15.

13 See Rick Fantasia, *Cultures of Solidarity: Consciousness, Action, and Contemporary American Workers* (Berkeley and Los Angeles: University of California Press, 1988), for a description of the contemporary possibilities.

14 See Joan Braderman's "Joan Does Dynasty: A Neopagan, Postsituationist, Socialist/Anarcho/ Feminist Expose," The *Independent Film and Video Monthly* 9 (August-September 1986): 14–19. This is the text of Braderman's wonderfully provocative video *Joan Does Dynasty,* pro-duced in March 1986. See also Jane Feuer's *Seeing Through the Eighties: Television and Reaganism* (Durham: Duke University Press, 1995), chap. 6 ("The Reception of Dynasty"). Specifying *Dynasty's* audience more carefully than I have done, Feuer writes, "the two groups that became obsessed with *Dynasty* in the mid-1980's were gay men and heterosexual women. These are, precisely, the two groups most connected to commodified beauty culture, to notions of femininity as a commodity to be purchased" (131).

15 Brown, *States of Injury,* 185.

16 See, for example, the destructively rigid, African American school principal in the film *Dangerous Minds.*

17 This is equally and as obviously true of the uneasy self-consciousness with which Hollywood now routinely depicts the subjects of race and class.

18 Thinking of the visual difference between Bette Davis, Joan Crawford, and Katherine Hep-burn films on the one hand, and Rita Hayworth, Jane Russell, and Marilyn Monroe films on the other, makes the distinction clear. Moreover, this is a distinction that encapsulates the otherwise equally decisive cleavage of race, so that Fred Williamson films are absolutely made for (mostly black) men, and TV sitcoms such as *Family Matters* for (mostly black) women.

19 "The Hollywood catechism has long been that 'women's movies' are problematic, for several reasons. Among them, there are no female stars who can match the box-office clout of big male stars. Men have to be dragged to women's movies. And when it comes to foreign sales, stories about women don't work as well as Sly and Arnold beating bad guys to a pulp." See Laurie Halpern Benenson, "Women's Ensemble Films Come of Age (Again)," *New York Times,* 18 December 1994, C36. It's particularly important to note that the preference of non-Americans for action films over domestic dramas says nothing more than that the latter are culturally more specific and therefore harder to identify with, or lose oneself in.

20 See her *Hard Core: Power, Pleasure, and the "Frenzy of the Visible"* (Berkeley and Los Angeles: University of California Press, 1989). Linda Williams is exceptional herself, even extraordinary, but for a different reason. To do what she did when she did it, was to defy an intimidating ideological consensus about "porn" that had been constructed within the feminist community—of which she certainly counts herself a member.

21 See the entry on Annette Haven in Danny Peary, *Cult Movie Stars* (New York: Simon and Schuster, 1991), 249. The career of Traci Lords, who has successfully graduated from hard-

core star to ass-kicking heroine of R-rated movies *(Ice, Not of This Earth, A Time To Die)*, gives some support to Haven's generalization.

22   The fate of "minority [a euphemism for "black"] -oriented" television is a good case in point. In the wake of NBC's incredibly successful and generally appealing *Cosby Show,* only the new Fox network really picked up on the possibilities of a new, primarily minority audience. By 1996 Fox had turned the big 3 into a big 4 and had dropped most of its "minority" programs, which now can be found almost entirely on two new upstart networks: Warner Broadcasting Company and United Paramount. See "The Transformation of the Television Industry and the Social Production of Blackness," in Herman Gray's *Watching Race: Television and the Struggle for "Blackness"* (Minneapolis: University of Minnesota Press, 1995).

23   The original and still perhaps the most influential analysis is that of Anthony Downs, *An Economic Theory of Democracy* (New York: Harper and Row, 1957). See also Robert Nozick's elegant demonstration, in his *Anarchy, State, and Utopia* (New York: Basic Books, 1974), 274ff., of how it is always in the interest of a centrist voting bloc to join a coalition with those above them socially, or to their Right politically.

24   Oil, steel, aluminum, cement, and so forth, are the most obvious cases of oligopoly, but they are not really what we think of as consumer products, as they are usually purchased by middlemen for processing or manufacture. Autos and other consumer durables, and consumer products such as pharmaceuticals, are better examples of how oligopoly works. One would think there was room for variation in the design of such products, but only marginal variation occurs. In the most famous instance, the American Big Three automakers proved absolutely impervious to the consumer demand for smaller cars, or the social demand for oil conservation, until German and Japanese competition—that is, competition exogenous to the oligopoly from equally large and powerful monopolies—brought about change.

25   Only in the last episodes of a canceled series does a more definitive narrative occasionally (very occasionally) surface, as in the politically paranoid ending of *Cagney and Lacey,* or the dark tragedy of *Under Suspicion.* On the other hand, the former was falsified—wiped out as though it had never been—by the production of a television movie sequel a few years later.

26   On movies of the week, see my comment above. It would be wrong to think that network television always remains the same; the explosion of same-sex weddings in the 1996 "season" is a case in point. But at no point will network television ever be truly pluralistic in the British sense. What I have said cannot be inserted into the schedule of commercial television is precisely what *is* inserted (only occasionally but often enough to be noteworthy) into the British television system's schedule. In the soap opera *Brookside,* for example, one 1993 episode featured both a political party debate on the National Health Service *and* a discussion between a teacher and her student about the latter's lesbianism, which concluded with the two going off to make love. Neither real politics nor uncensored female sexuality is permitted on American network television; either of those shocks to the system might prevent some element of the audience from being delivered to the advertisers who have footed the bill.

27   Movie channels, such as HBO/Cinemax, add the movie experience to the home via the television set. They are not part of the culture of television. And movies shown, with ads and cuts, on the networks, are not part of the culture of cinema.

6 Resistance and Opposition

1   For a fond, and fairly extensive account, see Paul Buhle's "The Hollywood Left: Aesthetics and Politics," *New Left Review*, no. 212 (July-August 1995): 101–119. The 1950s series *The Phil Silvers Show*, and the later *M*A*S*H* are examples of anti-authoritarian TV discussed by Buhle.

2   Victims and their relatives especially are treated in "news" (propaganda) culture as speaking in an uniquely authentic voice of anger: as though they've never watched television, nor learned any responses from it.

3   They don't, or at least not all of them do; an outcome that demonstrates how even (male) political radicals can fail to appreciate the equivocal position of women under "liberal" justice.

4   See Catharine A. MacKinnon, *Toward a Feminist Theory of the State* (Cambridge: Harvard University Press, 1989), chap. 9; and Carole Pateman, "Women and Consent," in *The Disorder of Women: Democracy, Feminism, and Political Theory* (Stanford: Stanford University Press, 1989), 71–89.

5   Just how much of the film's macho misogyny was intended as caricature or reflected Van Peebles's own ideology is open to question. On *Do the Right Thing* and *Malcolm X*, see bell hooks, *Yearning: Race, Gender, and Cultural Politics* (Boston: South End, 1990), 173–184; and *Outlaw Culture: Resisting Representations* (New York: Routledge, 1994), 155–64.

6   There is no difference between dominant cinema and "independent" cinema with respect to the desire to make money; producers of the latter at least wish to recoup their costs. The difference—and it is crucial—is between an organized financial structure in which films function primarily as commodities for exchange, and the more anarchic structure of small, entrepreneurial capitalism.

7   On the United States, see David Halle, *America's Working Man: Work, Home, and Politics among Blue-Collar Property Owners* (Chicago: University of Chicago Press, 1984); on Great Britain, see Nicholas Abercrombie, Stephen Hill, and Bryan S. Turner, *The Dominant Ideology Thesis* (London: Allen and Unwin, 1980).

8   *Strangers in Good Company* was made in Canada with assistance from the National Film Board of Canada. This public agency, which often provides support for non-mainstream films, illustrates the important point (see Chapter 5) that subsidization rather than competitive oligopoly is the only system under which genuine difference can survive.

9   In *Broken Mirrors*, the workers in a brothel hunt down and kill one of their johns, who is a serial killer of prostitutes.

10   In my experience, the appeal of *Sweetback* . . . to black women is equivocal and unpredictable.

11   On the distinction among various kinds of feminism, see Alison M. Jaggar, *Feminist Politics and Human Nature* (Totowa, N.J.: Rowman and Allanheld, 1983).

12   See Shannon Bell, *Reading, Writing and Rewriting the Prostitute's Body* (Bloomington: Indiana University Press, 1994).

13   Though the movie does not tell us this, some viewers might be aware that such women do really exist in 1990s America.

14   But see my comments about *Xena: Warrior Princess*, in Chapter 9.

15   My epithet "lonely town" is an example of the pathetic fallacy at work, since towns aren't lonely, only people are. I prefer it to more grammatically correct possibilities, however, for it captures exactly the feeling that is meant to be conveyed.

16   The "lonely town" is never in the South, for then the "mystery" is too obvious: there is only one hidden narrative in the American South, and thus the same tale told there is about race and racism from the moment we hear the first exchange of dialogue. As for New England, all small-town mysteries that take place there are, in the spirit of H. P. Lovecraft and Stephen King, horror stories: that is, the unearthing of a monstrosity concealed beneath the land. Why this should be so, what exactly is buried under the rocky New England soil, is a mystery worth exploring in its own right.

17   Marx, *Capital* (London: Lawrence and Wishart, 1970), 1:712.

18   This is perhaps unfair to Donohoe herself. She has gone on to produce two more "sequels" to *Shame*, one of them a passionate indictment of capital punishment that is far enough removed from her *L.A. Law* period as not to deserve this description. The apparent genuineness of her own commitment makes one suspect that any exploitation of her persona in *Shame* was not necessarily of her doing.

19   The director of *Shame*, Steven Jodrell, made the comment about its prospective audience at the London Film Festival in 1988.

20   Anne Glickman points out (in an unpublished paper) that "the most clearly voyeuristic gaze is seen through the blinds" of Esta's room, as her gaze "objectifies the father's grief and his inability to reach his frightened daughter."

21   See also, for example, the more or less amorous glances that pass between Vasquez and her male buddy Dietrich (along with her the most muscular of the Marines!) in *Aliens*. Even in British television's politically radical *Blind Justice*, an unnecessary heterosexual dalliance was inserted into the first episode, to reassure viewers that the female lead (and by implication the lawyer/creator of the series on whom everyone assumed she was based) was sexually okay.

22   See Joan Cocks, *The Oppositional Imagination: Feminism, Critique, and Political Theory* (New York: Routledge, 1989), chap. 10.

23   That is, it's hard to imagine either of them being subject to endless catcalls of "dyke," as Furness is in *Shame*.

24   To appreciate the full force of this conclusion, the viewer has to be aware of the cultural salience of the word "mate" in Australian society; it is a term that men apply to one another, and in context is suggestive of the continent's entire history as a penal colony and haven for exiles who together conquered it from nature and its indigenous inhabitants.

25   See Robert Jewett and John Shelton Lawrence, *The American Monomyth*, with a foreword by Isaac Asimov (Garden City, N.Y.: Anchor, 1977), xx.

26   One should also recognize Abe Polonsky here, but he was blacklisted for two decades, and never did recover the skills that make *Force of Evil* one of the greatest of all Hollywood movies.

27   The great document of racial liberalism is Gunnar Myrdal's *An American Dilemma: The Negro Problem and Modern Democracy* (New York: Harper and Bros., 1944); see especially 23–25 for Myrdal's discussion of "The American Creed" as an evaluative norm, based in American history, against which to measure deviations (e.g., racism).

28   See Chapter 9.

29   In *Thelma and Louise*, the policeman played by Harvey Keitel tries to do this, and this aspect of the film has been criticized by those who think it falls short of being a truly woman-oriented film. However, since he signally fails to persuade the protagonists that he is their appropriate moral judge, I would argue that his role is at worst equivocal. One imagines, of

course, that he is there to give "men" (that is, those persons assuming a "masculine" position of respect for authority) *someone* to identify with, and this is the kind of compromise that a non-Hollywood equivalent (e.g., any film by Marlene Gorris) would never make. In any event it's a meaningless compromise, since any men who are going to like this movie, or even see it, have already identified with Susan Sarandon (not Geena Davis), and will be bored to distraction, as I was, by the scene with Keitel. See my comments on Rita Hayworth, in Chapter 7.

7 "Put the Blame on Mame . . ."

1   The most notable exception to this generalization is the HBO movie *Criminal Justice*, with Forrest Whitaker as an accused and ultimately convicted murderer whose rights are given scant acknowledgment, but of whose guilt or innocence we are never certain. Here ambiguity achieves its genuine end, leaving us (as does *Prime Suspect* or *Between the Lines*) in a state of genuine unease about the very meaning of "law and order." In the Hollywood system, however, HBO is an exception by virtue of its institutional position. Since for any given film HBO has a guaranteed audience that has already "paid" for whatever films it is going to show in general, its projects do not have to pass the marketability test that the rest of Hollywood faces. Commercially dubious political projects are thus regularly brought to HBO; and HBO is receptive to them because its executives know that here they have a niche that no other Hollywood studio or network will fill (except on rare occasions). As long as the films get favorable reviews, and do not raise the kind of flak that can result in falling subscriptions, HBO can continue to be receptive to them. In this respect HBO is in a position comparable to that of BBC-TV in Britain.

2   The last (two-part) episode of *Cagney and Lacey*, referred to in Chapter 5, ends with its protagonists not only having failed but on the run. It was impossible not to feel that their victimization at the hands of the police, the mob, the CIA, and every other group even faintly connected with the "power elite," was a final comment by the show's creators on its own treatment by CBS rather than any literal theories about international conspiracy.

3   See Elayne Rapping, *The Movie of the Week: Private Stories, Public Events* (Minneapolis: University of Minnesota Press, 1992).

4   See, for example, *Pulp Fiction* or *The Usual Suspects*. I strongly suspect that the extraordinary popularity of the former film (to which a common response was, "I expected to hate it but I really liked it"), was due to the momentary exhilaration we all felt at seeing an American action film, perfectly accessible and belonging to a familiar genre, that had *absolutely no moral meaning.*

5   See Mark Crispin Miller, "Hollywood the Ad," *Atlantic Monthly* (April 1990): 41–68, for a litany of contemporary Hollywood productions that manage to achieve something resembling ideological or psychological simplemindedness.

6   The best account of this kind of slippage is probably Vito Russo's *The Celluloid Closet*, rev. ed. (New York: Harper and Row, 1987).

7   Again, the element of fantasy in cinematic commodities is crucial here. It's hard not to believe that if the creative and financial personnel involved with the making of *Dead Poets Society* had been fully conscious of what they were doing, they would never have done it.

8   *Double Exposure*, briefly described at the end of Chapter 6, deliberately brings this definition of ambiguity to life.

9   Richard Dyer, "Resistance through Charisma: Rita Hayworth and Gilda," in *Women in Film Noir*, ed. E. Ann Kaplan (London: British Film Institute, 1980): 91–99. Similarly, Molly Haskell writes about the androgynous allure of Garbo and Dietrich that they possessed "a natural force, a principle of beauty that, once set in motion, becomes autonomous." See *From Reverence to Rape: The Treatment of Women in the Movies,* 2d ed. (Chicago: University of Chicago Press, 1987), 107.

10   I should add that these students reach this conclusion without any help from me, and without having yet read Dyer's essay, which I tell them to read only after they have responded to the film in writing.

11   See Barbara Leaming, *If This Was Happiness: A Biography of Rita Hayworth* (New York: Viking, 1989).

12   In Judith P. Butler's words, "one might argue" that in such films "this displaced production and resolution of homosexual panic actually fortifies the heterosexual regime in its self-perpetuating task." See her *Bodies That Matter: On the Discursive Limits of Sex* (New York: Routledge, 1993), 126.

13   For a political criticism of *High Noon,* see Peter Biskind, *Seeing Is Believing: How Hollywood Taught Us to Stop Worrying and Love the Fifties* (New York: Pantheon Books, 1983), chap. 1.

14   The same feeling is conveyed in *The Naked Spur* and *Man of the West.*

15   This insight was suggested to me by Lisa Hix.

16   See, for example, the examples scattered throughout *The Celluloid Closet,* book or documentary: by far the greatest portion of them pertain to *male* homoeroticism.

17   As late as 1968, Robert Aldrich's *Too Late the Hero* recapitulates this theme.

8   "Women You Don't Mess With"

1   Throughout, my use of the term "disavowal" is *not* psychoanalyic, unless otherwise indicated, as in the discussion of voyeurism and castration anxiety below.

2   From this perspective, we can see that *Mrs. Doubtfire* and *Tootsie* are having it both ways. The camera's gaze is still a man's, and now the man can be a woman to boot—maybe we don't need women at all! Inversion of the conventional is only resistive when it questions the conventional; otherwise it's pure manipulation.

3   These arguments are explored by E. Ann Kaplan in her "Is the Gaze Male?" in *Powers of Desire,* ed. Ann Snitow, Christine Stansell, and Sharon Thompson (New York: Monthly Review Press, 1983), 309–27. The more recent examples were suggested to me by Gina Rourke.

4   In Griselda Pollock, *Vision and Difference: Femininity, Feminism and Histories of Art* (London: Routledge, 1988), 85.

5   George Mosse, *Nationalism and Sexuality: Middle-Class Morality and Sexual Norms in Modern Europe* (Madison: University of Wisconsin Press, 1985), 1.

6   The first feature film I can recall that starred a woman of action was Roger Corman's 1956 film, *The Gunslinger,* in which Beverly Garland becomes a town marshal after her husband, the previous marshal, is murdered; in a showdown she kills the murderer. In 1957 Garland also starred in the television series *Decoy,* as television's first police heroine, undercover cop Casey Jones. Nothing further came of either of these productions, though; and Garland's subsequent career does not seem to have owed anything to them. John Ford's 1966 film *Seven*

Women similarly came to nothing. In it Anne Bancroft as a doctor in prerevolutionary China, becomes the de facto leader of a group of missionaries besieged by bandits (and is recognized as such by the bandit chieftain) when the man who should be in charge turns out to be a coward. Barbara Stanwyck in two Westerns, *The Furies* and *Forty Guns*, Joan Crawford in *Johnny Guitar*, Rhonda Fleming in *Bullwhip*, and Maureen O'Hara as a sword-wielding pirate in *Against All Flags*, also played hard-riding or hard-fisted women; but in all those movies a man was ultimately the hero (or, in Stanwyck's case, the woman was a villain). *Seven Women* is the only one of these in which, long before Ripley, I recall feeling the thrill of excitement as a *woman* swung into action. The movie was a failure and is not to be found today in either video stores or on cable.

7   See Teresa de Lauretis, *Alice Doesn't: Feminism, Semiotics, Cinema* (Bloomington: Indiana University Press, 1984), chap. 5.

8   Burnett, Dern, Woodward, and Zuniga appear in made-for-TV movies; the last-named functions as the isolated hero (with a male sidekick, no less) uncovering a Ludlumesque plot within the CIA to destroy a crowded jetliner.

9   We will see in Chapter 9 what horrors may unfold when women are allowed to be sexually predatory. De Lauretis can therefore still insist on the essentially male *structure* of the quest; but as I suggest in this and Chapter 9 if gender roles become fluid within this structure, something ideologically different is happening.

10 Screenwriters and directors can read; therefore it's impossible to tell whether such heavy-handed symbolism is revelatory of the masculine unconscious or, lightheartedly, of self-consciously Freudian gamesmanship.

11 From *Manifesto of the Communist Party*, in *The Marx-Engels Reader*, 2d ed. (New York: Norton, 1978), 476; my emphasis, of course. The original German, *Menschen* rather than *Männer*, is actually gender-neutral.

12 In one episode of *Xena*, while the Greeks are preparing their Trojan gift horse, Xena counsels Helen of Troy [*sic*] not to let men define the meaning of her life for her. The ensuing action, in which with the help of Xena Helen evades both Paris and Menelaus, is carefully articulated to demonstrate that Helen is no longer the object of male exchange (see Chapter 3).

13 Interviewed in *Quest: A Feminist Quarterly* 2, no. 1 (Summer 1975): 42. Her novella, "Picnic on Paradise," which appears in *The Adventures of Alyx* (London: Women's Press, 1985), is probably the most famous sci-fi adventure featuring a woman. In the United States it is out of print, but can be found in *Alyx* (Boston: G. K. Hall, 1976), a collection of all the "Alyx" stories with an introduction by the sci-fi writer Samuel Delaney. Anyone who doubts the possibilities here should also read, say, Melissa Scott's *Trouble and Her Friends* (New York: Tor Books, 1994), a cyberpunk epic in which the protagonists are two women, sometime lovers, who "walk" the virtual realities of cyberspace like gunslingers in a traditional Western; this is probably the most exciting female adventure story since "Picnic." Lovers of "hard-boiled" writing should look as well at the Ace Books fantasy series by Laurell K. Hamilton, the best writer of such prose in the United States today, about "Anita Blake, Vampire Hunter."

14 To the extent possible, her considerable beauty is turned into athletic boyishness.

15 Maggie Greenwald is an independent director and it would be misleading to call this a "Hollywood" movie. It does, however, illustrate possibilities that even Hollywood will undoubtedly soon grasp; and its star, Suzy Amis, is herself a successful Hollywood actress.

16   In that film, Rutger Hauer symbolically fills the ideologically ambiguous role of the father who trains his daughter to be a superathlete.

17   This was hardly the first of its kind; it was preceded by, among others, the network series *Legwork*, starring Margaret Colin and Frances McDormand. *Legwork* was also original, but its location within the conventional television approach to "law and order" made it less ideologically deviant.

18   Robinson undoubtedly deserves much of the credit for this, in that her playing, like Rita Hayworth's in *Gilda*, is amusedly self-parodic.

19   She has not, so far as I know, had the opportunity to direct another one.

20   See my comment in Chapter 3 on *Physical Evidence*. "Vulnerability," a quality Russell visibly and totally lacks, is a word often used to describe actresses like, say, Marilyn Monroe; it has a pronounced ideological content. When we see a "vulnerable" actress with a strong-looking leading man, we are left in no doubt who's on top and who's on bottom. In *Physical Evidence*, the one major Hollywood movie to cast Russell opposite a leading man, even the macho Reynolds cannot credibly be projected into a narrative in which she would be the damsel in distress needing him to come to her rescue. In recent years Russell has been reduced to B-movie action or femme fatale roles.

21   Thereby reprising the triumphalist ending of *Texas Chain Saw Massacre II*. On the "final girl," see Carol Clover, *Men, Women, and Chain Saws* (Princeton: Princeton University Press, 1992), 48ff.

22   *Video Movie Guide*, ed. Mick Martin and Marsha Porter (New York: Random House, 1995), 6.

23   To the purist critics of Hollywood who will have nothing to do with mainstream culture because it is always fatally compromised, it's fair to reply that the alternative of withdrawal and separation is neither the arm of criticism *nor* the criticism of arms. On this point, see Alison M. Jaggar, *Feminist Politics and Human Nature* (Totowa, N.J.: Rowman and Allenheld, 1983), 293–96.

24   In Barbara Creed's summary (from which I've borrowed the image of *la femme castatrice*), "The archetypes of the phallic and castrating woman are quite different and should not be confused; the former ultimately represents a comforting phantasy [*sic*] of sexual sameness, and the latter a terrifying phantasy of sexual difference." See Creed, *The Monstrous-Feminine: Film, Feminism, Psychoanalysis* (New York: Routledge, 1993), 157–58.

25   An "exploitation" film is a film that has more violence and sex per dollar spent than a mainstream film, just as a "girlie" magazine is a magazine that has more erotic photographs in fewer pages than the *New York Times Sunday Magazine*.

26   Knox's original reference is actually not to a "regiment" of women (that is, a great number), but to what we would call a "regime": that is, the regime of Mary Tudor (later Stuart). However, his phrase has been used in the proliferative sense so often that there is none better to convey the impression that is not in fact the one he was trying to convey.

27   And largely unnoticed by cultural studies. To my knowledge, the first discussion of this genre by a female critic is Kirsten Marthe Lentz's, "The Popular Pleasures of Female Revenge (Or Rage Bursting in a Blaze of Gunfire)," *Cultural Studies* 7, no. 3 (October 1993): 374–403. Unfortunately her discussion is limited to the productions of mainstream Hollywood; as is that of Jeffrey A. Brown, "Gender and the Action Heroine: Hardbodies and the *Point of No Return*," *Cinema Journal* 35, no. 3 (1996): 52–71.

28   See Ben Singer, "Female Power in the Serial-Queen Melodrama: The Etiology of an Anomaly," *Camera Obscura* (Winter 1990): 91–130.

29 As to the latter, which in any event would have been totally impossible in the moral and aesthetic atmosphere of the time, one need only consult the many frames reproduced in Singer's essay.

30 It was briefly imitated on American television by the private-eye series *Honey West*, starring Anne Francis. *Honey,* though, was not nearly so successful as the import.

31 Lewis's complaint about *Modesty Blaise* (derived originally from a British comic strip) pertained not to Monica Vitti's campy performance in the title role as a female action heroine, but to a scene in which the Italian actress Rosanna Podesta strangled a man to death between her legs; this scene has been cut from the only version of *Modesty Blaise* now available in the United States. American audiences first saw *The Avengers* when the backup role, now "Mrs. Peel," had been taken over by Diana Rigg, whose RADA-bred air of hauteur and amused irony somewhat surmounted the part's fetishistic implications; as did the alternately kittenish and clunky behavior of Linda Thorson, who followed her (as "Tara King"). Only when the original series was released in the United States in the 1990s were the purely fetishistic origins of *The Avengers* plainly visible here.

32 Caffaro's movies, directed by her husband Don Schain, are the purest trash, and she plays them, to his evident enjoyment, like an escapee from a gas station office calendar. Dobson and Grier are both black, and it was the short-lived vogue of "blaxploitation" films that gave them their chance; they were shortly joined by Jeanne Bell in *T.N.T. Jackson* and *The Muthers*. Grier is a very good actress and a great beauty who has managed to eke out a limited "straight" career in films and on television. That Hollywood could rarely see her as a candidate for anything other than her roles of violence is a commentary on the primary place that race has in all of Hollywood's considerations of gender.

33 This speculation is strengthened by the cautionary financial history of *Sweet Sweetback . . .,* the only film of its time to address black power directly. *Sweetback* is still considered a "blaxploitation" film by many white critics who can't bear the thought of taking its politics seriously. The most unexploitative use of a black hero or heroine at the time was the 1974 TV pilot *Get Christy Love,* and subsequent series, with Theresa Graves as a female police inspector.

34 These movies are not, therefore, instances of what Kaplan calls gender reversal, by which she means men becoming the objects of the female gaze; see note 3 above.

35 The last-named of whom wrote and produced a movie, *Pushed to the Limit,* in which she also stars, as wrestler, exotic dancer (briefly), and hero. Any notion that the man she hired to direct this movie was expressing *his* fantasies in the course of that endeavor would be hard to defend. Heavily centralized television has not been so hospitable to such women, but the popular syndicated show *Hercules,* which with its spinoff *Xena* escapes many of the limitations of network televison, recently introduced body-building champion and video fitness expert Cory Everson as "Atalanta," and Cynthia Rothrock and Karen Shepard (the spelling of whose last name is indeterminate) as superstrong villains.

36 Sybil Danning is an ex-Playboy centerfold, a big, gun-toting, karate-chopping cult star: "the goddess of B action-adventure movies," in one admirer's phrase (Danny Peary, *Cult Movie Stars* [New York: Simon and Schuster, 1991], 132). An indication of her drawing power as a fetish for male viewers is that there is a movie described on its video cassette cover as "Sybil Danning in *The Tomb.*" In fact she appears for five minutes, before the credits, and then is never seen again. Actually, Danning's sexual persona is so strong that she is most often cast as a villain, but a villain we love to cheer.

37   Several of these movies are remakes: *No Contest* of *Die Hard, Seven Magnificent Gladiators* of its obvious namesake.

38   It may not be entirely coincidental that this is one of the few movies in the genre directed by a woman, Tanya Rosenberg. On the other hand, the same ending occurs in the later *Dangerous Prey,* directed by a man, in which the two female protagonists reprise the ending of *Casablanca,* including Bogart's line about "a beautiful friendship." Moreover, *Blood Games* is also the most visually erotic of the movies in this genre, the women all being dressed in the skimpiest of clothing (to play baseball?), and on one occasion being unclothed in a group shower scene. However, "the male gaze" is a social construct, not attached to any particular person or persons. As we learn from Linda Williams in her discussion of hard-core films produced by women, women can construct it just as well as men; sometimes even better. See her *Hard Core: Power, Pleasure, and the "Frenzy of the Visible"* (Berkeley and Los Angeles: University of California Press, 1989). Anyone who doubts this should see the "lesbian vampire" film *Blonde Heaven,* directed by Ellen Cabot (and also written by a woman), with its over-the-top gynephobia (perhaps intended satirically—perhaps).

39   Here I mean specifically nonsadistic female violence; see below.

40   Angela Bassett and Whoopi Goldberg have both played action leads, but only Bassett in Bigelow's *Strange Days* is also paired with a white man as the romantic duo.

41   *Red Sonja* is also interesting in that it has not only one of the first female fighters in a mainstream movie, but in Sandahl Bergman one of the first female action villains.

42   Mainstream Hollywood's sense of ideological propriety is sometimes wondrous to behold, and *The Money Train* is a perfect example of that sense in operation. The woman still functions as currency, and the terms of her exchange identify the hero: now the black man, rather than the embittered, poorly socialized white man. But she herself is "not white."

43   On the fringes this has already happened; see, for example, *Policewomen* with Sondra Currie and Jeanne Bell. In every way imaginable Bell is a more imposing and credible action hero—except, apparently, for the color of her skin.

44   Or the movie itself treated as a joke, for example, *Tank Girl.*

45   *Undercover Blues* manages to reduce one of Britain's greatest actresses, Fiona Shaw, to a villainous mud-wrestling partner for Turner.

46   Lentz, "Popular Pleasures of Female Revenge," 378.

47   Turner, Dickinson, Sharon Stone, and Alexandra Paul are among the actresses who've made this point.

48   Consider, for example, Bridget Fonda in *Point of No Return.*

49   Or consider Denise Crosby, who went in what male culture clearly considers a straight line, from *Arizona Heat*'s lesbian cop to a martial artist in *Star Trek II,* a dominatrix in Showtime's soft-core *Red Shoe Diaries,* to (inevitably) a butch killer in the movie *Dream Man.*

50   Kathleen Kinmont's *C.I.A. Code Name Alexa* is also a remake of *La Femme Nikita,* though not so rigorously faithful to the original. In 1997 "Nikita" was transported to cable's USA channel, but television's moral code, for reasons suggested in Chapter 5 (and also because of its susceptibility to government regulation), remains more stringent than cinema's. Nikita, who though she becomes a good woman is introduced to us cinematically as a cold-blooded killer, is transformed into a petty thief wrongfully convicted of murder—*The Desperate Trail* all over again.

51   In *Freeway* Fluegel is not physically tough, but merely determined, like "Veronica Clare." Her fate in *Breaking Point,* in which we frequently see her in tight gym clothes, suggestive nightwear, skimpy lingerie, and in which she engages in a lot of working out in gyms and

martial arts activity, gives one more demonstration that mainstream Hollywood has trouble fitting adventure heroines into the code described in Chapter 3.

52 And introduced by Paul with a lot of ad-break chatter about how much fun it was to play an action hero without using a stuntwoman, and so forth. *Private Obsession* is particularly interesting (though unfortunately not particularly good), in that it seems to be a purely misogynistic "beauty kidnapped and tortured by antifeminist psychopath" film for most of the story. We wait for "feminist leader" and "supermodel" Whirry (how Hollywood demonstrates "feminist" leadership does not bear too much, or even any, discussion) to give in to the kidnapper's sexual *and* political demands (by disavowing her feminism); and so she does, to our intense discomfort. But it has all been a ruse; while a tough private eye futilely scours the city looking for her, she turns the tables on the kidnapper all by herself.

53 Angie Dickinson's *Policewoman* was a fairly successful series of the 1970s, though.

54 Nowhere is this revealed so clearly as in the transition of *Jurassic Park* from novel to film, described in Chapter 3.

55 The only time Pam Grier did not play the lead in an action film, she was made sidekick to a white actress in the inaccurately titled *Naked Warriors*.

56 I have no idea whom he might have looked like, but I've always been certain that Walter Pidgeon is not it; Ronald Colman would have been just right. Still, there are limits to male as well as to female spectacle. Remake *Rogue Male* (or *Manhunt*, as the film is titled) a hundred times in a hundred different contexts, and still the protagonist can't be played by Mel Gibson or Sylvester Stallone without utter ruination.

57 On this point at least two of these martial arts films—Rothrock's *Guardian Angel* and Kathy Long's *Knights*—are deliberately "egalitarian" in an odd way: that is, each of them ends with the explicit statement that we can't tell who's better, the female hero or her male sidekick. In *Guardian Angel*, a policewoman and policeman, both martial arts experts, join forces to track down a murderous villain. They were once lovers but are now estranged, in large part because, according to her, he defeated her in the department's karate championship finals by cheating. At the end of the movie he proposes reconciliation to her and she accepts—"but first we've got something to settle." The film ends with a freeze frame of the two facing each other in combat stance. In the post-apocalyptic *Knights*, Kris Kristofferson plays a cyborg who teaches Long martial arts and swordplay, and is then himself amputated at the waist. After doing most of the ensuing heroics herself, she ties the rest of him to her back so that he can defend her rear in the final pitched battle; after which they ride off together, still back to back, toward the next film. Imagination has not completely deserted visual culture.

58 For a female hero who is not a fetishized male in disguise, see the discussion of television's *Veronica Clare* above. As Beth Greenleaf pointed out to me, we never see Sigourney Weaver, say, bringing enemies together around the negotiating table. Of course we never see male heroes in that role either, but this absence leaves women with nothing to do that is not an imitation of masculinity.

59 This is by no means to say these movies are *without* feminist subtexts. On the contrary, their feminism tends to be unabashedly didactic, on some occasions narrated in voice-overs by men who have "seen the light": a characteristic for which the post-apocalyptic *The Sisterhood* takes the prize hands down. On other genres, see Chapter 9.

60 It's important to remember that ideology is usually subordinate to profit in the milieus where capitalist production takes place, so that the best explanation for the explosion of "action women" on the big screen is the tiredness of the male action genre.

61 See chapter 5 for a more thorough discussion of this point.

62   I may be overinterpreting here. I find each Baldwin brother more sleazy than the last, but I assume, given their success, that mine is an isolated viewpoint. If I am wrong about this, if most people feel about the Baldwins as I do, then of course there's nothing shocking about the ending of *Sawbones* at all.

63   To be fair, on the evidence of his later work there's reason to doubt that Eastwood would ever incorporate such a scene into a movie again. Indeed *Unforgiven* can be read as, among other things, an apologia for *High Plains Drifter.*

64   In Jeffrey A. Brown's words, "The depiction of most action heroines as masculinized ... provides viewers with an example of masculine behavior that is not divorced from a feminine identity" ("Gender and the Action Heroine," 67). In some of these movies also, women and men ride equally to each other's rescue in a true confounding of social roles: most entertainingly and imaginatively in the 1983 version of *She;* see also *Barbarian Queen,* in addition to *Guardian Angel* and *Knights.*

65   Compare the analysis of James H. Kavanagh, "Feminism, Humanism and Science in *Alien,*" in *Alien Zone: Cultural Theory and Contemporary Science Fiction Cinema,* ed. Annette Kuhn (London: Verso Books, 1990), 73–82.

66   Though had they seen Anne Bancroft taking command of the missionary post from the cowardly Eddie Albert in *Seven Women,* it might not have seemed so new.

67   After one episode of *Xena,* I logged on to the "Xena Netforum" and scrolled through a few dozen messages. Fully three-quarters were clearly from female viewers, who ranged from a seven-year-old girl to an Australian lesbian collective signing on as "Amazon." Many of them gave vivid meaning to the phrase "role model." Coincidentally, the next day in a video store I overheard two teenage girls having a serious and intense discussion about whether Lucy Lawless is a lesbian "in real life"; this was a matter of importance to them. For a fuller description of *Xena,* especially its sexual politics, see Donna Minkowitz, "Xena: She's Big, Tall, Strong—and Popular," in *Ms.,* 7, no. 1 (July-August 1996): 74–77.

68   Eastwood's *The Gauntlet* is one of the few films in the male violence genre that avoids this outcome, by making him a drunken loser through most of the film. Here too a comparison with television's *Hercules* is useful. The latter never seems sadistic, because Hercules is, after all, not a man but a demigod: of course he's superhuman! As with *Xena,* departure from Hollywood's constrictive urban naturalism frees the imagination for genuine playfulness.

69   Fetishistic appeals aside, this may partially explain why, according to Rothrock (quoted in *Newsweek,* 7 June 1993) she gets "lots of letters from young men [that] say [she makes] Jean-Claude Van Damme look like a wimp." He beats up men; she beats up men. Whose is the more heroic accomplishment?

70   My impression, but it is only an impression based on a memory that I have been unable to check, is that the sexual code is generally ignored in these movies; the careful coding of "chastity" and "seductiveness" that dooms Darlanne Fluegel in *Breaking Point* (see Chapter 3, above) does not visibly apply to Cynthia Rothrock.

71   The margins of visual culture are certainly no more guilty of this kind of cultural imperialism than is mainstream Hollywood, though. The various adventures of Indiana Jones are just the most obvious offshoot of a new movement in what Renato Rosaldo calls "imperialist nostalgia." See "Imperialist Nostalgia," in Rosaldo, *Culture and Truth: The Remaking of Social Analysis* (Boston: Beacon, 1989), 68–87.

72   *Nemesis 2: Nebula* epitomizes this tendency. For no particular diegetic reason, the screenplay plants the extraordinarily muscular body-builder Sue Price in a tribal African setting full of

noble savages. There, as a combination of Tarzan, Sheena, and Schwarzenegger, she can be the strongest and most muscular of them all, defeating one young man (not so nobly ridden by jealousy of her strength) in brutal hand-to-hand combat. Of course she's a genetically programmed human from the future, and so on and so forth, but in visual culture what you see is what you get. Moreover, the cyborg terminator that pursues her, and is finally destroyed by her, is a literally black metallic monster. Overall, to say that the film is about the triumph of whiteness would be only a mild exaggeration.

73 Some of us might think that without this recuperation of traditional sexual norms, the sadistic villainess would be a large improvement on the prototypical passive heroine.

74 The present tense is slightly misleading; the show continues as of this writing, but now without Estes and Kapture.

75 It's possible, though perhaps a bit of a stretch, to say that by the very force—or nonforce—of his impersonation of a "new" man, Estes recuperates the old man to set off against Kapture's new woman. A few doses of Estes could make anyone long for Stallone. Kapture, on the contrary, radiates energy even when perfectly still.

76 The criminogenic are also extraordinarily photogenic, the women mostly parading around in skimpy bathing suits, as befits the Florida climate. This background voyeurism—the real subject of the series, a cynic might think—also helps root the attractive Kapture more firmly in her role as crimefighter, since she usually seems almost overdressed and underexposed by comparison.

77 In one late-1980s beer commercial, Rachel McLish hoists a bar stool over her head, with a disbelieving man sitting in it.

78 Though it hardly qualifies as mass culture, contemporary modern dance also offers evidence of the new tendency, as in the gender-bending partnering of the Mark Morris troupe; see Joan Acocella, *Mark Morris* (New York: Farrar, Straus and Giroux, 1993). Louise Lacavaliere, the sadistic, muscular killer of *Strange Days*, was originally the lead dancer of a Montreal-based dance group, La-La-La Human Steps. When I saw them in 1989, the program ended with the lead male dancer flinging himself into her arms, at which point she lifted him above her head and held him there like a weightlifter pressing a weight.

79 It's easy to miss this point because there are no equivalents of Norris or Bronson in mainstream cinema. Give Cynthia Rothrock the production values that Chuck Norris gets and the supposed difference in aesthetic intelligence will not be noticeable.

80 Appropriately enough, the first Pam Grier movie, *The Big Doll House*, is literally a movie of women's liberation: from a women's prison.

81 *Alyx*, xvii.

82 Clover's argument about slasher films, and above all their appeal to male masochism, is contained in "Her Body, Himself," chap. 1 of *Men, Women, and Chain Saws*. As she says of this new form of hero, "Abject terror may still be rendered feminine, but the willingness of one immensely popular current genre to represent the hero as an anatomical female would seem to suggest that at least one of the marks of traditional heroism, triumphant self-rescue, is no longer strictly gendered masculine" (60).

9 The Wrath of the Medusa

1 On the rape-revenge cycle, see Carol Clover, *Men, Women, and Chain Saws* (Princeton: Princeton University Press, 1992), chap. 3; and Barbara Creed, *The Monstrous-Feminine:*

Film, Feminism, Psychoanalysis (New York: Routledge, 1993), chap. 9. On the slasher movie, see Chapter 8, note 82.

2 On this figure, see Clover, *Men, Women, and Chain Saws,* chap. 1 ("Her Body, Himself").

3 Here, as often, "gynephobia" is a more accurate term than "misogyny."

4 See Creed, *Monstrous-Feminine,* 129.

5 When rapists are not rednecks or ethnically all-purpose city dwellers, they may be arrogant rich kids (or men); but the latter too are "deviant" in the populist perspective that Hollywood always adopts. In Clover's incisive description, "Raped and battered, the haves can rise to annihilate the have-nots—all in the name of feminism" (*Men, Women, and Chain Saws,* 163). For another discussion of several of these movies see Peter Lehman, "Don't Blame This On a Girl," in *Screening the Male: Exploring Masculinities in Hollywood Cinema,* ed. Steven Cohan and Ina Rae Hark (New York: Routledge, 1993), 103–15.

6 Compare Carol Clover's remark, note 5. Kirsten Marthe Lentz, in "The Popular Pleasures of Female Revenge (Or Rage Bursting in a Blaze of Gunfire)," *Cultural Studies* 7, no. 3 (October 1993): 377–403, has a much more thorough—and discomfiting—discussion of the intersection between "feminism" and the propaganda of guns and violence.

7 Lehman, "Don't Blame This On a Girl," argues that the genre is *particularly* voyeuristic, because the rape victims are always "beautiful." That is simply not true, though they are certainly attractive. Beyond that claim, Mulvey would correctly say that we are missing the point that cinema is *inherently* voyeuristic.

8 See Barbara Ehrenreich, *The Hearts of Men: American Dreams and the Flight from Commitment* (Garden City, N.Y.: Doubleday/Anchor, 1983), for a lengthy and persuasive (if perhaps exaggerated) discussion of this phenomenon.

9 Haskell, *From Reverence to Rape: The Treatment of Women in the Movies,* 2d ed. (Chicago: University of Chicago Press, 1987).

10 In her words, the right of privacy "keeps some men out of the bedrooms of other men." Catharine A. MacKinnon, *Toward a Feminist Theory of the State* (Cambridge: Harvard University Press, 1989), 194.

11 Of course it may be said that from my standpoint in the audience the victim is *my* possession; *I* am the man on whose behalf her violators are being punished. That is so; but to make too much of the point would be an example of the genetic fallacy at work. If we rejected every social vision that could be reduced to an impeachable psychic state, we wouldn't have a moral leg to stand on. This reductionist tendency in Freudianism, especially its naive American version, is the most questionable of its many methodological approaches.

12 In *The Stranger,* as noted in the previous chapter, he is positioned as a female avenger who in an earlier cinematic incarnation was a male rapist.

13 The prototype of these films is most probably Clint Eastwood's *Play Misty for Me,* which, fittingly, dates to the same period as the first action films discussed in Chapter 8.

14 In contrast, the bitch-villainess of soap operas is partly a figure of fun who mostly fouls up other people's sex lives or family relationships. When she becomes Catherine Trammell in *Basic Instinct,* she graduates to an entirely new level.

15 The real thing, though, is readily distinguishable, as in movies such as *Amazons,* which is about a secret society of women dedicated to seizing power from men—after which the Earth would presumably become the kind of planet that has to be rescued from matriarchy by the bold men and women of Starship Enterprise.

16 As pointed out in Chapter 3, there is a whole subgenre, in fact, of which *Wild Side* and *Bound*

are examples, about what might be called killer lesbians. *Basic Instinct* is the most notorious; *Dead On* and *Sins of the Night* are other examples. The former, in which two women who are secretly lesbian lovers successfully plot to get rid of the male protagonist who is the husband of one of them, is suggestive of a new and especially gynephobic tendency.

17 Archer then becomes the "final girl" of slasher movies. However, because of her rooted attachment to Douglas she remains a derivative figure, and lacks the independence to become a universal hero.

18 See Susan Faludi's *Backlash: The Undeclared War against American Women* (New York: Crown, 1991), 117–23, for a description of the original ending of *Fatal Attraction,* and how it got changed into the version that was theatrically released. A video of the first version ("the director's cut") is available.

19 There is such a film, in fact: the 1956 *Johnny Guitar*. But Sterling Hayden, the bystander to Joan Crawford's and Mercedes McCambridge's shootout, is not a hapless male, but a reformed gunman who pointedly decides not to interfere with Crawford's quest for revenge.

20 Anne Deutsch has pointed out to me that the first time Dan and Alex (Douglas and Close) are together, he struggles unsuccessfully to open his umbrella in the rain, whereas Alex then covers the two of them nicely with hers. At this point the call going out to Mama Beth (Archer) sounds loud and clear. For reasons Freud made perfectly clear, men may at some level profoundly enjoy this reduction to infancy—but not at the level of ideology.

21 In this sense Stone here achieves the reverse of Hayworth's accomplishment in *Gilda*. Hayworth persuades us of her essential innocence even when the evidence, and the very narrative itself, make her look most "guilty." Stone persuades us of her unrepentant guilt even while claiming innocence.

22 See, for example, Creed, *Monstrous-Feminine*, 155.

23 In *The Last Seduction* Peter Berg *intends* to rape Fiorentino. However, that is precisely what she wants him to do, for her own reasons, and she is manipulating him to that end. Of course she could not do that if he were not willing to be a rapist, and therefore that is certainly what he is.

24 As Gina Rourke again points out, Fiorentino says to the young man she has seduced, "Bet you never had a fuck like that"; and *Basic Instinct* is full of admiring references to "the fuck of the century."

25 See, for example, the discussion in *Vanity Fair* (April 1993, p. 202) by Naomi Wolf and Stone herself, as well as Camille Paglia. Paglia's remarks—"woman's domination of the sexual realm"—have to be taken with a very large grain of salt. Wolf does better in comparing Catherine Trammell to a "Nietzschean *Überfraulein* who owns everything about her own power." Similarly, on the 1996 TV special, *The Good, the Bad, and the Beautiful,* Molly Haskell refers to Close's performance in *Fatal Attraction* as "exhilarating." *Eve of Destruction,* another of Paul Verhoeven's (*Basic Instinct* and *Showgirls*) paeans to fetishism, was also received in the same way by some reviewers. In *Eve,* an unstoppable android, cloned from a dying woman, retraces her life in order to kill all the men who'd abused her. This movie manages to combine the female warrior, rape-revenge, and neo-noir genres all at once, in an apotheosis of masochistic gynephobia.

26 This remains true even in Mulvey's more recent "Some Thoughts on Theories of Fetishism in the Context of Contemporary Culture," *October* 65 (Summer 1993), 3–24. Here, dominant cinema has itself become fetishistic in its entirety: "feminist film theory has argued that the

eroticization of the cinema is a major prop for its successfully fetishized credibility." And it has also argued "that cinema finds its most perfect fetishistic object, though not its only one, in the image of woman" (7 and 12). What is being disavowed by fetishism in this logic is not simply castration anxiety, but a more general "threat that sets up a split between knowledge and belief" (20). That is, Hollywood uses the glamorized image of woman as the object of the voyeuristic gaze, to help us forget that we are seeing a *commodity* that has been *produced*, rather than an immediate image we've fantasized ourselves. This assimilation of the Freudian theory of fetishism (in its perfected feminist version) to Marx's theory of the fetishism of commodities, is compelling, but still leaves us unable to discuss fetishism in its particulars; that is, different varieties of fetishism. According to Sybil Danning, the exercise regime she engaged in to become a muscular action/adventure star took inches off a bustline for which she was previously famous, but her male fans prefer it that way. Why? If just seeing any seamlessly glamorized surface, regardless of content, draws us into the fetishized world of Hollywood commodities, then what are high-heeled shoes or whips or leather or firearms doing there? Perhaps something less, but certainly something different: it is this more Freudian, less Marxist, conception of fetishism that I employ in the discussion that follows.

27 Like Freud also, Mulvey conceptualizes fetishism only as *male*, which is reasonable enough when discussing dominant cinema. Freud was surely incorrect on this point, however. Outside the world of dominant cinema there is plentiful female fetishism as well: as can be verified by seeing the films of the German filmmakers Ulrike Ottinger and Monika Treut, or by attending any gay and lesbian film festival, or reading the erotic horror stories of, say, Lucy Taylor and Kathe Koja. On this point, see Lorraine Gamman and Merja Mekanin, *Female Fetishism: A New Look* (London: Lawrence and Wishart, 1994).

28 This aspect of voyeurism is brought out most clearly, perhaps, in Manet's classic anti-voyeur paintings, *Olympia* and *Le Dejeuner sur l'Herbe*.

29 Creed, *Monstrous-Feminine*, 155.

30 See Joan Cocks's discussion of the "subversive" male role, in *The Oppositional Imagination: Feminism, Critique, and Political Theory* (New York: Routledge, 1989), for a major break with the tradition of this tactful avoidance of the concrete in feminist theory. In much feminist theory (not only in that, of course), though happily less than used to be the case, terms like "man," "masculine," "male power," and so forth, are still used as though they have a clear and singular meaning.

31 The way was paved for them, however, by the pioneering work of Kaja Silverman, most notably in her "Masochism and Male Subjectivity," *Camera Obscura* 17 (1988): 30–67.

32 In one interpretation: "In their secret society of the spectacle, male 'slaves' enact with compulsive repetition the forbidden knowledge of the power of women. In cultures where women are the child-raisers, an infant's first identification is with the culture of femininity, which enters the child's identity as its first structuring principle. But in these same societies, boys are tasked with identifying away from women. . . . Masculinity thus comes into being through the ritualised disavowal of the feminine. . . . Nonetheless, identification with the culture of women survives in secret rites—taboo and full of shame." Anne McClintock, "Maid to Order: Commercial S/M and Gender Power," in *Dirty Looks: Women, Pornography, Power*, ed. Pamela Church Gibson and Roma Gibson (London: British Film Institute, 1993), 213.

33 Sut Jhally's compilation video, *Dreamworlds 2*, available from the Center for Media Studies

in Northampton, Massachusetts, is the best source for those who don't want to immobilize themselves in front of one of the music video channels.

34 In addition to those already mentioned, see for example *Roots of Evil, Out of the Dark, Stripped to Kill, Baby Doll Murders, Jennifer 8, Last Dance, Relentless,* and *Midnight Tease.* All of these movies are post-*Fatal Attraction,* and most of them post-*Basic Instinct.*

35 See Elizabeth Young, "*The Silence of the Lambs* and the Flaying of Feminist Theory," *Camera Obscura,* 27 (September 1992): 5–35.

36 See Susannah Radstone on "Theda Bara," in *The Women's Companion to International Film,* ed. Annette Kuhn with Susannah Radstone (Berkeley and Los Angeles: University of California Press, 1994; originally published, London: Virago, 1990), 35–36.

37 Karen Horney, from her essay "The Dread of Woman," reprinted in *Feminine Psychology: Papers,* ed. and with an introduction by Harold Kelman (New York: Norton, 1967), 134.

38 I have personally never known a man who was anything like the heros and villains of the male action movies that this genre imitates; presumably they are out there somewhere.

39 Paul Goodman, *Growing Up Absurd: Problems of Youth in the Organized System* (New York: Random House, 1960); and Betty Friedan, *The Feminine Mystique* (New York: Dell, 1963).

40 There are screenplays written by women that feature superwomen in action roles. As far as I can recall, though, none of these carries a gynephobic subtext.

41 For an updated, contemporary version of Goodman's thesis, see Carol Lee, *Talking Tough: The Fight for Masculinity* (London: Arrow Books, 1993). Lee interviewed boys and men in Great Britain and the United States; the most disturbing aspect of her findings is that young men on, say the streets of New York, *oppose* violence, but feel powerless to avoid or prevent it.

42 See Yvonne Tasker, *Spectacular Bodies: Gender, Genre and the Action Cinema* (London: Routledge, 1993). This book is to the action genre what Clover's is to horror movies and Williams's to hard-core. Another interesting version of the same theme is Susan Jeffords, *Hard Bodies: Hollywood Masculinity in the Reagan Era* (New Brunswick: Rutgers University Press, 1994).

43 Mariah B. Nelson, *The Stronger Women Get, the More Men Love Football* (New York: Avon Books, 1995). Like Stephanie Coontz's *The Way Things Never Were;* this book deserves immortality for its title alone. The quotation is from Marina Warner, *Six Myths of Our Time: Little Angels, Little Monsters, Beautiful Beasts, and More* (New York: Vintage Books, 1995), 25.

44 Or are done so comically, as in the movies of Andy Sidaris.

45 Compare the discussion in Dennis Bingham's *Acting Male: Masculinities in the Films of James Stewart, Jack Nicholson, and Clint Eastwood* (New Brunswick: Rutgers University Press, 1994).

46 For a discussion of these films, see Joan Smith, *Misogynies* (New York: Fawcett Columbine, 1991), 21–35.

47 One can see the effect of this cultural deformity, again so to speak in its absence, by watching Sharon Stone, as an ambitious photojournalist, dominate the international co-production *The Year of the Gun* (a movie about the kidnapping of Aldo Moro) as fully as she does *Basic Instinct,* without any fetishization of her role, and without even being the female lead. When Stone says in interviews that until *Total Recall* all her parts were career detours, she presumably includes *The Year of the Gun* in this litany of waste. Yet in a cultural universe that could accept women's energy in its own right, that role would have catapulted any movie actress to the top of her profession. The best discussion of the great female icons of the classical period is Molly Haskell's discussion of "The Thirties" in *From Reverence to Rape.* Haskell makes the

important point that many of the great women's films of the period were made by exiles from Europe (e.g., Lubitsch, von Sternberg), who were free of the puritanical American association of sex with death, and therefore had an uninhibitedly positive attitude toward sexually powerful women.

48   Dyer, "Resistance through Charisma: Rita Hayworth and Gilda" in *Women and Film Noir*, ed. E. Ann Kaplan (London: British Film Institute, 1980).

49   See Clover, *Men, Women, and Chain Saws*, chap. 1, for her discussion of transformations in bodily recognition and identification; she herself is greatly influenced by Linda Williams's *Hard Core: Power, Pleasure, and the "Frenzy of the Visible"* (Berkeley and Los Angeles: University of California Press, 1989), and especially Kaja Silverman's *The Acoustic Mirror: The Female Voice in Psychoanalysis and Cinema* (Bloomington: Indiana University Press, 1988). In general, such transformations take place most easily in cinema, where film and audience stand (or sit) in a sadomasochistic relationship. That is certainly the case for *Gilda*.

50   On female spectatorship of cultural genres created primarily by men, see Jane Gaines, "Women and Representation: Can We Enjoy Alternative Pleasure?" in *American Media and Mass Culture: Left Perspectives,* ed. Donald Lazere (Berkeley and Los Angeles: University of California Press, 1987), 357–72.

51   From his "Introduction to the Contribution to the Critique of Hegel's *Philosophy of Right,* in *The Marx-Engels Reader,* 2d ed. (New York: Norton, 1978), 60.

INDEX